Risk, Governance and Society

Volume 21

The book series "Risk, Governance, and Society" is devoted to interdisciplinary and cross-cutting studies addressing comprehensive risk analysis and risk management strategies. The focus is on integration: risk is viewed from scientific, economic, social, and cultural perspectives. The series addresses all types of risks -- technological developments, natural hazards, chemical and biological threats, human activities at work and at home, as well as social risks such as terrorism. Although wide in scope and diversity, the series emphasizes the common elements of risks. The series highlights the interaction between natural and social sciences, governmental regulation, and societal actors from industry and civil society. It encourages the building of bridges between the disciplines and provides a home for both empirical research and theoretical analyses that can contribute practical advice for risk governance in plural societies and is able to advance our knowledge in the conceptualization and analysis of risks.

Allan S. Benjamin

Integration of Project, Infrastructure, and Enterprise Risk Management

How to Evaluate, Aggregate, and Manage High-Tech Performance Risks

Springer

Allan S. Benjamin
Allan Benjamin Company
Albuquerque, NM, USA

ISSN 2512-3076 ISSN 2512-3084 (electronic)
Risk, Governance and Society
ISBN 978-3-031-85069-1 ISBN 978-3-031-85070-7 (eBook)
https://doi.org/10.1007/978-3-031-85070-7

This Springer imprint is published by the registered company Springer Nature Switzerland AG
The registered company address is: Gewerbestrasse 11, 6330 Cham, Switzerland

Preface

There have been many books, journal papers, and online submittals written about risk management. A few of these have concentrated on large *high-tech* organizations, but most have focused on institutions and businesses whose interests are mainly oriented toward profit, financial stability, and customer satisfaction. Of those that have ventured into the realm of high technology, few if any (in my opinion) have taken the truly holistic approach that is needed from risk management in order to balance business priorities with the broader goals that emanate from promoting and successfully implementing new technology in new settings.

What exactly is implied by the terms "large high-tech organization" and "truly holistic approach" in the context of mission-oriented risk management? Basically, the strategic mission of large high-tech organizations is to explore new worlds and possibly to go where no one has gone before (to quote the opening of the Star Trek movies and television series). Whether the means to that end is traveling to distant galaxies on the spaceship Enterprise or creating a better life on Earth through effective enterprise management, such lofty goals have to be tempered by existential necessities. Among them are not having to endure a financial collapse, not killing innocent people, not ending up in jail, and not disappointing stakeholders (all of which have some degree of mutual dependency).

In the context of balancing mission exploration goals with existential necessity, a truly holistic approach would look long and hard at all the types of risks and potential benefits that could accompany the efforts of the organization in all its areas of endeavor, and would do so in a truly integrated fashion. That's a large bite to swallow, and so to lessen the amount of food in one's mouth at one time, large organizations have opted to divide the risk management landscape into smaller bits. These bite-sized bits are called PRM, IRM, and ERM, or as I sometimes like to call it, PIE-RM. The "P" in the PIE stands for program or project risk management, the "I" for infrastructure or institutional risk management, and the "E" for enterprise risk management. Traditionally, when someone is writing a book about risk management, he or she selects which part of the pie to swallow, i.e., either the P, the I, or the E. That's all well and good, but the reality is that "P" risks, "I" risks, and "E" risks are strongly interrelated, or as we say in risk management, cross-cutting. So if we want to make truly good decisions, we have to treat them as interacting parts of an integrated whole—i.e., the whole PIE.

To look at it from beneath the clouds, infrastructure or institutional risks, such as a loss of critical staff or aging of a critical test facility, could cause failure of a program or project; the risk of several program or project failures could ruin the enterprise, particularly if the program/project failures reveal critical safety flaws; and the risks from an unstable or malfunctioning enterprise, causing a rapid turnover of upper management or a flawed safety culture, could jeopardize the success of programs, projects, and institutional initiatives. On top of that, certain types of risks, such as cybersecurity risks, can span across the P, I, and E risk management domains (since all three rely on IT networks, and sometimes each has its own network). Therefore, cyber risks need to be considered in an integral manner with risks from accidents caused by hardware or software failures, or by human error, or by "acts of God".

All of this leads to a need for risk management to be conducted consistently and communicatively across the entire organization, which brings communication processes and internal controls into the array of concerns that need to be pursued within the integrated risk management ecosphere.

In light of these observations, it is easy to see why the challenges of formulating and conducting an integrated and holistic risk management game plan for large high-tech organizations are so much greater than those for organizations that are strictly financial or business-oriented. To reiterate, the main reasons are the much greater breadth of goals and objectives for high-tech organizations and the much greater impact of uncertainties associated with developing and implementing new technology or extending the use of existing technology to new applications.

The intent of this book is to build upon the works of a few prescient previous authors, who are referenced throughout this book, to expand their thinking on integrated risk management and the use of Monte Carlo techniques for financial institutions and businesses to large high-tech organizations. To support this effort, the book is based on the experience and knowledge I was fortunate enough to acquire as a consultant for NASA for the last 15 years in the areas of risk management and system safety and derives as well from my prior 40 years of direct work with the Nuclear Regulatory Commission, the Department of Energy, the Department of Defense, the Lockheed Martin Corporation, the Boeing Company, the Northrop Grumman Corporation, Sandia National Laboratories, Los Alamos National Laboratory, Idaho National Laboratory, and the Pantex Plant for nuclear weapon assembly and disassembly. I hope to share what I have gained from these endeavors so as to benefit other managers, professionals, and practitioners who support risk-informed integrated decision making directly related to large high-tech organizations.

Albuquerque, NM
February 22, 2025

Allan S. Benjamin

Acknowledgements

In writing this book, I relied on the insights and assistance of many people. First among them is Homayoon Dezulfi, the Technical Fellow for System Safety and Risk Management at NASA's Office of Safety and Mission Assurance, who has been the project lead for the preparation of NASA's procedural requirements and associated handbooks on these two subjects. Also, Sergio Guarro and Chris Everett were co-authors with me on several versions of these handbooks. Thanks are also in order for Prof. Emeritus Ortwin Renn, University of Stuttgart, who reviewed an early version of this book and provided comments that proved to be very useful. I also wish to acknowledge the many people (too numerous to mention individually) who worked with me over the years when I was either leading or performing risk analyses and writing about it for various government agencies and commercial contractors. Finally, I want to thank my wife Gail, daughter Corinna, and her fiancé Frank, who allowed me the latitude to work on this book at home more-or-less full time for several months with relatively few interruptions by doing most of the household chores and keeping the hubbub to a minimum.

Competing Interests The author has no competing interests to declare that are relevant to the content of this manuscript.

Key Terms and Concepts Introductory Table

The following table of key terms and associated concepts is presented at the outset of this book because there are varying definitions of the same terms provided by other authors in other books, journal publications, and conference papers. It is intended as an introductory table, with Appendix A giving further details, explanations, and justifications for these definitional choices compared to those of other authors, thereby providing additional perspective. Readers may choose to scan this table for reference purposes initially and later consult both this table and Appendix A as needed to provide clarification when the topics are encountered later in this book. As is usually the case, providing details in an appendix is intended as a means for relieving readers from the headaches that can be produced by overloading the book with too many details up-front.

Key term	Definition and associated concept summary	Refer to
Performance Measure (PM)	A quantitative metric used to evaluate the extent to which a system, process, or activity fulfills an intended objective, in effect acting as a surrogate for the objective. For example, the expected frequency of a severe accident involving loss of life, calculated through verified and validated models, might be defined as the performance measure for the objective of achieving a safe operation.	§1.1.3 and A.1
PM Measure Marker (PMM)	A particular value of a PM that the organization sets, such as a constraint or a target.	§3.1.1, 3.1.2, and A.1
Constraint	A PMM that stakeholders, including managers, funding authorities, and others at risk, specify as not to be breached with a high level of confidence (e.g., the maximum allowable cost of a project, the minimum required service life of an engineered system, or the minimum acceptable revenue from a service).	§3.1.1, 3.1.2, and A.1
Target	A less restrictive PMM which can be interpreted as a relaxed constraint that includes a designated margin or reserve.	§3.1.1, 3.1.2, and A.1
Risk Tolerance Level (RTL)	A risk threshold that expresses the *maximum limit* of probability of shortfall with respect to a PMM that the organization is willing to accept in order to pursue the achievement of a particular objective. If the risk of not achieving the PMM is evaluated to be higher than the corresponding RTL (or equivalently, the confidence level for achieving the PMM is lower than 1 – RTL), the organization tries to identify and implement control or mitigation actions.	§1.1.2 and A.2
Risk Acceptance Level (RAL)	A risk threshold that expresses the maximum level of probability of shortfall with respect to a PMM that the organization requires in order to provisionally retire the risk as an area of concern requiring control or mitigation. If the risk is not fully eliminated, the organization continues to monitor it so as to ensure that it does not rise above the RAL.	A.2
Risk Tolerance Posture (RTP)	The full set of RTLs that an organization seeks to apply across the range of organizational objectives, expressing the organization's view of how the tolerable risk levels for any one objective balance against the tolerable risk levels for the other objectives.	§1.1.2 and A.2
Risk Acceptance Posture (RAP)	The full set of RALs that an organization seeks to apply across the range of organizational objectives, expressing the organization's view of how the acceptable risk levels for any one objective balance against the acceptable risk levels for the other objectives.	A.2
Individual Risk Scenario	A defined sequence of events, starting from an initiating event or perturbation, and leading after some set of pivotal events to an undesirable effect on one or more performance measures. The characterization of an individual risk includes the scenario itself, the likelihood of the scenario occurring, and the consequence resulting from the scenario.	A.3

Key term	Definition and associated concept summary	Refer to
Known Risk	The category of individual risks for which there is (1) a defined scenario leading to degraded performance with respect to one or more performance measures, plus (2) a known occurrence likelihood for the defined scenario (either single-valued or with a well-characterized uncertainty distribution), and (3) a known consequence with respect to the severity of performance degradation (with a well-characterized uncertainty distribution).	§1.1.2 and A.6
Underappreciated Risk	The category of individual risk contributors for which there is again (1) a well-defined scenario leading to degraded performance, but for which (2) either the scenario likelihood or the accompanying consequence, or both, is not well characterized. The incomplete or erroneous characterization is caused usually by a lack of dependable information about the realm of possibility, but may also be caused by a misinterpretation of available information.	§1.1.2 and A.6
Unknown Risk	The category of risk contributors for which there is *no* well-defined single scenario leading to the degraded performance, but rather a set of unknown scenarios whose existence is implied by a set of *leading indicators*.	§1.1.2 and A.6
Aggregate Risk	The cumulative risk associated with a given performance measure, accounting for all significant risk contributors and their interactions with one another. The individual contributors may include known risks that are determined through analytical means, such as probabilistic risk analysis, as well as underappreciated and unknown risks that are estimated through the analysis of leading indicators.	§1.1.3 and A.4
Risk Undesirability (RU) Score	A normalized aggregate risk for each objective, and for each PMM associated with the objective, as determined from the following equation: RU Score = (Aggregate Risk – RAL) / (RTL – RAL).	A.5
Risk Posture	The combination of risk tolerance posture, risk acceptance posture, and aggregate risk status. In terms of the RU score, the risk posture is considered intolerable if the score is greater than 1.0 for any PMM associated with any objective, acceptable if it is less than or equal to 0.0 for all PMMs associated with all objectives, and marginal otherwise.	§1.1.2 and A.5
Optimal Balancing of Risks	The risks are considered to be optimally balanced if the maximum RU score over all PMMs for all objectives is as low as reasonably achievable (ALARA).	A.5
Risk-Informed Decision Making (RIDM)	The process of evaluating both individual and aggregate risks for the purpose of informing deliberations toward decision making regarding the selection between alternative initiatives, concepts, designs, processes, and/or modes of operation.	A.7
Continuous Risk Management (CRM)	A systematic and iterative process that (1) identifies, (2) analyzes, (3) plans responses to, (4) tracks, (5) controls, and (6) communicates/documents all individual and aggregate risks associated with the implementation of initiatives, designs, and processes within and across the PRM, IRM, and ERM activity domains.	A.7

About the Book

This book develops the holistic approach that is needed from risk management in order to balance business and regulatory priorities with the broader goals that emanate from advancing and successfully implementing new technology, including the promotion of long-term strategic opportunity in a business sense and fostering of broad human benefit in a societal sense. It approaches the problem from many directions including: the treatment of strategic risk and tactical risk; evaluation of individual risks and aggregate risk; integration of programmatic, infrastructure, and enterprise risk; use of qualitative heuristic analysis in combination with quantitative probabilistic analysis techniques; evaluation of known risk, unknown risk, and underappreciated risk; treatment of leading indicators in additon to well-defined scenarios; elicitation of stakeholder risk tolerance and acceptance levels; risk mitigation through broad defensive strategies and specific internal controls; special considerations for evaluating and managing cybersecurity risks; application of Monte-Carlo-based risk analysis methods; establishment and maintenance of organizational and operational resilience; application of artificial intelligence to risk analysis and management; and use of various types of informative risk displays such as spider charts. It caters first to management entities who wish to have a broad view of the principal concepts, then to practitioners who need to have detailed guidelines for implementating the concepts. It also provides examples of the principal mathematical underpinnings for those who are more academically minded. All in all, the reader will appreciate being exposed to a comprehensive view of the tenets of integrated risk management presented in a style that is both witty and very readable.

Contents

1 Concepts of Risk Management for Large High-Tech Organizations 1
1.1 Implications for Risk Management of the Expanding Presence of New Technology and New Applications of Existing Technology 2
1.1.1 Special Features of Large High-Tech Organizations Relevant to Risk Management 2
1.1.2 Synopsis of the Distinguishing Features of Risk Analysis Methodologies and Risk Management Processes that Are Pertinent to Large High-Tech Organizations 3
1.1.3 Synopsis of the Features of Risk Analysis Methods and Risk Management Processes that Are Common to High-Tech Organizations and Financially Oriented Businesses 6
1.1.4 The General Relevance of Monte Carlo Sampling and Multi-Criteria Decision Analysis 7
1.1.5 Synopsis of Risk Leadership Principles and Corresponding Risk Management Attributes 7
1.2 Risk Management Activity Domains and Corresponding Types of Risk 8
1.3 Integration of Internal Control, Risk Management, and Governance 9
References 11

2 Handling Cross-Domain, Cross-Function, and Cross-Organization Interfaces and Communications 13
2.1 Combatting the Silo Mentality 13
2.2 Interactions Between Risk Management Activity Domains 14
2.2.1 Example 1: Cyber Protection 15
2.2.2 Example 2: Opportunity for Partnership 16
2.2.3 Example 3: Staffing 16

2.3 Interactions Between Functional Entities in the Program/Project Domain ... 19
2.4 Interactions Between Organizational Levels ... 20
2.5 Establishment of an Enterprise-Wide Repository of Risk Models and Results ... 21
References ... 24

3 Articulation of Aggregate Risk, Risk Tolerance Posture, and Risk Posture ... 25
3.1 Specification and Characterization of Mandated Requirements and Performance Markers ... 25
3.1.1 Mandated Requirements, Performance Constraints, and Associated Confidence Levels ... 25
3.1.2 Performance Targets, Other Markers, and Associated Confidence Levels ... 26
3.1.3 Short-Term and Long-Term Performance Measures ... 27
3.2 Specification and Characterization of Risk Tolerance and Acceptance Levels ... 29
3.2.1 Direct Elicitation of Risk Tolerance Levels: Financial Institutions and Customer-Oriented Businesses ... 29
3.2.2 Direct Elicitation of Risk Tolerance and Acceptance Levels: Large High-Tech Organizations ... 30
3.2.3 A Note on Expert Calibration and more Rigorous Elicitation Methods ... 33
References ... 34

4 Development and Implementation of Integrated Models for the Calculation of Aggregate Risks and Determination of Risk Drivers ... 35
4.1 Integrated Multi-Domain Analysis Models and Monte Carlo Sampling Processes Leading to the Calculation of Performance Measure Exceedance Risks ... 35
4.2 Summary of Special Provisions for Cybersecurity Objectives ... 40
4.3 Determination and Display of the Organizational Risk Posture ... 42
4.3.1 Calculation of Risk Undesirability Scores ... 42
4.3.2 Management-Friendly Displays Showing How Risk Undesirability Scores for Various Decision Alternatives Compare ... 44
4.4 Determination of Risk Drivers and Identification of Mitigation and Control Options ... 45
References ... 47

5 Adjusting the Predicted Aggregate Risks to Account for Unknown and Underappreciated Risks, Part 1: General Considerations, Cost, and Schedule . . . 49
5.1 Introduction . . . 49
5.2 Identification and Categorization of Leading Indicators of U/U Risk . . . 51
5.2.1 General Design Factors . . . 51
5.2.2 Organizational Factors . . . 52
5.2.3 Work Environment Factors . . . 52
5.2.4 External Factors . . . 53
5.3 Example U/U Risk Correlations for Project Cost and Schedule . . . 53
5.3.1 Robotic Space Missions and the James Webb Space Telescope . . . 53
5.3.2 Private Sector Projects and the Nelson Complexity Index . . . 56
5.4 Adjustments to Predicted Total Project or Activity Cost to Account for Unknown and Underappreciated Risks . . . 56
References . . . 58

6 Adjusting the Predicted Aggregate Risks to Account for Unknown and Underappreciated Risks, Part 2: Safety and Reliability . . . 59
6.1 Case Studies . . . 59
6.1.1 Launch Vehicle Failures . . . 59
6.1.2 Space System Loss-of-Crew-and-Vehicle Accidents (the Space Shuttle) . . . 62
6.1.3 Commercial Nuclear Reactor Fuel Melting Accidents . . . 64
6.1.4 Commercial and Military System Reliability Growth . . . 66
6.1.5 Human Reliability and Performance Shaping Factors . . . 67
6.2 Adjustments to Predicted Probability of a Life-Threatening Accident to Account for Unknown and Underappreciated Risks . . . 68
6.3 Closing Thought on U/U Risk Correlation Uncertainty . . . 70
References . . . 71

7 Processes for Optimally Balancing Risks Against Opportunities in Strategic Portfolio Planning . . . 73
7.1 The Similarities and Differences Between Risk Analyses Needed for Strategic Portfolio Planning vs. Design, Development, and Operation of a System . . . 74
7.2 The Augustine Committee Assessment of Alternative Human Spacecraft Programs for NASA . . . 74

7.3 Going Beyond the Augustine Committee Assessment of Relative Benefits to Risk-Inform the Selection of a Comprehensive Portfolio of Programs 77
7.3.1 Introduction 77
7.3.2 Defining Benefit Significance Scores as Performance Measures for the Enterprise-Level Aspirational Objectives 79
7.3.3 Expanding the Monte Carlo Analysis for Individual Programs to Apply to Program Portfolios Containing Multiple Program Elements 80
7.3.4 Strategic Portfolio Planning Elicitations (and Felicitations) 81
7.3.5 Displays Comparing the Risk Postures of Different Portfolio Alternatives 86
References 87

8 Continuous Risk Management, Part 1: Models and Simulation Processes 89
8.1 The Fundamentals of Continuous Risk Management (CRM) 89
8.1.1 CRM in the Traditional Sense 89
8.1.2 CRM in an Expanded Sense 91
8.2 The Distinction Between Mandated Requirements and Objectives in CRM 91
8.3 Summary of CRM Models for Analyzing Risks Initiated by Random Events 93
8.3.1 Risk Scenario Diagrams 93
8.3.2 Performance Modeling and Simulation 96
8.3.3 Fault-Tree-Based Risk Aggregation Models 99
8.3.4 The Importance of Accounting for Dependencies During Risk Aggregation 101
8.3.5 Making Adjustments for U/U Risk 103
8.4 Putting It Together 104
References 105

9 Special Considerations for Risks Associated with Cyberattacks 107
9.1 Use of Conditional Probabilities 107
9.2 Performance Measure Markers and Risk Tolerance Levels for Cybersecurity Aggregate Conditional Risk 108
9.3 Performance Measure Probability Distribution and Level of Acceptability 109
9.4 Societal Integration Approach for Scenarios Initiated by Cyberattacks 111
References 112

10 Continuous Risk Management, Part 2: Internal Controls, Risk Mitigations, and Mission-Advancing Opportunities 115
10.1 Introductory Remarks 115
10.2 CRM and Risk-Informed Internal Controls 116
10.2.1 Hierarchical Control Loops 116
10.2.2 RACI Matrices 118
10.2.3 An Example 118
10.3 CRM and Risk-Balancing Mitigations 119
10.3.1 Introduction to Risk Mitigation 119
10.3.2 Identifying Mitigation Alternatives that Address Risk Drivers 119
10.3.3 Evaluating Mitigation Alternatives and Making the Case for a Particular One 122
10.3.4 Re-baselining the Program, Project, or Activity Plan When Necessary 123
10.4 CRM and Mission-Advancing Opportunities 124
10.4.1 Introduction to Tactical and Strategic Opportunities 124
10.4.2 Demonstration of the Analysis of Alternative Portfolio Re-Baselining Options to Take Advantage of Emerging Strategic Opportunities 125
References 128

11 Graded Analysis and Screening Analysis Approaches 129
11.1 Graded Analysis Approaches 129
11.1.1 Introduction 129
11.1.2 How Activity Importance and Timeframe Affect Choices Concerning the Scope, Inclusiveness, Completeness, and Rigor of Analyses that Support Risk Management 131
11.2 Analysis-of-Alternatives Screening Analysis Approach 133
11.2.1 Method Overview 134
11.2.2 Simplifications to Performance Modeling and Analysis 134
11.2.3 For Equation Nerds Only 135
References 136

12 Example No. 1 on Accounting for Dependencies Between Risk Scenarios 137
12.1 Setup 137
12.2 Analysis 137
12.3 Common Cause Treatment 141
References 142

13 Example No. 2 on Multi-Year Milestone Risk Analysis 143
13.1 Setup 143
13.2 Analysis 144
13.2.1 Calculation of Aggregate Schedule Risks 145
13.2.2 Calculation and Display of Schedule Risk Undesirability Scores 147
References 149

14 Example No. 3 on Designing for Optimally Balanced Risks 151
14.1 Flow of Activities within Design for Optimally Balanced Risks 151
14.2 Principles Concerning the Conduct and Use of Trade Studies in Design for Optimally Balanced Risks 154
14.2.1 Starting from De-Minimis, De-Maximus, and Hybrid Reference Designs 154
14.2.2 Narrowing the Trade Space in the Search for Optimal Balance by Identifying and Acting upon Risk Drivers 155
14.2.3 Simplified Synthetic Models for the Trade Space 156
14.3 Fundamentals Concerning Communication, Evaluation, and Assurance in Design for Optimally Balanced Risks 157
14.3.1 Coordination Between Designers and Risk Analysts 157
14.3.2 Evaluation and Display of Results from the Trade Studies 157
14.3.3 Performance Metrics Considered Jointly 159
14.3.4 Formulation of a System Design Case for Optimally Balanced Risks 159
References 161

15 Advanced Concepts for Evaluating, Aggregating, and Managing High-Tech Performance Risks and Promoting Resilience 163
15.1 Evaluating Societal and Environmental Tipping Point Likelihoods and their Effects on the Aggregate Risks to Organizational Objectives 164
15.1.1 Agent-Based Modeling (ABM) 165
15.1.2 Tipping Points 165
15.1.3 The Use of ABM to Predict Tipping Points 166
15.1.4 The Use of Empirically Derived Leading Indicators as Monitoring Aids for Tipping Points 167
15.2 Utilizing Artificial Intelligence to Better Evaluate and Manage Cybersecurity Risk 167
15.2.1 Using AI Proactively in Conjunction with the Use of Red Teams 168
15.2.2 Using AI to Improve Both Resistance and Response to Cyberattacks 169

15.3 Utilizing Artificial Neural Networks and Genetic Algorithms to Derive more Accurate Correlations Between Leading Indicators and Performance Risks 170
15.3.1 Neural Networks............................... 171
15.3.2 Genetic Algorithms 172
15.3.3 Accommodating Data Sparsity and Epistemic Uncertainty.................................. 173
15.4 Use of AI in Support of Organizational and Operational Resilience... 173
References.. 176

Appendix A. Explanation and Characterization of Key Concepts....... 179

References 189

Index.. 191

List of Figures

Fig. 1.1 OMB Circular A-123 conception of the relationship between governance, risk management, and internal control 10
Fig. 2.1 An example of enterprise, programmatic, and institutional risks propagated from an enterprise initiative and the delegation of responsibility 15
Fig. 2.2 An example of enterprise, programmatic, and institutional risks propagated from a new program opportunity and the delegation of responsibility 17
Fig. 2.3 An example of programmatic and institutional risks propagated from an institutional initiative and the delegation of responsibility 18
Fig. 2.4 DFOBR process flow and interactions between systems engineering, safety and mission assurance, organizational management, and non-management stakeholders 21
Fig. 2.5 The principal activities and transfer of planning, performance, and risk information within and between organizational levels 22
Fig. 2.6 A representative integrated risk management organizational chart for a large high-tech organization 23
Fig. 3.1 Example elicited risk tolerance levels for financial loss due to the aggregated effect of individual risks 30
Fig. 3.2 Example elicited risk tolerance and acceptance levels for the probability of loss of crew 33
Fig. 4.1 Performance measure histogram determination using integrated model simulation within a Monte Carlo sampling procedure 37
Fig. 4.2 Specific example showing how performance models may interact with one another during the risk aggregation process 38
Fig. 4.3 More detailed list of inputs, models, and outputs for the example of Fig. 4.2 39
Fig. 4.4 Illustration of a method for calculating risk undesirability scores 43

Fig. 4.5 Notional spider chart display comparing risk undesirability scores across P, I, and E risk management domains for each of two hypothetical decision alternatives ... 44
Fig. 5.1 Schematic representation of the results from an aggregation of known risk contributors and U/U risks ... 50
Fig. 5.2 Aerospace Corporation's correlation of project cost for satellite missions with a derived complexity index ... 54
Fig. 6.1 Failure histories for the Molniya/Soyuz, Atlas, and Delta launch vehicles ... 60
Fig. 6.2 Correlations of loss probability from all risks with chronological flight number ... 62
Fig. 6.3 Results of a retrospective analysis of P(LOCV) for the Space Shuttle compared to earlier PRA predictions ... 63
Fig. 6.4 Comparison of retrospective analyses of shuttle risks accounting for versus not accounting for revealed LOC accidents ... 65
Fig. 6.5 Commercial and military system reliability growth data, from Duane (1964) ... 66
Fig. 7.1 Spider charts showing results obtained by the Augustine committee and reported in "Seeking a Human Spaceflight Program Worthy of a Great Nation" ... 77
Fig. 7.2 Aerospace Corporation Methodology Used for Estimating Cost Uncertainty Distributions for the Program Options Evaluated by the U.S. Human Spaceflight Plans (Augustine) Committee ... 78
Fig. 7.3 Determination of histograms for aggregate risk performance measures and benefit significance opportunity measures using integrated model simulation and expert input within a Monte Carlo sampling procedure ... 82
Fig. 7.4 Illustration of the method for calculating risk undesirability scores when there are both programmatic objectives and aspirational objectives ... 86
Fig. 7.5 Notional spider chart display comparing risk undesirability scores for programmatic and aspirational objectives at enterprise or agency level for each of two hypothetical portfolio alternatives ... 87
Fig. 8.1 Schematic of the CRM process ... 90
Fig. 8.2 An example RSD showing the effects of each pathway on the organizational unit's objectives ... 94
Fig. 8.3 An expanded RSD showing the consequences for each pathway, with each consequence related to a performance measure, an RM activity domain, and a risk type ... 95
Fig. 8.4 Interfacing of risk scenario diagrams for different organizational units ... 95
Fig. 8.5 An example objectives logical decomposition diagram, showing where individual risk scenarios and leading indicators of U/U risk interface with the objectives ... 100

Fig. 8.6 Fault tree counterpart of the example objectives logical decomposition diagram, including additional higher-level objectives ... 102
Fig. 8.7 Aerospace Corporation's correlation of project development time for satellite missions with a derived complexity index ... 104
Fig. 9.1 Example results for three red-team simulations ... 110
Fig. 10.1 Standard control loop form ... 117
Fig. 10.2 Example form of a hierarchical system of internal control loops ... 117
Fig. 10.3 Flow diagram of CRM aggregate risk result deliberations and management decisions regarding their acceptance or mitigation ... 120
Fig. 10.4 Notional spider chart display for six organizational objectives comparing risk undesirability scores for two hypothetical mitigation alternatives and the corresponding base case ... 122
Fig. 10.5 Notional spider chart showing risk acceptability results for each original mission objective, for the baseline portfolio ... 127
Fig. 10.6 Notional spider chart showing risk acceptability results for each original mission objective and the new objective, for the baseline portfolio and the re-baselined portfolio ... 127
Fig. 11.1 An equation-based form of the integrated performance analysis flowchart that is suitable for screening analyses ... 135
Fig. 12.1 Fault tree representation for the example ... 138
Fig. 13.1 Example inputs, models, and outputs to apply to the analysis of key milestone risks ... 144
Fig. 13.2 Schematic of key milestones and planned achievement dates ... 145
Fig. 13.3 Example risk posture results for aggregate schedule risk and evaluation of schedule risk undesirability scores ... 148
Fig. 13.4 Example spider chart display for the aggregate schedule risk to objectives caused by slippages of key milestones ... 149
Fig. 14.1 DFOBR process flow ... 152
Fig. 14.2 Spider chart for the example comparing risk rankings for a de-maximus design, an intermediate design, and the final balanced risk design ... 158
Fig. 14.3 Spider chart for the example comparing risk rankings for a de-minimis design, an intermediate design, and the final balanced risk design ... 159
Fig. 15.1 Conceptual depiction of a neural network with inputs and outputs applying to an integrated analysis of program/project, institutional/infrastructure, and enterprise risk analysis ... 170
Fig. 15.2 Conceptual depiction of a genetic algorithm plus neural network crossover operation ... 172
Fig. A.1 Schematic representation of an individual risk scenario ... 182
Fig. A.2 Schematic representation of the results from an aggregation of risk contributors ... 184

Fig. A.3 Schematic representation of the relationships between probability density functions, cumulative distribution functions, and complementary cumulative distribution functions 185
Fig. A.4 High-level conceptualization of the relationship between RIDM, CRM, and management 188

List of Tables

Table 1.1 Common risk types typically assigned to the enterprise, institutional, and program/project risk management activity domains 9

Table 5.1 Example guidelines for estimating the mean value of the adjustment of the total project or activity cost to account for U/U risks 57

Table 6.1 Modification of assessed probabilities of the top LOC accident scenarios at the time of the first shuttle flight assuming the Challenger and Columbia accidents had not occurred; originally assessed probabilities are shown in brackets 64

Table 6.2 Example guidelines for estimating the mean value of the adjustment of the loss probability, at the time of operational start-up, to account for U/U risks 69

Table 8.1 The steps of CRM relative to individual and aggregate risks 92

Table 8.2 Analysis methodology guidance chart 97

Table 10.1 Example form of a RACI matrix 118

Table 10.2 A set of example risk drivers and corresponding example mitigation options 121

Table 11.1 Suggested activity-execution graded approach levels for various importance classes and timeframe categories 133

Table 13.1 Itemization of dimensions and discrete values for the example 146

Table 14.1 Questions addressed and arguments developed for the system design case for optimally balanced risks 160

List of Tables

Chapter 1
Concepts of Risk Management for Large High-Tech Organizations

This chapter introduces the reader to the implications on risk management of the expanding presence of new technology along with new applications of existing technology. It's specific purposes are as follows:

- To outline the differences between the objectives of traditional corporate enterprises (e.g., most financial institutions and consumer-focused businesses) and pioneering high-tech institutions;
- To synopsizes the distinguishing features of risk analysis methodologies and risk management processes that are pertinent to large high-tech organizations;
- To identify the features of risk analysis methodologies and risk management processes that are common to both large high-tech organizations and financially oriented businesses;
- To relate the foundational attributes of integrated risk management to key risk leadership principles;
- To introduce and discuss the relevant risk management activity domains that contribute to integrated risk management (i.e., the program/project, institutional/infrastructure, and enterprise domains);
- To identify the classifications of risk that are associated with each risk management activity domain; and
- To define and characterize the integration of risk management with an organization's internal control and governance functions.

A. S. Benjamin, *Integration of Project, Infrastructure, and Enterprise Risk Management*, Risk, Governance and Society 21,
https://doi.org/10.1007/978-3-031-85070-7_1

1.1 Implications for Risk Management of the Expanding Presence of New Technology and New Applications of Existing Technology

In today's world and the world of tomorrow, new technologies and new applications of existing technology are taking an increasingly important role. We see this in the burgeoning development and implementation of new information technologies (e.g., artificial intelligence), new energy sources (e.g., commercial fusion power), new ventures into space (e.g., the mission to inhabit other planets and moons), new weapon systems (e.g., totally autonomous drones with directed energy capability), and new transport systems (e.g., flying taxis).

New technologies offer the potential for great benefit (i.e., opportunity) and also the potential for unwanted ramifications (i.e., risk). They also generally require a large collaborative effort involving multiple, integrated organizational entities (e.g., Government agencies, educational institutions, and commercial enterprises), each with their own individual objectives together with the common objectives that define the purpose of the overall mission. For the mission to be performed successfully, there is a critical need for enlightened risk analysis methods and risk management practices that can lead to an optimal balancing of risk and opportunity across multiple competing objectives.

1.1.1 Special Features of Large High-Tech Organizations Relevant to Risk Management

There are several obvious major differences between the objectives of traditional corporate enterprises (e.g., most financial institutions and consumer-focused businesses) and pioneering high-tech institutions (e.g., Government entities like NASA, DOE, DoD, and others, educational institutions like MIT, Caltech, and others, and commercial companies like SpaceX, NVIDIA, and others). Thus, it is not surprising that there are some important differences in the modeling of risk and the choice of risk analysis methods that each type of organization pursues. On the other hand, there are also many similarities in the modeling techniques and analysis methods used by traditional corporate enterprises and pioneering high-tech institutions. One of the purposes of this book is to edify and demonstrate both the similarities and the differences.

In summary form, the high-tech organizations holding the spotlight in this book have the following attributes and characteristics that are relevant to the formulation and practice of risk management:

- They have a substantial portfolio of programs that develop new technology and/or explore new applications for existing technology. In space exploration, for example, new technologies are currently being developed within both the public and private sectors in the areas of nuclear cryogenic propulsion, radioisotope electric power generation, remotely controlled robotic systems, fluidic telescopes, increasingly powerful recoverable launch vehicles, and highly maneuverable suits for extravehicular activities (EVAs), to name a few.

- They have to balance ambitious exploration goals with both internally and externally specified constraints. These constraints regularly occur in project areas such as schedule, cost, safety assurance, physical security, and cyber protection; in areas involving infrastructure such as the development and maintenance of core competencies; and in enterprise areas such as liability protection, concern for reputational integrity, and community involvement.
- They have a diverse institutional structure, generally including technical organizational units, project units, administrative support units, high-level administrative offices, research laboratories, testing facilities, and manufacturing facilities. Large high-tech organizations typically have tens of thousands of employees at different field locations.
- They contract with or otherwise collaborate with a variety of extra-organizational entities, either through an acquisition process or through partnership agreements. Many of them establish contracts with a few main commercial entities who are generally involved to some extent in technology development and who themselves subcontract with other entities. Many, as well, have partnerships with universities, U.S. Government agencies, and international agencies who develop and/or utilize new technologies.

1.1.2 Synopsis of the Distinguishing Features of Risk Analysis Methodologies and Risk Management Processes that Are Pertinent to Large High-Tech Organizations

In general, large high-tech organizations have a broader range of objectives than financial institutions and consumer-oriented businesses that include technology development and application for the betterment of society and/or a client base, and that also include infrastructure alignment with a corresponding set of core competencies. This makes the organizational structure more diverse, leading to an increased premium on integrating risk analysis and risk management across different domains.

One of the first major differences pertains to the tasks involved in setting up a risk tolerance posture that establishes the stakeholders' view of risk parity across the full set of objectives that the organization is committed to achieve. I use the term "risk tolerance posture" here in the sense of specifying a complete set of individual risk tolerances, each of which applies to a particular objective, and the combination of which establishes the stakeholders' consensus on how to balance the risks overall and achieve risk acceptability across the multiple, often competing, objectives. I correspondingly use the term "risk posture" to include both the risk tolerance posture and the actual risk, the combination of which determines the organization's risk health.

Note that my combination of the terms "risk", "tolerance", and "posture" as just defined is not really original, because several sources use this terminology in the same sense as defined here (e.g., Mathias et al., 2017; Kelly, 2024; Tsing, 2020; Graham, 2010; Peasley et al., 2017). Others, however, use different combinations of these terms. For example, the fresh-off-the-press new version of NASA's risk management handbook (NASA, 2024a, 2024b), of which I was one of the co-authors, defines "risk posture" in the same way that I, in this book, define "risk tolerance posture". Others use the term "risk appetite", to express what I refer to here as "risk tolerance posture" (e.g., COSO, 2004; Rittenberg & Martens, 2012). The problem is that there is presently no agreed-upon consensus terminology and many different proposals. Appendix A Sects. A.2 through A.5 discuss this question in more detail.

For large high-tech organizations, the elicitation of the risk tolerance posture involves establishing the organization's view of parity between developing and implementing new technology for the benefit of mankind or clientele vs. meeting deadlines or making a financial profit. This necessitates an elicitation process that first minimizes the participants' unconscious biases and perception inconsistencies, and then reconciles different positions and viewpoints. Means for achieving a suitable consensus risk tolerance posture will be explored in Sects. 3.2.1, 3.2.2, and 7.3.4.

Furthermore, to the extent that large high-tech organizations become involved with developing new technology or implementing existing technology in new circumstances, a large fraction of their risk is related to scenarios that are not known at the time decisions have to be made, or if known, cannot be quantified based on experience prior to their implementation in the field. Such undefined or unquantifiable risk scenarios, referred to in the book as "unknown/underappreciated risks", or "U/U risks", can often be the result of unpredictable human behavior, unexpected operational behavior stemming from a lack of experience using a new technology, or non-inclusive management practices.

For example, the Chernobyl nuclear reactor meltdown in 1986 was attributed to technicians attempting a poorly designed experiment during which standard safety measures were ignored (Chernobyl, 2024). The Soviet Union had only 25 reactor years of experience operating RBMK reactors up to that point, a reactor type (used for the first time at Chernobyl) that was known to have several safety shortcomings, including a large positive void coefficient, a positive control rod scram effect, and instability at low power levels.

While the fact that the operation of the facility was risky could be inferred from certain leading indicators, such as inadequate training, poor quality control, and poor safety design, it is fair to say that most practitioners would not have been able to identify the specific scenario prior to its actual occurrence.

For large high-tech organizations, therefore, it is necessary to pay special attention to leading indicators and incorporate them into the analysis of risk rather than simply rely on a list of risk scenarios consisting of defined sequences of events. This runs counter to most risk analysis guidelines for financial institutions and consumer-oriented businesses, where it is suggested that the solution to better risk analysis is to continually strive to identify a more comprehensive set of risk scenarios and find data that can be used to help quantify them (see, for example, Hubbard, 2020; Vose, 2008). It is also outside the scope of most risk analysis guidelines previously published for large high-tech organizations (see, for example, Rasmussen et al., 1975; Bedford & Cooke, 2001; Stamatelatos & Dezfuli, 2011). The subject of estimating the potential magnitude of U/U risks from leading indicators will be taken up in Chaps. 5 and 6 and in Sect. 8.3.5.

A related distinguishing feature of risk analysis for large high-tech organizations is the need to consider a broader spectrum of uncertainty sources, including not only uncertainties in the input variables to the risk analysis models but also uncertainties in the models themselves. Model uncertainty is a direct consequence of the fact that new technologies and new implementations of existing technologies do not have a backlog of empirical data from which model verification and model validation can ensue. This is particularly true in early phases of the technology development process when portfolio selection decisions have to be made on the basis of risk vs. opportunity, but can be true even after the technology readiness level (TRL) advances to greater maturity, owing to the fact that a true understanding of how the technology behaves in the field is lacking. It may be necessary to include alternative sets of models in the risk analysis process, each weighted according to the experts' degree of belief, until sufficient field experience is gained to justify converging to a single set of models. Further elucidation on this point will be provided in Sect. 4.1.

Another related feature is the need to integrate quantitative risk analysis with expert judgment from technical subject-matter experts, some of whom have in-depth expertise in specialized technical areas and others with broad insights about all the technical areas of interest and the interfaces between them. While quantitative analysis needs to be combined with expert judgment from management for both large high-tech organizations and financially driven businesses, the difference is in the level of emphasis on technical subject matter expertise for organizations that develop and implement new technology solutions vis-à-vis finance and consumer driven businesses. More on this subject will be presented throughout the book, and in particular in Chap. 7, Sects. 8.3.3, and 10.3.3.

A final distinguishing feature is the need to scope the technical rigor of the risk analysis to the technical maturity level. When the technology is immature, the level of rigor that can be exercised is necessarily lower than when the technology is mature, if for no other reason that the level of design maturity is likely to be compatible with the level of technology maturity. Of course, several other factors have to be taken into account in determining the level of rigor that is appropriate to exercise. Most crucial of these is the importance of the project or initiative to the enterprise, with a higher level of rigor being required for high-importance, high-cost projects and initiatives and a lower rigor level for low-importance, low-cost ones. In general, the demand for a graded analysis approach is higher for large high-tech organizations than for financial institutions and consumer-oriented businesses, owing to the influence of technical maturity. Specific guidance on graded analysis options for practitioners at large high-tech organizations is provided in Sect. 8.3.2 and in Chap. 11.

1.1.3 Synopsis of the Features of Risk Analysis Methods and Risk Management Processes that Are Common to High-Tech Organizations and Financially Oriented Businesses

While there are certain important differences between the formulation and implementation of risk analysis methods and risk management processes for large high-tech organizations vs. financial institutions and consumer-oriented businesses, there are also many areas of commonality. First and foremost is the need for risks to be framed in terms of the success or failure of well-defined organizational objectives with well-defined measures of performance. The purpose of risk analysis is to estimate the probability that an organization's objectives may not be achieved (and complementarily, the confidence that they *will* be achieved); to identify which objectives are most threatened and how greatly they are threatened; to highlight the particular vulnerabilities and sources of uncertainty that most significantly threaten the achievement of the objectives; and to aid in the identification of controls, retrofits, or other actions that could help fix the problem. Performance measures are quantifiable metrics that are capable of gauging the degree to which each objective is being threatened. Sections 3.1.3 and 7.3.2 and Appendix A (Sect. A.1) will provide much more detailed descriptions and characterizations of performance measures and their relationship to objectives.

Implicit in the rationale of the above paragraph is the need for risks to be aggregated from lower to higher level objectives and from lower to higher level organizational levels. For example, a risk scenario that results in the failure of a component in a system consisting of multiple subsystems, each with multiple components, contributes to the risk of failure of the entire system; but so do other risk scenarios that could threaten the system. The failure of the system could contribute to the failure of an entire mission, which in turn could threaten the organization's strategic goals, which subsequently could lead to legal or reputational liability. The determination of risk to an enterprise at the strategic and existential levels requires a means of aggregating lower level risks to higher functional levels, and by natural extension, to higher levels in the organizational hierarchy.

The same logic of lower-level risks aggregating with other lower-level risks to threaten failures of higher-level objectives applies to financial risks, cybersecurity risks, software error risks, supply chain risks, and others. For example, bankruptcy risks in financial institutions may occur as the result of a variety of scenarios which aggregate to the potential for undercapitalization, insufficient liquidity, safety and soundness deficiencies, and fraud (Bennett & Unal, 2014). The subject of risk aggregation will be greatly expanded upon in Sects. 4.1, 7.3.3, and 8.3.4 and in Appendix A (Sect. A.4).

1.1.4 The General Relevance of Monte Carlo Sampling and Multi-Criteria Decision Analysis

Also common to both large high-tech organizations and financially-oriented businesses is the need to rely on Monte Carlo sampling processes to determine the probabilistic outputs of the risk analysis. It is the most common quantitative method used in risk analysis, followed by statistical analysis of historical data (which is only plausible as a stand-alone alternative when there is directly applicable historical data). In the words of Philippe Jorion, "Monte Carlo is by far the most powerful method to compute value at risk" (Jorion, 1997). Jorion, however, also expresses some reservation about the computational cost of very large Monte Carlo simulations. Douglas Hubbard, while affirming Jorion's assessment about the value of Monte Carlo, refutes the reservation about computational costs as follows: "I've been running Monte Carlo simulations on a variety of risk analyses since the 1980s ... [and] my most complex Monte Carlo models were always *far* simpler than the systems I was modeling" (Hubbard, 2020).

Statements about the importance of Monte Carlo simulation methods are also iterated by many other risk management experts with reference to both large high-tech organizations and financially-oriented institutions and businesses (see for example, Krose et al., 2014). In this book, discussions and examples on applications of the Monte Carlo technique will be taken up in Sects. 4.1 and 7.3.3, and references to that material will appear frequently in later sections.

Another set of processes commonly used in the decision making aspect of risk management collectively falls under the tent of multi-criteria decision analysis (MCDA), sometimes also called multi-criteria decision-making (MCDM). Multi-attribute utility theory (MAUT) falls under the umbrella of MCDA (see, for example, Keeney & Raiffa, 1993; Weirich, 2012; Mullen & Roth, 2002; Kleindorfer et al., 1993; Ellis, 2006), and is sometimes taken to be synonymous with it, although the tent also includes processes that do not rely on utility theory. One or more of these processes may be used to help establish the risk tolerance posture (as defined in Appendix A Sect. A.2) by eliciting and organizing the risk tolerance levels of stakeholders with respect to a set of competing organizational objectives. The use of MCDAs will be taken up again in Sects. 3.2.1 and 3.2.3 and in Appendix A.

1.1.5 Synopsis of Risk Leadership Principles and Corresponding Risk Management Attributes

Risk Leadership is a term that has been gaining prominence as a fundamental aspect of enterprise management. As described in NASA's Policy Directive for Governance and Strategic Management (NASA, 2020) and in NASA's most recent risk management handbook (NASA, 2024a), risk leadership can be thought of as the application of a risk culture that is implemented from the highest levels of management and that has the goal of increasing both decision effectiveness and decision velocity at all levels by ensuring that decisions are made within the framework of a "proper risk posture". Risk leadership is expressed and enabled via the unequivocal identification and communication by higher-level organizational leaders of the strategic and institutional objectives of the concerned entity or institution, and of accompanying operational guidelines on how to pursue the achievement of an appropriate balance between speed and effectiveness in risk related decision making (NASA, 2022). A complementary and enabling element of risk leadership is the feedback of appropriately prioritized risk information and risk management results from the execution levels to the higher managers and leaders of the organization and enterprise.

For risk management to be of maximal benefit within a culture that espouses risk leadership, it should adhere to the features of integrated risk management that have been mentioned above, and which will be elaborated upon in Chap. 2, and Sect. 14.3, so as to facilitate effective and timely decision making by management authorities.

In the United States, various organizations have established or joined into "risk leadership councils" to help implement the principles of risk leadership. For example, current membership in the Supply Chain Risk Leadership Council, formed in 2009, includes Boeing, Cisco, FedEx, General Motors, John Deere, the Logistics Management Institute, the MIT Center for Transportation and Logistics, McDonald's, Proctor & Gamble, Rand Corporation, the University of Michigan Ross School of Business, and Zurich North America (SCRLC, 2024).

1.2 Risk Management Activity Domains and Corresponding Types of Risk

While enterprise-wide risk management requires an integrative approach that crosses over program/project, infrastructure/institutional, and enterprise boundaries, the character of the risk to each organizational objective is a function of the particular objective to which it applies and the organizational level at which the objective is allocated. Objectives allocated to executive-level entities are *enterprise objectives*; those allocated to infrastructure and mission support entities are *institutional objectives*; and those allocated to programs and projects are *programmatic objectives*, sometimes also referred to as *program/project objec*tives or *mission objectives*.

In like manner, *risks* to objectives can be characterized as being *enterprise risks*, *infrastructure/ institutional risks*, or *program/project risks*, and the management of those risks can be organized into buckets. Such bucketing has led to the separate disciplines of *Enterprise Risk Management* (*ERM*), *Infrastructure/Institutional Risk Management* (*IRM*), and *Program/Project Risk Management* (*PRM*). NASA's latest risk management handbook (NASA, 2024a, 2024b) refers to ERM, IRM, and PRM as constituting *RM activity domains*.

Table 1.1 Common risk types typically assigned to the enterprise, institutional, and program/project risk management activity domains

Enterprise	Infrastructure/Institutional	Program/Project
• Strategic risk	• Staffing risk	• Safety risk
• Operations risk	• Training risk	• Technical risk
• Compliance risk	• Maintenance risk	• Physical security risk
• Acquisition risk	• Supply chain risk	• Cybersecurity risk
• Cybersecurity risk	• Cybersecurity risk	• Cost risk
• Fraud risk	• Facility safety risk	• Schedule risk
• Reputational risk	• Facility availability risk	• Etc.
• Etc.	• Etc.	

The objectives, risks, and risk management activities within a given organizational entity can be further characterized in terms of performance categories. For example, NASA defines seven performance categories within the PRM activity domain, namely *safety, mission success, technical performance, physical security, cybersecurity, cost,* and *schedule.*[1] Thus, risks that affect safety objectives can be referred to as *safety risks*, and so on.

Common types of risks that are traditionally assigned to the ERM, IRM, and PRM categories are listed in the Table 1.1. The assignment of risk types to RM activity domains helps ensure that all significant risks are considered under the risk management umbrella. In actuality, however, many risk types span at least two and sometimes all three of the activity domains in the table. For example, cybersecurity risks that affect the integrity of an IT network can occur within enterprise-level networks, institutional networks, or program/project networks, as shown in Table 1.1. Additionally, technical risks, cost risks, acquisition risks, and supply chain risks can occur in any of the RM activity domains, although not specifically shown in the table.

1.3 Integration of Internal Control, Risk Management, and Governance

An internal control is any action or set of actions initiated by management, and assigned to an organizational entity reporting to management, for the purpose of providing a means to manage significant contributors to risk and increase the likelihood that established objectives and goals will be achieved.

[1] To be precise, NASA groups mission success and technical performance into a single category, and likewise for physical security and cybersecurity, and they refer to these as five *mission execution domains* in their procedural requirements and policy documents, but they are equivalent to the seven program/project performance categories cited above.

The relationship between internal control, risk management, and organizational management in Government agencies is discussed in OMB Circular A-123, which views internal control as being a part of program/project risk management, PRM as being a part of enterprise risk management, and ERM as being a part of governance (OMB, 2017). This hierarchical concept is illustrated schematically in Fig. 1.1, which I have slightly amended from the form in the OMB circular by combining PRM and ERM into a single entity called "RM." This is done for the sake of simplifying the exposition that follows while maintaining the holistic philosophy of risk management.

It has been common practice for internal controls to be associated with the effectiveness and efficiency of operation, the reliability of financial reporting, compliance with applicable laws and regulations, and especially protection against fraud (see, for example, OMB, 2017; COSO, 2013; Seaman, 2022). Several books by Nancy Leveson provide a framework for applying internal controls to safety risk (see, for example, Leveson et al., 2005; Leveson, 2012, 2013). Also, my earlier book (Benjamin, 2017) extends the purview of internal controls to include the control of risks in all the activity domains of ERM, IRM, and PRM and all the associated risk types, as summarized earlier in Sect. 1.2.

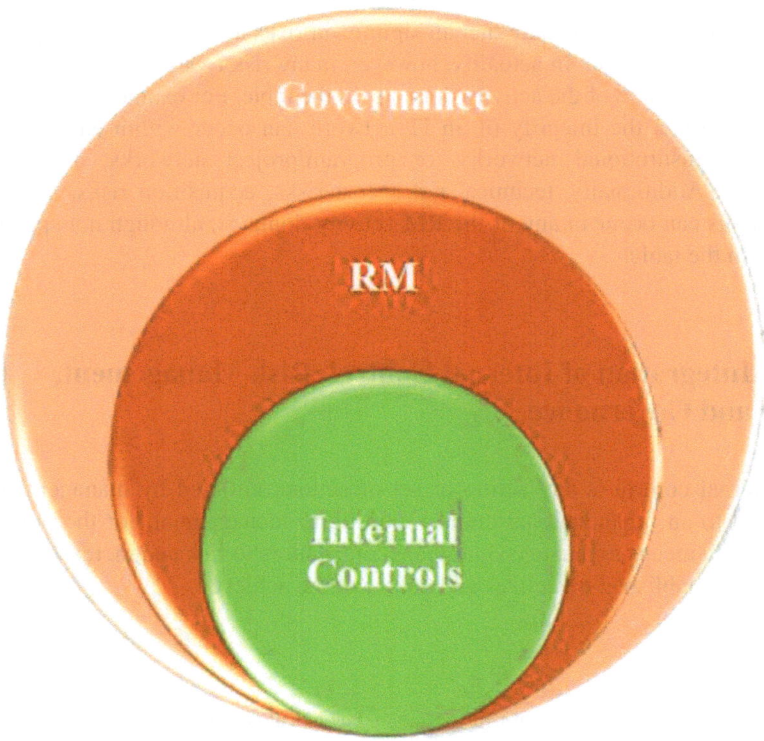

Fig. 1.1 OMB Circular A-123 conception of the relationship between governance, risk management, and internal control

The works by Leveson, and later by me, posit that two of the primary reasons for establishing and monitoring and enterprise-wide internal controls function are (1) to ensure that the assumptions made in selecting a particular risk response alternative and formulating an implementation plan remain applicable, or if necessary are updated and communicated so that the risk management team can accommodate changes and (2) to correct any weaknesses that need to be addressed for the aggregate risks and opportunities to be effectively and efficiently controlled within the decision maker's risk posture (based on the characterization of internal controls in Leveson, 2013). Those works develop the framework for internal controls using control loop methodology, starting first from the development of single control loops and progressing thereafter to the development of multiple hierarchical control loops; demonstrate by example how task delineation and process diagrams are used to assist the development of these nested control loops, and how they result in the identification of the specific monitoring and control activities that are needed to ensure that the aggregate risks in all domains stay within the enterprise's risk posture; and demonstrate how the achievement of this objective is aided by the use of RACI matrices (Smith & Erwin, 2005), which identify those who are Responsible, Accountable, Consulted, and Informed. Finally, they identify the ways in which the formulation aligns with the standard approach developed by the Committee of Sponsoring Organizations of the Treadwell Commission (COSO) for interfacing internal controls with enterprise risk management within commercial companies (COSO, 2004, 2013), and how it differs from the COSO approach in extending the purview of internal controls beyond financial and operational domains into all mission execution and risk activity domains.

A discussion on how to extend these earlier analyses to formulate hierarchical control loops that focus on assumptions and potential weaknesses will be provided in Sect. 10.2, along with a reference to a specific example that clarifies and elucidates the processes.

References

Bedford, T., & Cooke, R. (2001). *Probabilistic risk analysis: Foundations and methods*. Cambridge University Press.

Benjamin, A. (2017). *Enterprise risk and opportunity management: Concepts and step-by-step examples for pioneering scientific and technical organizations* (Finance Series). Wiley.

Bennett, R. L., & Unal, H. (2014, July). *Understanding the component of bank failure resolution*. Federal Deposit Insurance Corporation, FDIC CFR WP 2014-04.

Chernobyl. (2024). *Chernobyl disaster*. en.wikipedia.org/wiki/Chernobyl_disaster

COSO. (2004). *Enterprise risk management – Integrated framework*. Committee of Sponsoring Organizations of the Treadway Commission (updated in 2017).

COSO. (2013). *Internal control – Integrated framework*. Committee of Sponsoring Organizations of the Treadway Commission (updated to include sustainability in 2023).

Ellis, S. (2006). Multiple objectives: A neglected problem in the theory of human action. *Synthese, 153*, 313–338.

Graham, J. D. (2010). *The emergence of risks: Contributing factors*. International Risk Governance Council, Infoscience-EPFL.
Hubbard, D. W. (2020). *The failure of risk management: Why it's broken and how to fix it* (2nd ed.). Wiley.
Jorion, P. (1997). *Value at risk: The new benchmark for managing financial risk* (5th ed.). McGraw Hill.
Keeney, R. L., & Raiffa, H. (1993). *Decisions with multiple objectives*. Cambridge University Press.
Kelly, M. (2024, June). *The risk management process: How to do more with less during challenging economic times*. Hyperproof Blog.
Kleindorfer, P., et al. (1993). *Decision sciences*. Cambridge University Press.
Krose, D. P., et al. (2014, June). Why the Monte Carlo method is so important today. *WIREs Computational Statistics, 6*(6), 386–392.
Leveson, N. G. (2012). *Engineering a safer world: Systems thinking applied to safety*. MIT Press.
Leveson, N. G. (2013). *An STPA Primer (Systems-Theoretic Process Analysis, Version 1)*. MIT Press.
Leveson, N. G., et al. (2005). *Risk analysis of NASA independent technical authority*. MIT Press.
Mathias, D. L., et al. (2017, June). *A probabilistic asteroid impact risk model*. NASA Ames Research Center, Elsevier Icarus.
Mullen, J., & Roth, B. (2002, September). *Decision-making: Its logic and practice*. Rowman & Littlefield.
NASA. (2020, January). *NASA governance and strategic management handbook*. NASA NPD 1000.0C.
NASA. (2022, April). *Agency risk management procedural requirements*. NASA NPR 8000.4C.
NASA. (2024a, November). *NASA risk management handbook (Version 2, Part 1)*. NASA/SP-2024-3422 (first made available online 2–3–2025).
NASA. (2024b, November). *NASA risk management handbook (Version 2, Part 2)*. NASA/SP-20240014326 (first made available online 2–4–2025).
OMB. (2017, June). *Management's responsibility for enterprise risk management and internal control*. OMB Circular A-123.
Peasley, S., et al. (2017). *Cyber risk in consumer business*. Deloitte University Press.
Rasmussen, N. C., et al. (1975, October). *Reactor safety study. An assessment of accident risks in U. S. commercial nuclear power plants*. U. S. Nuclear Regulatory Commission, WASH-1400.
Rittenberg, L., & Martens, F. (2012, January). *Enterprise risk management: Understanding and communicating risk appetite*. Committee of Sponsoring Organizations of the Treadway Commission.
SCRLC. (2024). *Supply chain risk leadership council website*. scrlc.com
Seaman, J. (2022, October). *A beginner's guide to internal controls*. Government Finance Officers Association.
Smith, M. L., & Erwin, J. (2005). *Role & responsibility charting (RACI)*. PMForum.org
Stamatelatos, M., & Dezfuli, H. (2011, December). *Probabilistic risk assessment procedures guide for nasa managers and practitioners* (2nd ed.). NASA/SP-2011-3421.
Tsing, W. (2020, March). *Securing the MSP: Best practices for vetting cybersecurity vendors*. Malwarebytes Labs.
Vose, D. (2008, April). *Risk analysis: A quantitative guide* (3rd ed.). Wiley.
Weirich, P. (2012). Multi-attribute approaches to risk. In S. Roeser et al. (Eds.), *Handbook of risk theory*. Springer.

Chapter 2
Handling Cross-Domain, Cross-Function, and Cross-Organization Interfaces and Communications

The purposes of this Chapter are as follows:

- To discuss the tendency for organizations to promote a silo mentality, and to introduce the need for an enterprise-wide mentality of integration and communication;
- To provide examples showing how the various risk-management activity domains cross-connect with one another in practice;
- To demonstrate the need for close communication between systems engineering and project risk management and their interfaces with organizational management as part of designing systems for optimally balanced risks;
- To describe and demonstrate the transfer of planning, performance, and risk information that needs to take place within and between organizational levels;
- To identify the purposes and functions of risk management boards and risk management working groups, and to describe their roles in facilitating enterprise-wide risk communication; and
- To highlight the need for an enterprise-wide repository of risk models and results, and to discuss the relevance to model-based systems engineering (MBSE) and model-based mission assurance (MBMA) paradigms

2.1 Combatting the Silo Mentality

The term "silo mentality" conveys the tendency for many practitioners to inadequately consider risks consistently and in an integrated manner across all risk management activity domains, across all functional entities, across all intra-organizational levels, and across all partnerships. As stated by Hubbard, "there is a huge silo effect at organizations" (Hubbard, 2020). Risk models at all levels need to "reach across organizational silos." Many others express the same thought.

A. S. Benjamin, *Integration of Project, Infrastructure, and Enterprise Risk Management*, Risk, Governance and Society 21,
https://doi.org/10.1007/978-3-031-85070-7_2

In the real world, where any one activity can spawn risks that cross over into other risk management activity domains, risk management cannot be performed within silos. Rather, there has to be free and open communication between all the organizational entities involved in the integrated risk management process. This sometimes goes against the grain in organizations where cultural resistance to change and unwillingness to share information viewed as negative prevail. It is not always easy to convince people to adopt a process that is part of the bigger organization and to share information regarding their ability to achieve organizational objectives (Holzer, 2006).

In general, new attitudinal and operational perspectives are needed to accomplish a satisfactory implementation of integrated risk management. Specifically, managers within each of the organizational entities need to be convinced that making risk known to all participants will be positively recognized and at times rewarded, e.g. with an allocation of risk mitigation funds. Entities dealing with overlapping risks that affect other entities need to be convinced that it is to their benefit to collaboratively and cooperatively manage risks evolving from the integrated relationships. When entities managed by distinctly different organizations join to create an extended partnership, diverse leaderships, objectives, motivations, and other cultural views (and ways of doing risk management) need to be melded in accordance with proprietary, export control, and other considerations.

The single most important factor for achieving buy-in among risk management partners is for senior leaders of each partnering organization, especially at the top level, to repeatedly voice their support and enforce accountability for an integrated risk management process across the partnership.

2.2 Interactions Between Risk Management Activity Domains

As a rule, an initiative that is undertaken by a sizable, multi-faceted organization originates in one of the three risk management activity domains and is managed by an entity within that domain. Most such initiatives, however, introduce risks that propagate into other activity domains as well, so it is important that some aspects of the risk management responsibility be delegated to organizational entities that lie within those domains. The results obtained from the various entities must then be integrated into an assessment of risk acceptability that includes consideration of the multi-domain risk posture. Normally an initial integration is performed by the organization that is assigned responsibility for the new initiative. The final integration of results and assessment of acceptability, however, may be elevated to a higher level organization that has a broader purview over all the risk management elements and all the involved organizational entities.

The following three examples will demonstrate some of the risk analysis and risk management interfaces that can occur across the PRM, IRM, and ERM activity domains. The cross-cutting nature of many risks over various activity domains and the need for a systematic process for integrating ERM, IRM, and PRM activities will also be addressed in Sects. 4.1, 4.3.2, and 4.4, and throughout this book.

2.2.1 Example 1: Cyber Protection

The first example illustrating this need for delegation and integration is shown in Fig. 2.1. In this example, top management of a company has decided to implement a new software patch designed to identify, protect against, and recover from cyber-attacks upon the company's IT network. This initiative lies within the enterprise RM activity domain because the IT system in question serves the whole enterprise, and because the initiative serves the enterprise-wide objective of providing effective security against external and internal threats. The new initiative, however, spawns risks that span not only the enterprise domain but also the program/project and insitutional domains. For example, there may be unanticipated difficulties in implementing an effective cyber patch that is compatible with the company IT system, an enterprise risk, but the IT patch may also slow the IT system operation and thereby impede work flow in programs and projects. In addition, the increased software

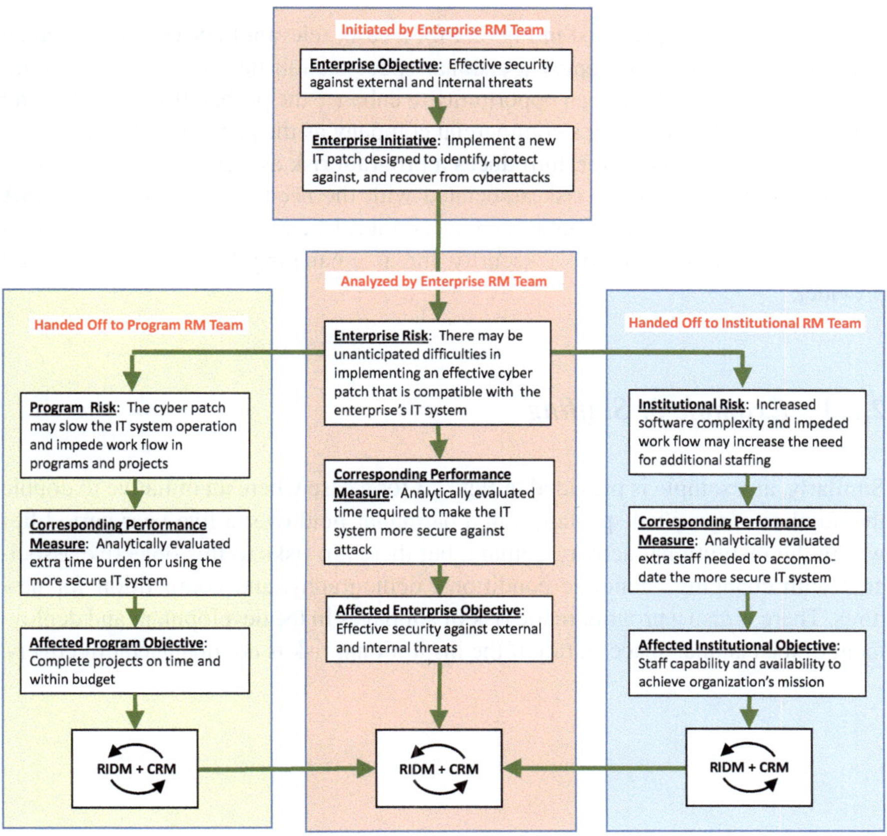

Fig. 2.1 An example of enterprise, programmatic, and institutional risks propagated from an enterprise initiative and the delegation of responsibility

complexity and impeded work flow may increase the need for additional staffing, an institutional risk.

The performance measures determined to be appropriate for these risks are analytically evaluated quantities. For the enterprise risk, the selected performance measure is the time required to make the IT system more secure against attack, which affects the ability to satisfy the objective of providing effective security against external and internal threats. For the program/project risk, it is the extra time burden on programs and projects for using the more secure IT system. For the institutional risk, it is the extra staff needed to provide the capability and concomitant availability needed by the company. Each individual risk is handed off to the organizational entity appropriate for handling it, but it is still the responsibility of the entity that manages the enterprise risk to integrate the results into the overall case for making a decision about what kind of risk responses should be undertaken for this initiative.

2.2.2 Example 2: Opportunity for Partnership

The next example is provided in Fig. 2.2 for a case, relevant to NASA, in which an initiative to develop and deploy a cislunar space station lies within the program/project domain, and there is an opportunity to enhance the probability of succeeding in the initiative by engaging a commercial company as the principal provider.

The opportunity, however, introduces a program risk associated with using new technology, an institutional risk associated with the need to transition the NASA technical support from an insight to an oversight role, and an enterprise risk associated with the possibility of a security threat emanating from the commercial provider.

2.2.3 Example 3: Staffing

Similarly, an example is provided in Fig. 2.3 for a case where an initiative to double the number of qualified specialists in a particular field over a five-year period lies within the institutional activity domain, but there are risks to this objective associated with changing economic conditions, demography, and competition for new hires. There is also a programmatic risk of slippages in the development and deployment of the cislunar space station if the institutional risk is not managed effectively.

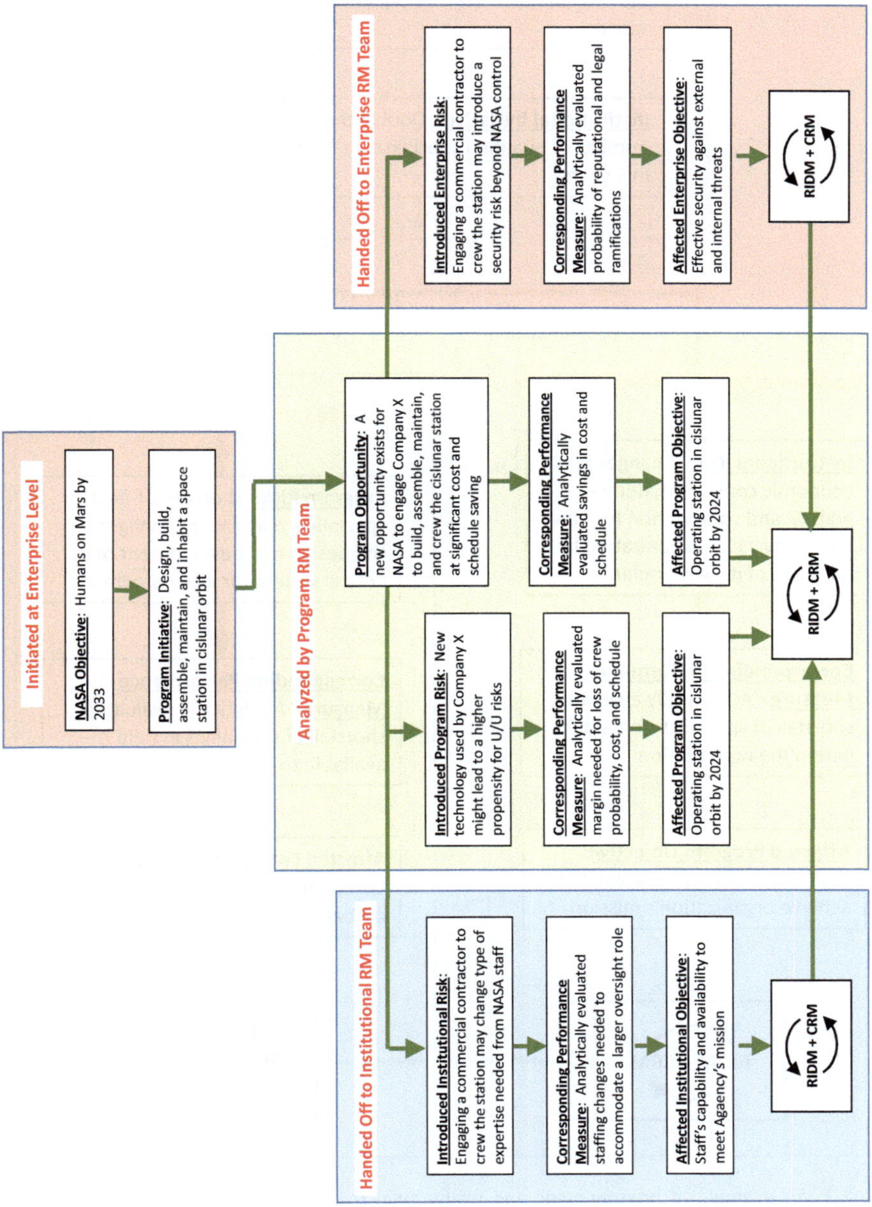

Fig. 2.2 An example of enterprise, programmatic, and institutional risks propagated from a new program opportunity and the delegation of responsibility

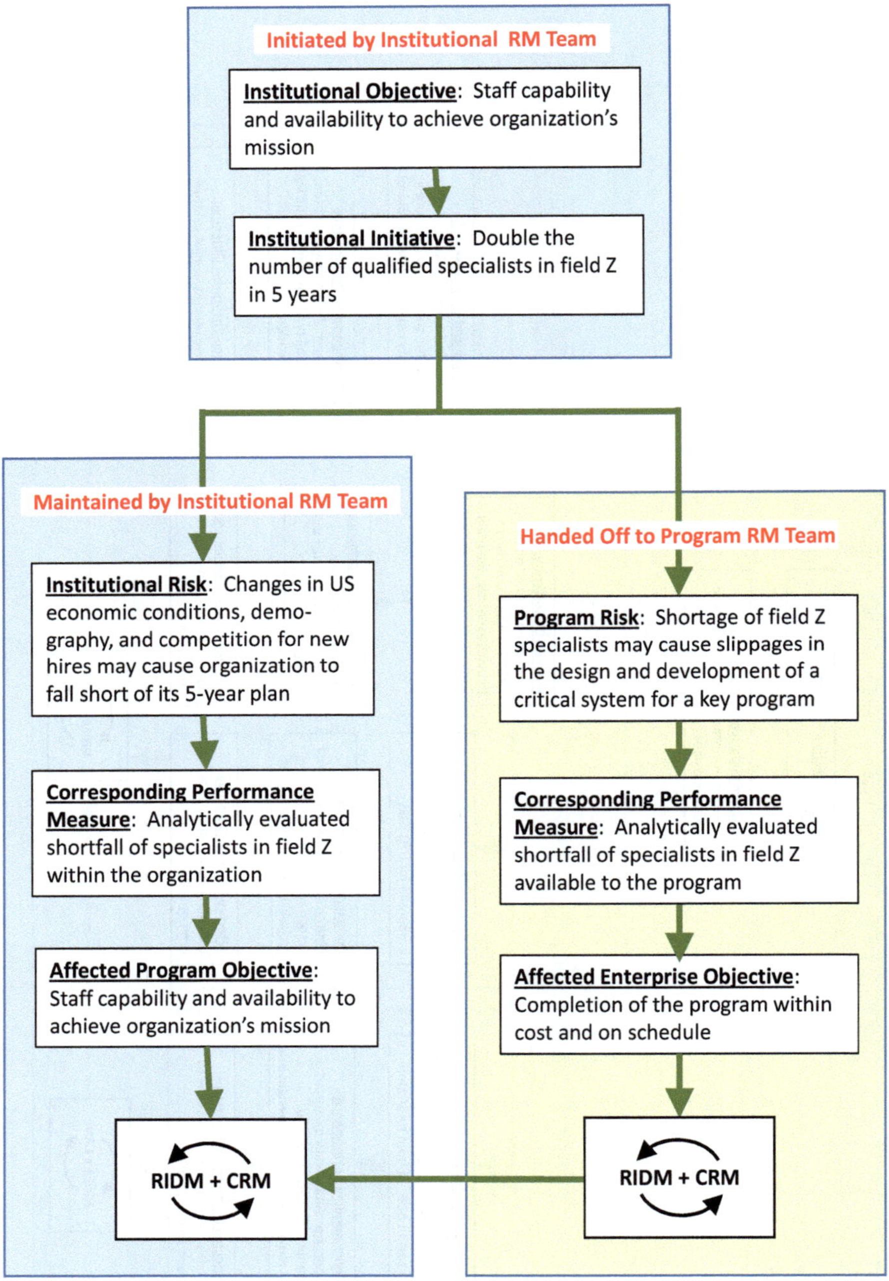

Fig. 2.3 An example of programmatic and institutional risks propagated from an institutional initiative and the delegation of responsibility

2.3 Interactions Between Functional Entities in the Program/Project Domain

As an example of the interactions that need to occur between different functional entities in a program or project setting, a risk-informed development of concepts and design of systems within various projects requires a fully coordinated effort between the design teams (usually associated with the organization's systems engineering, or SE, function) and risk teams (usually associated with the organization's safety and mission assurance, or SMA, function). A coordinated risk-informed process is needed to achieve designs that balance risks against opportunities, not only within individual projects but also across different projects that have cross-cutting interests. I refer to the process of developing designs that balance risks against opportunities as Design for Optimally Balanced Risks (DFOBR).

In a fully coordinated effort, the designers and risk analysts work together in real time as part of a technical team integrated across organizations to simultaneously understand the system and create the risk models (Mattenberger, 2010). This allows the risk analysts to capture knowledge and insights into system behavior directly from the designers without having to transfer the knowledge solely via design documents, thereby reducing the possibility of errors in communication or bad assumptions. Moreover, designers who are intimately involved in the development of the risk models gain much deeper insight into the inherent risk of the design (NASA, 2008). The result is better risk models, better designs, results more quickly obtained, and significantly fewer resources expended. The coordinated effort allows the integrated technical team to consider the risk implications of design decisions much earlier in design development, thus enabling risk informed design during the conceptual design phase as well as the preliminary and final design phases.

In addition to performance-based objectives, each functional entity typically has to satisfy a set of mandated requirements that usually derive from lessons learned from past experience. Though usually beneficial, under some circumstances it may be found that one or more of the mandated requirements is acting in opposition to the DFOBR intent because of circumstances unique to the project that differ from past experience. For example, a mandated requirement for component redundancy may be having an outsized negative cost impact while having a minimal positive safety benefit because of the unusually high reliability of the individual components. If that is the case, the integrated SE-SMA team may submit to management a request for changes to the mandated requirements, and if that is not sufficient to rectify the problem, a request for changes to the allocation of objectives and risk tolerances may also be entertained.

Regarding requests for changes to requirements, allocated objectives, or risk tolerances, large government organizations usually have formal means for seeking waivers and deviations from the previously assigned values (e.g., NASA, 2012). They also have stated (though less precisely defined) provisions for re-baselining programs and projects when objectives and requirements are not being met (e.g., NASA, 2011). The management of the organization is empowered to approve or reject requests for waivers, deviations, or re-baselines. If a reject decision is made and there is no other way to satisfactorily achieve the objectives within the stated risk posture, a decision may be made to suspend the project.

A schematic of the overall DFOBR process is shown in Fig. 2.4. Further elucidation on the interactions between the SE and SMA functions during the design for optimally balanced risks will be provided in Chap. 14 and particularly in Sect. 14.3.1.

2.4 Interactions Between Organizational Levels

Most large enterprises have at least three organizational levels: high, mid, and low. As shown in Fig. 2.5, the organizational entities at each level all share the basic cyclical tasks of developing a plan, implementing the plan, and assessing past performance and present risks that occur during the execution of the plan. Information about contents of the plans flows downward from high to mid to low, while information about performance and risks flows upward from low to mid to high.

While the detailed organizational and management structures of individual enterprises differ, it is common for large high-tech organizations, at the middle level, to have directorates that manage large programs, and enterprise support offices that manage the sharing of resources across the enterprise. At the lower level, it is typical for such organizations to have numerous organizational units responsible for implementing projects, developing and maintaining core competencies, and operating supporting test facilities. These functional entities and their interactions are illustrated in the pyramidal structure of Fig. 2.5.

With respect to integration of the risk management function across the enterprise, there are again various paradigms that suit the needs of various organizations. Figure 2.6 shows one paradigm that has proved effective for large multi-purpose agencies, and especially for Department of Defense programs and projects that involve many actors (DoD, 2023; NASA, 2016). In this paradigm, there is a risk management board and a risk management working group within each organizational entity.

The responsibilities of the RM board are to prepare RM plans applicable to its organizational level; schedule and conduct regular meetings with the corresponding RM working group and with lower-level RM boards; participate in meetings with higher level RM boards, review groups, and management councils; identify and monitor cross-cutting risks and opportunities applicable to its organizational level; assign ownership for cross-cutting risks and opportunities and elevate them to higher levels when warranted; integrate risk and opportunity responses applicable to its level, including mitigations and internal controls; advise management on the acquisition, allocation, and retirement of resources applicable to its level; and ensure that requirements at the next level up are being met.

The responsibilities of an RM working group are to implement RM plans applicable to its level; schedule and conduct regular meetings with lower-level RM working groups; participate in meetings with the corresponding RM board and with

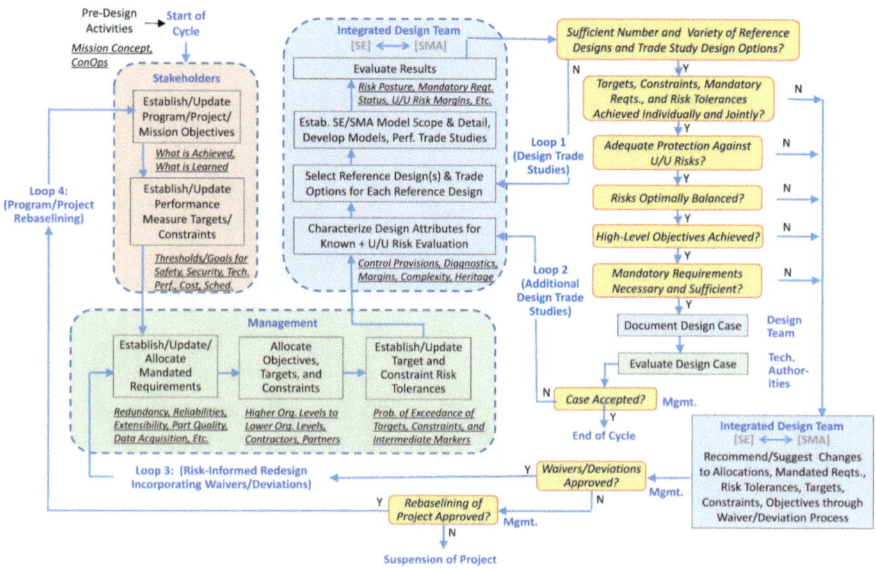

Fig. 2.4 DFOBR process flow and interactions between systems engineering, safety and mission assurance, organizational management, and non-management stakeholders

higher level RM working groups and technical authorities; identify and analyze risks and opportunities applicable to its organizational level; oversee the integration of risk and opportunity analyses from lower levels; advise the RM board on the budgeting of resources among supporting entities; and maintain a database of risk and opportunity information applicable to its organizational level.

The entities comprising the enterprise in Fig. 2.6 include not only the organizational units that are inside the parent organization, but also outside organizations (e.g., international partners, university partners, government agencies, contractors, and subcontractors). Correspondingly, the assemblage of these organizational entities is referred to as an "extended enterprise."

The principal goal with respect to participation is for all entities involved in the extended enterprise to have technical representation in a working group and/or managerial representation in a management board. This far-reaching intent is necessary to achieve the buy-in that is needed in all parts of the extended organization.

2.5 Establishment of an Enterprise-Wide Repository of Risk Models and Results

Implicit in the establishment of an enterprise-wide communication process is the need for a single repository for analyses of decisions under uncertainty (e.g., Hubbard, 2020), i.e., one that is available to all organizational entities. Expanding

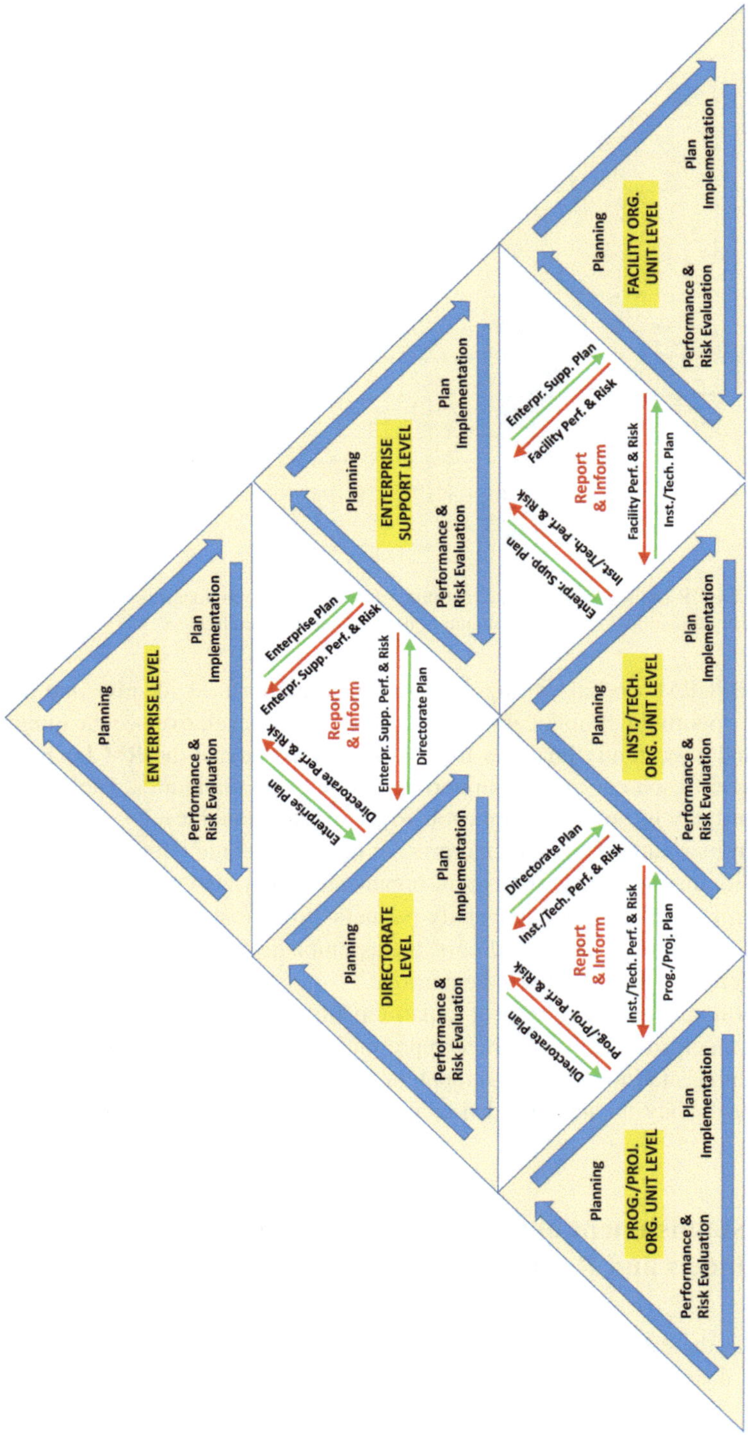

Fig. 2.5 The principal activities and transfer of planning, performance, and risk information within and between organizational levels

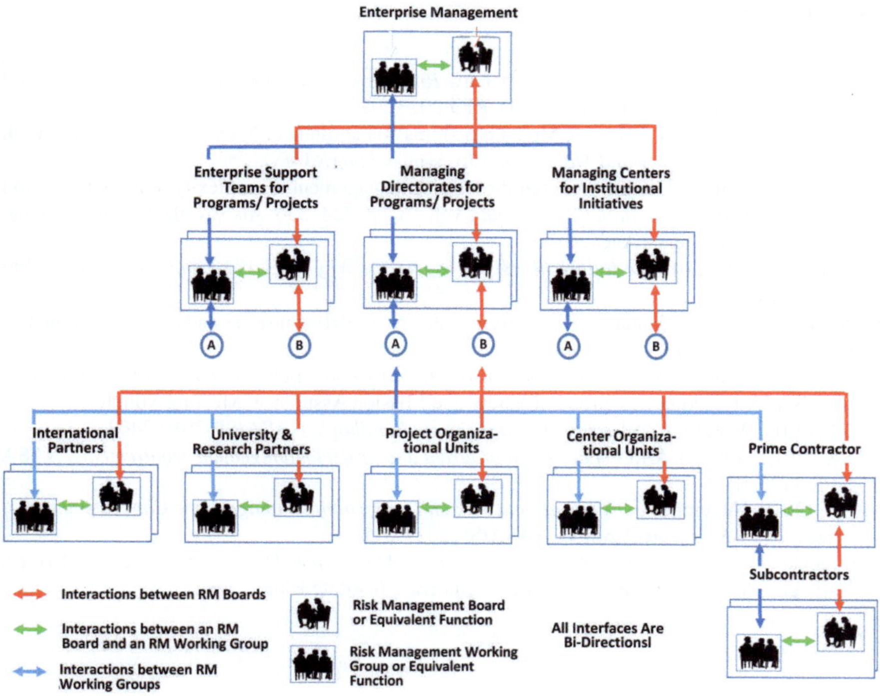

Fig. 2.6 A representative integrated risk management organizational chart for a large high-tech organization

on this, many (including myself) advocate for a single enterprise-wide repository of *aggregate risk models*, including associated uncertainty distributions for the models and their inputs and for the leading indicators of U/U risk. The risk models and model input repository should be available to all members of the extended organization, including systems engineers, risk managers, and decision makers, to ensure consistency and transparency across the organization.

This mode of communication and integration of risk information is analogous to the concepts of Model-Based Systems Engineering (MBSE) and Model-Based Mission Assurance (MBMA). In MBSE, integrated models are the primary currency for intra-organizational communication, and documents that merely summarize the models and present the results are secondary (Shevchenko, 2020). MBMA is similar to MBSE but applied within the realm of safety and mission assurance (Evans et al., 2016). I believe that a model-based risk management repository, which could accurately be referred to as "Model-Based Risk Posture Assessment," would extend the MBSE/MBMA concepts further so that the integrated models for multi-domain risk management would become the currency for communications pertaining to the organization's overall risk posture.

References

DoD. (2023, September). *Department of Defense Risk, Issue, and Opportunity (RIO) Management guide for defense acquisition programs*. RIO-2023-2-2.

Evans, J. W., et al. (2016, January). Model based mission assurance: NASA's assurance future. In *2016 Annual Reliability and Maintainability Symposium (RAMS)*.

Holzer, T. (2006, July). Uniting three families of risk management–Complexity of implementation × 3. In *INCOSE International Symposium*, Vol. 16, pp. 324–336. Also available from National Geospatial-Intelligence Agency.

Hubbard, D. W. (2020). *The failure of risk management: Why it's broken and how to fix it* (2nd ed.). Wiley.

Mattenberger, C. (2010, January). Risk informed design modeling process and design team-analyst interaction. In *RAMS Symposium*.

NASA. (2008, August 7). *Altair risk-informed reliability and safety buy-back analysis presentation*. NASA Headquarters Office of Safety and Mission Assurance, Meeting Minutes.

NASA. (2011, March). *NASA schedule management handbook*. NASA/SP-2010-3403.

NASA. (2012, August). *NASA space flight program and project management requirements*. NASA NPR 7120.5E.

NASA. (2016, November). *Organizational risk and opportunity management: Concepts and processes for NASA's consideration*. NASA/SP-2014-615.

Shevchenko, N. (2020, September). *An introduction to Model-Based Systems Engineering (MBSE)*. Carnegie Mellon University, Software Engineering Institute Blog.

Chapter 3
Articulation of Aggregate Risk, Risk Tolerance Posture, and Risk Posture

The purpose of this chapter is to provide more detailed guidance on the following subjects:

- The characterization of mandated requirements, performance constraints and targets, performance measure timeframes, and confidence levels;
- How to elicit information from stakeholders, decision authorities, and subject matter experts about performance constraints and targets, risk tolerance levels, and risk acceptance levels; and
- Where to find references on how to calibrate expert judgment and how to perform more rigorous elicitations

3.1 Specification and Characterization of Mandated Requirements and Performance Markers

3.1.1 Mandated Requirements, Performance Constraints, and Associated Confidence Levels

The primary focus of risk management during the execution of activities within the PRM, IRM, and ERM activity domains is to meet mandated requirements and to satisfy performance constraints, as defined in Appendix A Sect. A.1, within specified risk tolerances. Since it is the organization's overall risk posture that governs the determination of whether the performance constraints have been met satisfactorily, the specified constraints will normally apply both within and across all three RM activity domains.

Mandated requirements, as defined in Sect. 2.3, are usually absolute, whereas constraints may be non-absolute and subject instead to confidence levels. For example, a mandated requirement for there to be redundant components in a given system to provide defense-in-depth is an absolute requirement. The requirement is either met or not met; there is no uncertainty. On the other hand, a constraint that the total cost of the activity be less than a stated monetary value is initially a confidence-based requirement. At the beginning of the activity, subject matter experts might

A. S. Benjamin, *Integration of Project, Infrastructure, and Enterprise Risk Management*, Risk, Governance and Society 21,
https://doi.org/10.1007/978-3-031-85070-7_3

assess with justification that they have very high confidence that the constraint will be met by the time the activity is completed, but assuredness is only possible when the final result is in and all costs have been tallied. More perspective on this definition of mandated requirements will be provided in Sect. 8.2.

Some constraints are not directly observable and so can never be guaranteed. For example, a constraint that the reliability of a system over its term of performance be greater than a specified value, say 0.95, can never be proven, even after the term has expired, because the reliability could well be considerably lower than 0.95 and still no failure might occur. At the beginning of the activity, we might state that we have high confidence that the reliability is greater than or equal to 0.95, and at the end of the project we might have even higher confidence that that was the case, but there is no absolute assurance of such. These are constraints for which we can only talk about risk and not assuredness.

When expressing their views on performance constraints, the authorities give an indication of not only the constraint value, per se, but also the minimum level of confidence that they require for the constraint to be considered satisfied. For example, if the activity in question employs a mechanical system whose reliability is supposed to be at least 0.95, those in authority might additionally state that they want to feel 70% confident that that reliability will be achieved in order to continue funding the effort. Furthermore, the minimum acceptable confidence level might be expressed as a function of time. Demonstration of a 70% confidence level might be satisfactory when the project is first funded and the system is under development, but a 90% confidence level might be more appropriate when the system is mature and has been operating for some time.

Confidence levels are the complement of risk tolerance levels. For example, a confidence level of 70% implies a risk tolerance level of 30%, and a confidence level of 90% implies a risk tolerance level of 10%.

3.1.2 Performance Targets, Other Markers, and Associated Confidence Levels

In addition to mandated requirements and specified constraints, along with the latter's associated confidence levels, a risk management activity might include within its focus the specification of aspirational targets, as defined in Appendix A, Sect. A.1. For example, it might be desirable for a newly funded system development initiative to include the possibility for the system to be extendable to other uses beyond those that are specifically required. Or it might be desirable for the system to have higher reliability than the required value, simply to provide a margin against unexpected exigencies.

Like performance constraints, performance targets and other performance markers should have their own specified levels of achievement, and each target should have a corresponding expression of a desirable confidence level. Performance targets and their associated confidence levels may be stipulated in some cases by organizational management and in other cases by the risk management team leadership. In general, however, they are best settled upon through a collaboration between stakeholders, organizational management, and risk management professionals. Stakeholders such as funding agencies and users of the product or process being developed bring to the table what they consider to be the necessary attributes of the product or process; organizational management provides its view about the desirable attributes considering the overall objectives of the organization; and risk management professionals bring their view of how realistic the targets and associated confidence levels are, and how consistent they are with the already established constraints and their corresponding confidence levels.

In the example for system reliability, for instance, organizational and risk management professionals might select a target value of 0.99, higher than the constraint value of 0.95, in case the operational life of the system is extended beyond the current plan, or in case an unexpected condition results during the design and development phases of the activity. For example, the outcome of an integrated test prior to deployment might indicate the existence of a new failure mode, which while unlikely to occur during the lifetime of the activity, still might degrade the achievable system reliability.

In accordance with the fact that the target is aspirational rather than requisite, it would be natural to accept a lower confidence level (higher risk tolerance level) for the target than for the constraint. For example, those specifying the target might accede to a confidence level of 50% rather than 70% at the onset of the activity, and 60% rather than 90% at the conclusion.

In cases where greater discrimination is needed, moreover, it is possible and often desirable for the risk management team to specify additional performance markers and associated confidence levels. Intermediate performance measure markers that lie between the target and constraint values, with associated confidence levels, may provide the greater resolution needed for making close decisions about which of several risk mitigation options to pursue when the aggregate risk exceeds a tolerable value, or about whether or not to exploit a new opportunity that offers an expansion of existing objectives but introduces competing risks. More on this subject will be provided in Sects. 3.2.1, 3.2.2, and 9.2.

Theoretically, there is no limit to the number of performance markers one may include in the analysis of aggregate risk, although at some point, the benefit of adding new markers will reach diminishing returns.

3.1.3 Short-Term and Long-Term Performance Measures

Many multi-year projects or activities are funded on an annual basis and are reviewed by the funding authorities at least once a year. Accordingly, many objectives that are monitored yearly (e.g., cost, schedule, technical milestones, company profit, etc.) are divided into short-term and long-term components (e.g., projected cost during the next year and projected cost over the entire duration of the activity). Long-term objectives are sometimes referred to as fundamental objectives or top-level objectives, and short-term objectives of the same type are correspondingly sometimes referred to as means objectives or annual performance goals (NASA, 2011).

Robust risk management processes consider both fundamental and means objectives of the same type (e.g., long-term cost and short-term cost) to be separate but related objectives that each have their own performance measures, constraints, targets, and associated confidence levels. The processes for assuring that cross-cutting effects between the PRM, IRM, and ERM activity domains are rationally accounted for apply to both.

In many cases, the process for managing long-term cost and schedule risks, as well as (for commercial enterprises) risks to profits, has to be tuned to political and existential realities. This is most often the case for Government agency projects that are annually funded by the Federal legislative and executive branches and for commercial projects that are partially funded through bank loans. History tells us, for example, that many long-term estimates of performance submitted to Congress and/or to the Office of Management and Budget by Government agencies, or to Government agencies by commercial contractors, have been notably optimistic (Freaner et al., 2008; SpaceNews, 2021). The ultimate realized cost has sometimes exceeded the original cost estimate by as much an order of magnitude (e.g., the NASA James Webb Space Telescope project and the DOE Clinch River Breeder Reactor project, to name just two). Evidence of this will be presented in Chap. 5.

In simple terms, the initial estimates for long-term performance have failed to account for all potential sources of risks. In somewhat more subtle terms, however, it is a recognized fact of life that optimistic estimates for long-term costs may have an ulterior purpose: they may encourage funding which would not have had been attainable had the estimates included adequate consideration of all potential risk sources. The challenge for organizational management, working with the integrated risk management team, is to establish realistic, rather than inflated, constraints, targets, and associated confidence levels so that the cost and schedule risks can be controlled effectively by the organization responsible for executing the project or activity.

Typically, this means that initial optimistic estimates for the total long-term cost, schedule, or profit margin should be treated as targets but not constraints, and the risk tolerance level for not exceeding or under-shooting the target, whichever is appropriate, should have a higher value than for a constraint, reflective of an acceptance of lower confidence. A second estimate accounting for the potential actual cost, schedule, or profit margin based on historical experience should form the basis for establishing the constraint value, and the risk tolerance level for that constraint should be much lower than the risk tolerance level for the target.

3.2 Specification and Characterization of Risk Tolerance and Acceptance Levels

As alluded to in Sect. 1.1.2 and stated in Appendix A Sect. A.5, determination of the risk posture of an organization requires, for each performance measure, a specification of risk tolerance levels and risk acceptance levels together with an evaluation of the aggregate risk. This enables a determination to be made of where the actual risk lies with respect to the risk tolerance and acceptance specifications.

The specification of risk tolerance and acceptance levels starts at the top level of the enterprise and proceeds progressively to lower levels, so that eventually RTLs and RALs are determined for all organizational units.

3.2.1 Direct Elicitation of Risk Tolerance Levels: Financial Institutions and Customer-Oriented Businesses

In the case of financial institutions and customer-oriented businesses, Douglas Hubbard has described in detail the processes that need to be followed in order to elicit the information regarding risk tolerances that is needed from the pertinent authorities (Hubbard, 2020). This subsection summarizes Hubbard's observations on this subject regarding financial risks, and the next extends Hubbard's approach to cover risks that are especially important for large high-tech organizations. (Hubbard alludes to risks that apply to large high-tech organizations, such as the risk of core melting in nuclear reactor facilities and the risk of loss-of-crew during human spaceflight, but does not extend his methodology to explicitly cover them.)

In his section in Chap. 4 entitled "Establishing Risk Tolerance", Hubbard states that it is possible to canvass executives and use the results to draw a "risk tolerance curve" to compare to the loss exceedance curve, or LEC. He shows how the data to generate the risk tolerance curve can be gathered in a meeting with a level of management that is in a position to state, as a matter of policy, how much risk the organization is willing to accept. In his words, it involves simply explaining the concept to management, and then asking them to establish a few points on the curve. He gives an example of the dialogue that could occur between analysts and executives to obtain the necessary data for constructing the curve. (Generally, the dialogue consists of the analyst explaining to the executive the evaluated risk of not meeting given financial objectives, asking what chance per year the executive could accept of losing a specified amount of money in order to provide near-total protection against the financial risk, and repeating the question for different specified amounts of money.)

Figure 3.1 provides my interpretation of what Hubbard means by a risk tolerance curve, using his interview results as the example. It is important to note that because of the dangers of extrapolation, the curve should not extend beyond the limits of the range of performance markers covered by the elicitation (although the figure shows a slight amount of extension for visual purposes only).

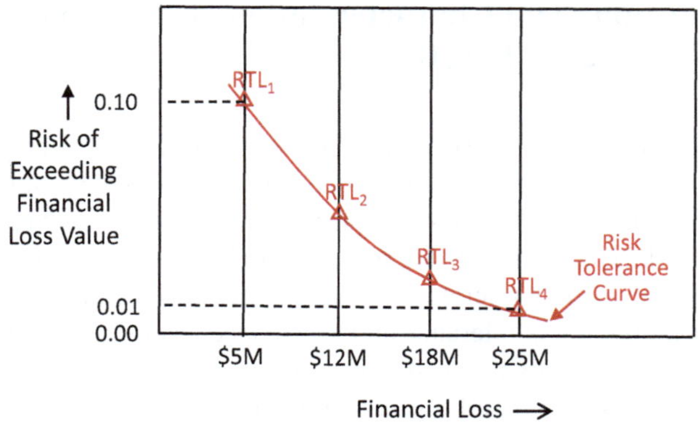

Fig. 3.1 Example elicited risk tolerance levels for financial loss due to the aggregated effect of individual risks

3.2.2 Direct Elicitation of Risk Tolerance and Acceptance Levels: Large High-Tech Organizations

In this section I will develop a modified version of Hubbard's elicitation technique to explore how risk tolerance levels and risk acceptance levels might be deduced for a performance measure that is especially applicable to large high-tech organizations that develop new technology and use it in new applications. The example will pertain to the organization's desire to avoid severe life-threatening accidents, especially during the early stages of operation when there is little experience to shed light on how the new technology will fare in the field. The specific setting for the example will be NASA's human spaceflight program, but the lessons to be learned will be applicable to all large high-tech organizations that take risks in order to pursue opportunity.

By way of background, NASA's Human-Rating Procedural Requirements stipulates that for all programs involving human spaceflight, there must be "Administrator-approved safety goals and thresholds defining [respectively] long-term targeted and maximum tolerable levels of risk. … Safety goals and thresholds must match the type of mission being conducted and are used in addition to other safety criteria, such as the requirement for the system to be failure tolerant and provide crew escape and survival capabilities (NASA, 2017)."

The performance measure for safety in this case is the likelihood of a severe accident occurring during a flight, which for crewed spaceflight equates to P(LOC), the probability of loss-of-crew per flight. On closer look, there are two performance measures implied here: a short-term one and a long-term one. The threshold applies to values of P(LOC) applicable to initial operation before enough experience has been gained to eliminate most of the U/U risks, and the goal applies to later operation after most of the U/U risks have shaken out and corrected for. Normally this is accomplished through observations of precursors and other unusual behavior during actual operation.

I should mention in passing that NASA's use of the term "threshold" (see NASA, 2017) is synonymous with my use of the term "constraint" in the preceding subsections, and their use of the term "requirement" is synonymous with my use of the term "mandated requirement". Also, their use of the term "goal" is equivalent to what I would call a "long-term constraint." These minor differences in terminology are indications of personal preference ("different strokes for different folks"), but are not critical in a formative sense.

It is also pertinent to note that in addition to specifying safety thresholds and goals as short-term and long-term markers for P(LOC), NASA's Technical Requirements for Human Rating require that there be accompanying analyses to determine the associated uncertainty in the determined P(LOC) values (NASA, 2023). The aggregate risk for initial operation is the risk that P(LOC) initially exceeds the threshold marker because of uncertainty from all sources that apply, including known sources, unknown sources, and underappreciated sources. Similarly, the aggregate risk for long-term operation is the risk that P(LOC), after a long period of operation, exceeds the goal marker because of uncertainty from the known and U/U sources that remain.

To demonstrate the elicitation process, suppose that a particular program involves a relatively large number of crewed spaceflights using new technology. Suppose also that the safety authorities have recommended, and the Administrator has accepted, a safety threshold of no more than one accident per 50 flights (i.e., a likelihood of 0.020 per flight) and a safety goal of no more than one severe accident per 200 flights (i.e., a likelihood of 0.005 per flight). The ratio of the likelihoods (4 to 1) reflects the technical authorities' views of the amount of safety improvement that should be achievable when enough experience has been gained to pare down the U/U risk (the unknown and/or underappreciated risk).

The discussion between a senior risk analyst and a designated safety authority might conceivably start as follows:

<u>Analyst</u>: First we are going to try to deduce your risk tolerance level for not meeting the safety threshold of no more than one fatal accident per 50 flights. How confident would you have to be about meeting that safety threshold at the time of the first launch in order to state that you are willing to proceed without change to the current plan? Would you say that 90% confidence is sufficient for you to make that decision? <u>Decision Authority</u>: Not really. I think I would want to feel at least 95% confident. <u>Analyst</u>: So you are saying that you would be willing to proceed if the risk of not meeting the safety threshold at the beginning of operation was no more than 5%? <u>Decision Authority</u>: Yes, I believe so. But at the same time, I would want to research ways to further reduce the risk at reasonable cost. <u>Analyst</u>: Great. Now let's try to deduce your risk acceptance level. How confident would you have to be about meeting the safety threshold of no more than one fatal accident per 50 flights at the beginning of operation in order to state that you are willing to conclude that the risks that contribute to not meeting the safety threshold do not need to be reduced any further? Would you be comfortable with making that conclusion if your confidence level was,

say, 97%? Decision Authority: No, that would not do it. I would have to be at least 99% confident. Analyst: Okay. So you would accept a 1% risk. Decision Authority: Yes.

After establishing an RTL and an RAL for the threshold marker during initial operation, or in other words the P(LOC) constraint for initial operation, the conversation might proceed as follow:

Analyst: Let's talk about your risk tolerance levels for other P(LOC) values for initial operation. Having a high confidence of not exceeding the constraint of one in 50 flights is necessary for the operation to be conditionally approved. At the same time, meeting a value of, say, one in 100 flights would give you greater peace of mind. What would be the value and associated confidence level that would provide you that peace of mind? Safety Authority: Well, I think a P(LOC) of zero with 100% confidence would allow me to sleep very well at night. Analyst: True, but as we both know that's impractical. Would you be able to sleep very well if you had 50% confidence that P(LOC) is no greater than one in 100 flights? Safety Authority: No, I think I would still need a sleeping pill or a stiff drink. However, I might sleep very well without medicinal help if I could be 80% confident that the probability of loss of crew was no greater than one in 125 flights. Analyst: Okay, then. Your risk tolerance level for a P(LOC) target marker of 1 in 125 is 20%. Safety Authority: I would think so, although my opinion might change if you ask me tomorrow. Analyst: Good point. I will ask you again in maybe a week or two to see if you've had a change of heart, and if you have, we'll revise your risk tolerance level accordingly. But we're not quite done with this question. I also need to establish your risk acceptance level for a P(LOC) value of 1 in 125 by having you tell me the level of confidence you would need in order to conclude there is no point in trying to find ways to reduce the risk any further. Safety Authority. I would have to be at least 95% confident to agree to that. Analyst: Okay then. A 5% risk of P(LOC) exceeding 1 in 125 is your risk acceptance level for P(LOC) at the time of initial operation. Incidentally, your answers are all logically consistent, so we don't have to explore further. Safety Authority: Good. My head was starting to spin.

The interview for determining risk tolerance levels and risk acceptance levels for the initial value of P(LOC) continues the next day by asking the decision authority the same questions for two intermediate performance markers. For example, the two performance markers for the initial P(LOC) value that are equally spaced between the target of 0.008 (one in 125) and the constraint of 0.020 (one in 50) are 0.012 (one in 83) and 0.016 (one in 63). Then the whole process is repeated for long-term value of P(LOC), which starts out with a constraint value of 0.005 (one in 200).

Figure 3.2 shows what the risk tolerance and risk acceptance curves might look life after completion of the elicitation.

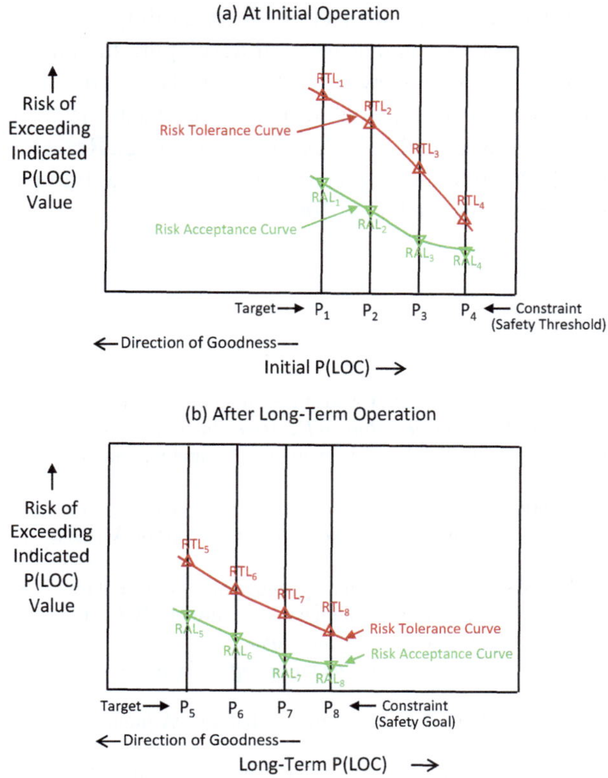

Fig. 3.2 Example elicited risk tolerance and acceptance levels for the probability of loss of crew

3.2.3 A Note on Expert Calibration and more Rigorous Elicitation Methods

In his aforementioned book, Hubbard goes on to state that in practice, direct elicitation without calibration often allows inconsistencies and unintended biases to take hold. He cites the work of Khaneman and Tversky in the psychology of judgment and decision making (DJM), and describes how calibration training can improve the ability of subject matter experts to eliminate inconsistencies and biases from their thinking (Kahneman & Tversky, 1972, 1973). He also points out the value of weighting the responses of multiple experts based on their past performance in correctly identifying likelihoods and avoiding biases.

In addition to Hubbard's book, more detailed information on the elicitation of risk tolerance levels and risk tolerance postures, particularly with respect to the use of multi-attribute utility theory, may be found in Weirich's book (Weirich, 2012)

and the related references cited in Sect. 1.1.4. Regarding multi-criteria decision analysis techniques, Saaty's seminal work in developing the analytical hierarchy process (AHP), a popular but somewhat controversial type of multi-criteria decision analysis, may be found in various publications (e.g., Saaty, 1980, 1987; Forman, 2001), as may explanations of other MCDA techniques (e.g., Rezaei, 2015; Salabun, 2015; Garnett et al., 2008; Mahmoudi et al., 2021; Edwards & Baron, 1994; Khazaei et al., 2021; Serafim & Gwo-Hshiung, 2007).

References

Edwards, W., & Baron, F. H. (1994). Improved simple methods for multi-attribute utility measurement. *Organizational Behavior and Human Decision Processes, 60*, 306–325.

Forman, E.H., & Gass, S.I. (2001, July). The analytical hierarchy process: An exposition. *JSTOR, Operations Research, 49*, 469-486.

Freaner, C., et al. (2008, May). *An assessment of the inherent optimism in early conceptual designs and its effect on cost and schedule growth*. European Aerospace Cost Engineering Working Group.

Garnett, H. M., et al. (2008, September). Reliable, repeatable assessment for determining value and enhancing efficiency and effectiveness in higher education. In *IMHE Conference on Outcomes of Higher Education–Quality, Relevance and Impact*.

Hubbard, D. W. (2020). *The failure of risk management: Why it's broken and how to fix it* (2nd ed.). Wiley.

Kahneman, D., & Tversky, A. (1972). Subjective probability: A judgment of representativeness. *Cognitive Psychology, 3*, 430–454.

Kahneman, D., & Tversky, A. (1973). On the psychology of prediction. *Psychological Review, 80*, 237–251.

Khazaei, M., et al. (2021). Creating shared value to redesigning IT-service products using SYRCS; Diagnosing and tackling complex problems. *Information Systems and E-Business Management, 19*, 957–992.

Mahmoudi, A., et al. (2021, January). Sustainable supplier selection in megaprojects: Grey ordinal priority approach. *Business Strategy and the Environment, 30*, 318–339.

NASA. (2011, November). *NASA risk management handbook (Version 1)*. NASA/SP-2011-3422.

NASA. (2017, July). *Human-rating requirements for space systems*. NASA NPR 8705.2C.

NASA. (2023, December). *NASA technical requirements for human-rating*. NASA-STD-8719.29.

Rezaei, J. (2015). Best-worst multi-criteria decision-making method. *Omega, 53*, 49–57.

Saaty, T. L. (1980). *The analytical hierarchy process: Planning, priority setting, resource allocation*. McGraw-Hill.

Saaty, R. W. (1987). The analytic hierarchy process—What it is and how it is used. *Mathematical Modeling, 9*, 161–176.

Salabun, W. (2015). The characteristic objects method: A new distance-based approach to multicriteria decision-making problems. *Journal of Multi-Criteria Decision Analysis, 22*, 37–50.

Serafim, O., & Gwo-Hshiung, T. (2007). Extended VIKOR method in comparison with outranking methods. *European Journal of Operational Research, 178*, 514–529.

SpaceNews. (2021, May). *Cost and schedule overruns continue to grow for NASA programs*. SpaceNews Article.

Weirich, P. (2012). Multi-attribute approaches to risk. In S. Roeser et al. (Eds.), *Handbook of risk theory*. Springer.

Chapter 4
Development and Implementation of Integrated Models for the Calculation of Aggregate Risks and Determination of Risk Drivers

The purpose of this chapter is to provide guidance on the following subjects:

- How to develop and implement integrated multi-domain analysis models and Monte Carlo sampling processes leading to the calculation of aggregate risks;
- How to treat the question of modeling and simulation of risks emanating from cyberattacks;
- How to calculate risk undesirability scores;
- How to display the results in a management-friendly format; and
- How to deduce risk drivers and identify control and mitigation options

4.1 Integrated Multi-Domain Analysis Models and Monte Carlo Sampling Processes Leading to the Calculation of Performance Measure Exceedance Risks

Because in many cases performance risks are highly correlated with one another, risk analysis must employ integrated risk models. The correlations between performance risks often occur because they emanate from the same root cause(s). For example, lack of trained staff may lead to safety problems, technical shortfalls, security lapses, high costs, slipped schedules, and legal liability. This is an example of how an infrastructure/institutional risk (staff shortage) can lead to both program/project and enterprise risks.

Correlations between performance risks also occur when the calculated value of one performance measure is a necessary input to the calculation of another performance measure. For example, a calculated schedule slippage will often serve as an input to a model that calculates cost overruns, and may also be an input to a model that calculates the probability of having to enact a mission downscoping. Similarly,

A. S. Benjamin, *Integration of Project, Infrastructure, and Enterprise Risk Management*, Risk, Governance and Society 21,
https://doi.org/10.1007/978-3-031-85070-7_4

a calculated value of the probability of a severe accident exceeding a specified constraint may be an input to a model that calculates the likelihood and consequences of legal ramifications and reputational damage. Monte Carlo sampling processes are valuable for such situations because they enable the risk resulting from these and other performance measure interfaces to be quantified in a direct and intuitively satisying manner. They provide outputs that are full probability distributions rather than just point estimates, and they can be implemented for complex systems without requiring closed-form analytical solutions.

Fig. 4.1 illustrates the basic structure of a Monte Carlo simulation process that uses repeated random sampling of the uncertainty distributions of input variables, leading to execution of the integrated performance models and generation of a histogram of results for each of the performance measures. A schematic showing the integration of performance models is presented in Chart B of that figure. Figures 4.2 and 4.3 provide specific examples of the linkages between individual-domain models and the relationships between performance parameter inputs and performance measure outputs.

Regarding Chart A in Fig. 4.1, the uncertainties that may be sampled in the Monte Carlo process emanate from a variety of sources. First, there may be uncertainties about which of several alternative models best describes a system response or a physical process. Uncertainties in modeling are an important contribution to the overall uncertainty in the calculation of performance measure risks that is unfortunately left out of many risk analyses. The easiest way to account for it, when modeling uncertainty is considered to be significant (as it would be when new technology is being developed and implemented), is to propose several models that have the backing of subject matter experts, and let the experts weight them based on their judgment. The weights form a probability scale from which different models can be selected for different Monte Carlo iterations. The sampling of alternative models is shown schematically in the upper left graphic in Chart A.

The model inputs that are applicable for a particular Monte Carlo iteration depend on the models that are selected, and may include (for example) system design parameters, environmental parameters, material properties, event occurrence probabilities or frequencies, and leading indicator values for the determination of the contribution from U/U risks. Uncertainty distributions for each of these are established by the risk analysts in conference with subject matter experts. The sampling of model input distributions is illustrated in the top right graphic within Chart A.

For most of the model inputs, uncertainty distributions are generated through statistical analysis of relevant data, resulting in the determination of means, standard deviations, and/or percentile values to guide the formulation of the distributions. Often, expert judgment guided by experience in a broader setting may be needed, in addition to or in place of statistical analysis, to generate realistic uncertainty distributions when there is a lack of reliable data directly relevant to the project or activity being analyzed.

Once event occurrence probability uncertainty distributions have been sampled for a particular Monte Carlo iteration, these may be applied as inputs to models that determine the state of the system for the calculation of the performance measure values. Similarly, once leading indicator uncertainty distributions have been

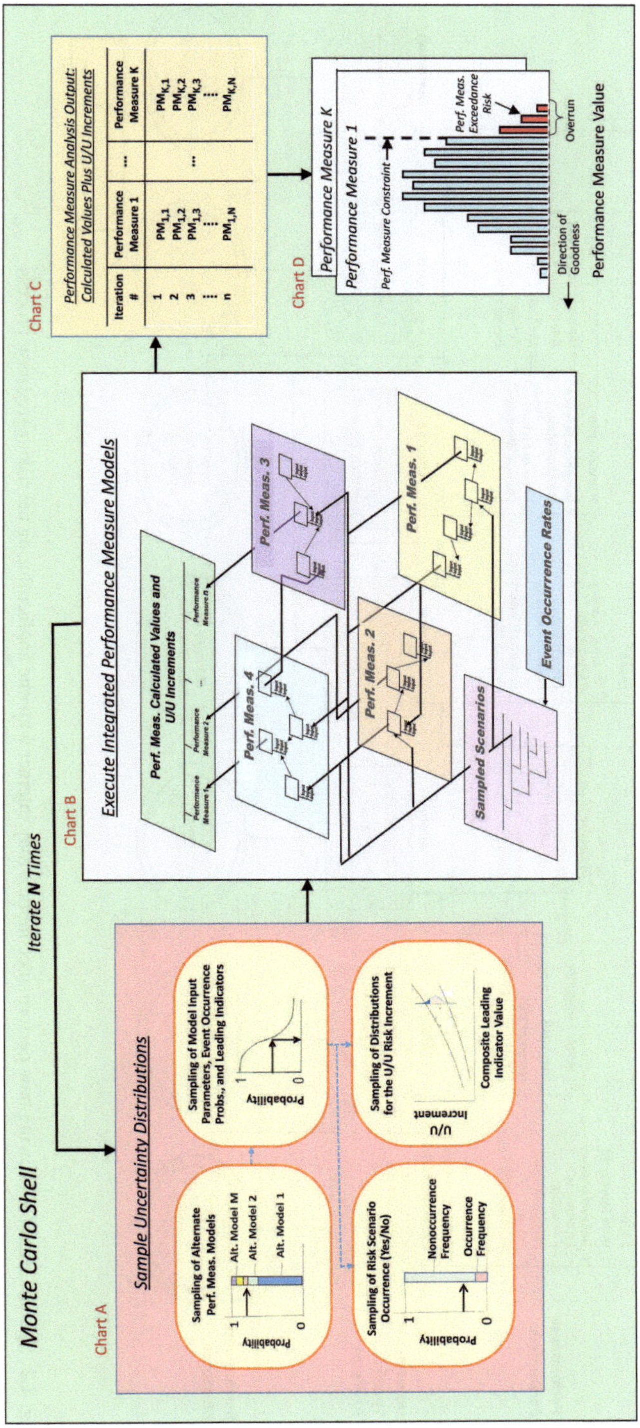

Fig. 4.1 Performance measure histogram determination using integrated model simulation within a Monte Carlo sampling procedure

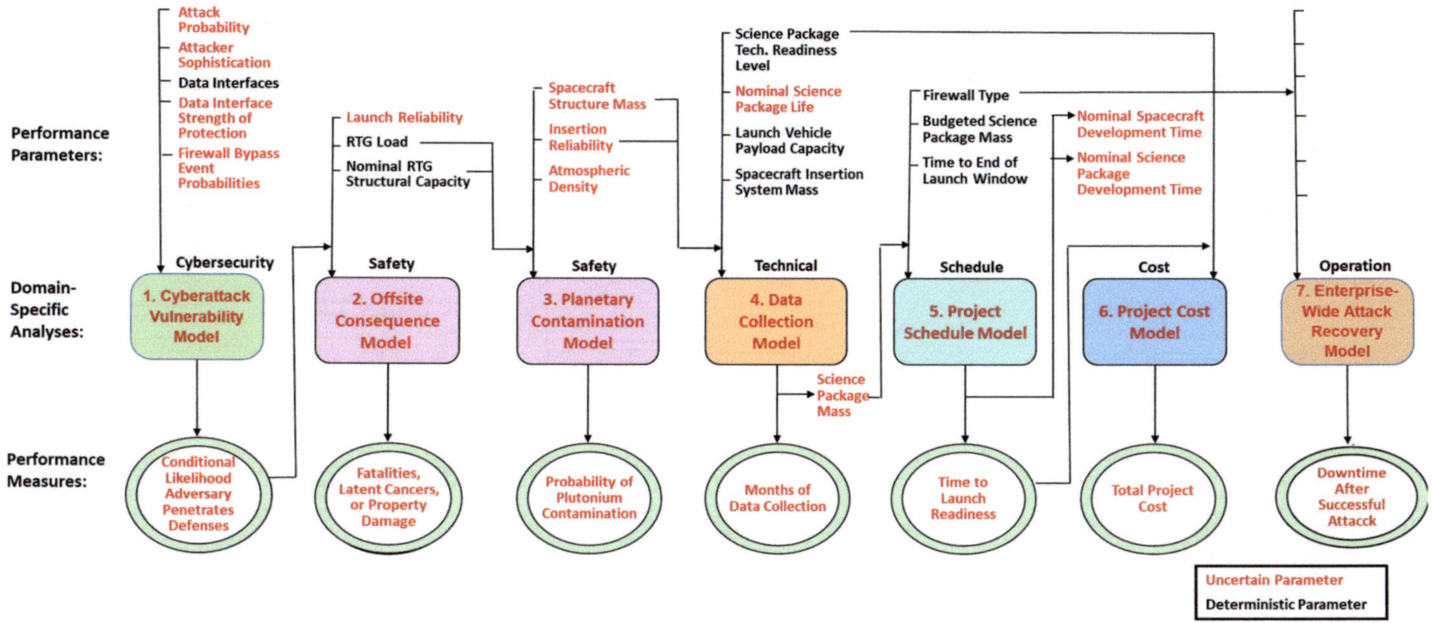

Fig. 4.2 Specific example showing how performance models may interact with one another during the risk aggregation process

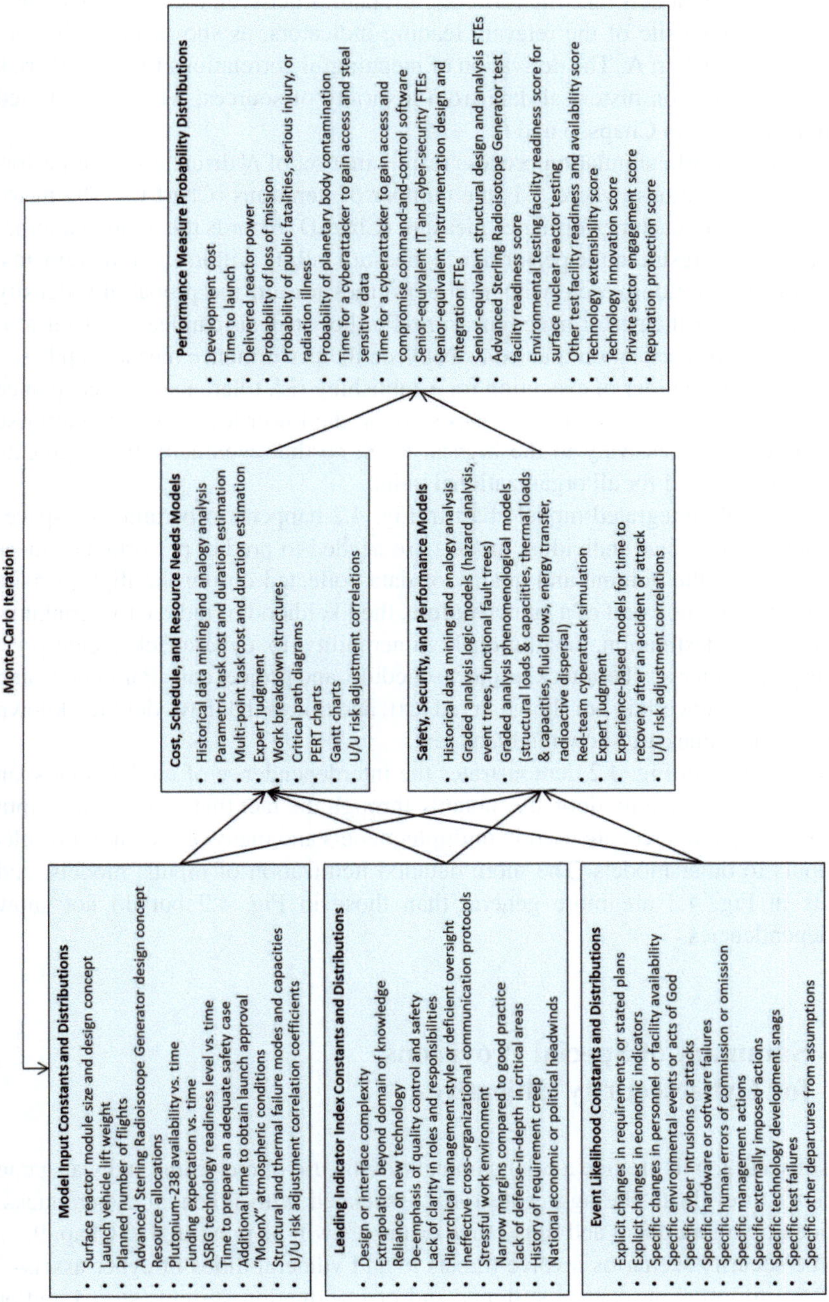

Fig. 4.3 More detailed list of inputs, models, and outputs for the example of Fig. 4.2

sampled, they may be applied through the use of analogous but different models to determine the incremental effect from unknown and underappreciated (U/U) risk scenarios. These models take the form of correlations between the U/U risk adjustment and a composite of the relevant leading indicators, as shown in the bottom right graphic of Chart A. The derivation of meaningful correlations for the U/U risk adjustment, based on historical data from a variety of sources, will be illustrated through examples in Chaps. 5 and 6.

The Monte Carlo simulation process results in a set of *N* discrete sets of performance measure values, where *N* is the number of iterations (Chart C). The histogram resulting for each performance measure (Chart D) records the relative number of iterations that result in the performance measure falling within equal increments. With enough iterations, each histogram converges toward the probability density function (pdf) for the performance measure. Further analysis can lead to determining the degree of correlation that exists between the performance measures pdf's.

Opposite to the order of execution for establishing risk tolerance and acceptance levels, the calculation of aggregate risks starts at the lower levels of the enterprise and proceeds progressively to the highest level, so that eventually the aggregate risks are determined for all organizational units.

The example integrated model chart in Fig. 4.2 happens to pertain to a spaceflight activity in which individual models are needed to predict performance measures related to the volume and quality of data collected during the flight, offsite consequences in the event of a launch failure, the likelihood of radioactive contamination at the destination, institutional vulnerability to cyberattacks, enterprise recovery time after a cyberattack, project schedule, and project cost. Parameters and models that are uncertain are shown in red text, and others that have definite, known deterministic values are shown in black text.

The example in Fig. 4.2 demonstrates the interdependence of models that span risk management activity domains, notably through the fact that many of the input performance parameters are used in multiple models and many of the output results are inputs to other models. The more detailed itemization of inputs, models, and outputs in Fig. 4.3 are more general than those in Fig. 4.2 but do not show interdependencies.

4.2 Summary of Special Provisions for Cybersecurity Objectives

This subsection will provide a brief summary of the use of red-teams and war-game processes to evaluate the aggregate risks associated with potential cyberattacks. Considerably more detail and illustrative examples will be presented in Chap. 9.

Cybersecurity scenarios involve threats to and vulnerabilities of cyber-assets—i.e., data, information, control systems, and or information systems stored and/or implemented in digital form. Example types of threat-consequence combinations that can result from cyberattacks include: (1) bypass of cyber controls resulting in the theft of sensitive data from an IT storage system, (2) the insertion of rogue software into an IT network that defeats its function and interrupts work flow, or (3) the corrupting of on-board software for an in-flight control system resulting in catastrophic failure of a space system before or during flight, to name just three.

Over the last few years, costly cybersecurity breaches, such as the "NotPetya" ransomware attack on the Maersk company's Ukraine operation in 2017 (McQuade, 2018; LogRhythm, 2017), and the "Solar Winds" hacking attack of the American company of that name in 2020 (Temple-Raston, 2021), have shown that highly determined and knowledgeable adversaries can exploit obscure vulnerabilities in highly connected IT networks to achieve massive penetration across globally connected entities.

Because of the many ports of entry that exist in large interconnected networks, it is generally agreed among cybersecurity experts that a determined and knowledgeable adversary will be able to find a way to gain access and perpetrate a successful attack *if they have enough time* (e.g., Rosencrance, 2011; Mitnick, 2024). The key to combatting that threat is to identify the points of access that an adversary can attack without being discovered before the adversary is able to identify and exploit those access points themselves.

Arguably, the most effective way of doing that is to form a set of red teams and have them perform war-game type exercises designed to estimate the least amount of time it would take for a knowledgeable adversary to succeed without being detected, and to uncover the corresponding pathway or scenario (Mitnick, 2024; Bailey et al., 2012). The red teams would be doing what a knowledgeable adversary would be doing: experimenting with ways to compromise the system starting with approaches that have worked in the past. Ideally, the red teams would include not only IT and cybersecurity personnel from the organization that is trying to protect itself against cyberattacks, but also personnel from Federal agencies charged with identifying and assessing cyber threats, acting in a supporting manner.

The use of red teams to perform actual simulations is superior to relying on analytical models that require knowledge about the scenarios, because most organizations are not inherently aware of the vulnerabilities of their system to remote access through ports of entry that may seem innocuous or may not be under their control. The difficulty, however, is that the statistical precision achieved from a Monte Carlo analysis of accident scenarios cannot be obtained for scenarios initiated by intentional acts, without presumptions about the nature of the probability distribution, unless a similar number of trails is undertaken. Obviously, this would be impractical when the method of simulation relies on human trial and error rather than integrated modeling, since it is impossible to think in terms of executing hundreds (if not thousands) of red-team trials.

As a fallback, use can be made of the fact, based on ample evidence in the literature, that the time to solve a difficult puzzle for the first time generally adheres to a particular kind of distribution, namely a *lognormal* distribution. For instance, probability distributions for the time it takes knowledgeable people to complete a chess game, perform repairs on a maintainable system, or solve Rubik's cube for the first time are typically lognormal (GeeksforGeeks, 2023; Chegg, 2024). If the assumption is made that the distribution for a red team's time-to-succeed is indeed lognormal (or, if shown to be more appropriate, a different type of distribution with a few quantifiable parameters), the number of red-team simulations needed to obtain a reasonably reliable distribution is drastically reduced. Section 9.3 will provide a demonstration of how an assumption of lognormality (or theoretically any other preferred distribution type) can be used to advantage in this process.

4.3 Determination and Display of the Organizational Risk Posture

4.3.1 Calculation of Risk Undesirability Scores

As described in Appendix A Sect. A.5, I use the term *risk undesirability score* to refer to the risk analysts' ranking of the degree to which each organizational objective is vulnerable to risk, given the current state of affairs. It is calculated based a collection of risk tolerance and acceptance levels (see Appendix A Sect. A.2) and calculated aggregate risks (see Appendix A Sect. A.4).

Suppose that risk tolerance and acceptance levels have been established per Chap. 3 and aggregate risks have been calculated for each objective that an organization has to satisfy and for each of several performance measure marker values. One way to derive a *risk undesirability score* from that information is illustrated in Fig. 4.4. A separate score is derived for each objective.

In the upper chart of Fig. 4.4, the risk tolerance and acceptance levels and the calculated exceedance risk are plotted for each of the several performance measure values that have been assigned a risk tolerance and a risk acceptance level (a total of four in this example). For visual purposes, the RTLs and RALs and the calculated exceedance probabilities are fitted to separate curves, the former referred to as the risk tolerance and risk acceptance curves and the latter being a portion of the aggregate risk CCDF.

To obtain the lower chart, the exceedance risk is normalized by subtracting RAL from it and dividing it by the difference between RTL and RAL, as described in Appendix A Sect. A.5. (In other words, the normalized risk is zero when $Risk = RAL$ and one when $Risk = RTL$.) Next, the normalized exceedance risk is plotted for each of the performance measure values, $PM_{1,k}$ through $PM_{4,k}$. Again, the results have been fitted to a curve for visual purposes. The risk undesirability score, then, is taken to be the maximum value of the normalized exceedance risk over the four PM values for which RTLs and RALs have been provided. (The corresponding equation is shown on the lower chart.)

It should be obvious that the means of calculating a risk undesirability score has to be tailored to the manner in which the stakeholders, managers, and committee of experts have provided their risk tolerance and risk acceptance postures. Other possible entry formats might necessitate other corresponding risk undesirability scoring metrics, some more complex than the one just described. For many purposes,

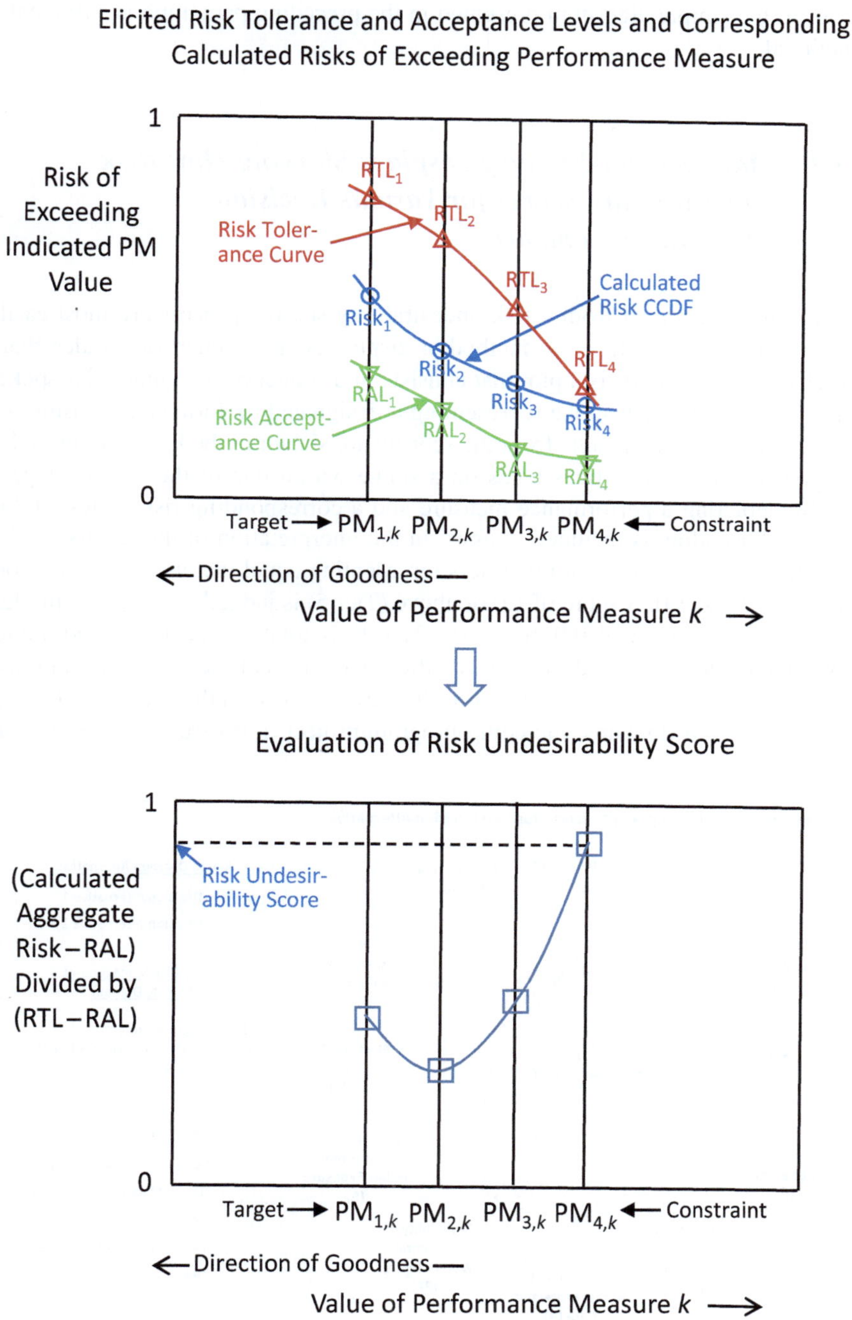

Risk undesirability score for $PM_k = \max(\rho_{1,k}, \rho_{2,k}, \ldots, \rho_{n,k})$,

where $\rho_{i,k} = (Risk_{l,k} - RAL_{i,k}) / (RTL_{l,k} - RAL_{i,k})$

Fig. 4.4 Illustration of a method for calculating risk undesirability scores

however, the simple algorithm presented in the preceding paragraph is sufficiently functional.

4.3.2 Management-Friendly Displays Showing How Risk Undesirability Scores for Various Decision Alternatives Compare

The results determined from a risk undesirability scoring process are most easily envisioned using a spider-chart method of display. A spider chart (aka radar chart, star chart, or web chart) is a plot that consists of a sequence of equiangular spokes (a.k.a. radii), with each spoke representing a designated performance measure. As shown in Fig. 4.5, the results from the scoring are shown in the form a multi-sided polygon. Each of its vertices lands on a spoke within one of the circular layers, thereby depicting a performance measure and a corresponding risk undesirability score. Color coding is included to assist in the interpretation of the results. In this case, the score is divided into five tiers representing equal increments in the score between 0.0 and 1.0. A score of 1.0 or above (Tier 5) is judged to be totally intolerable, whereas a score of 0.0 or below (Tier 1) is totally acceptable, and values between 0.0 and 1.0 are judged to have different degrees of marginal acceptability.

In Fig. 4.5, the performance measures that are shown span the entire spectrum of risk management domains, including program/project, infrastructure/institutional,

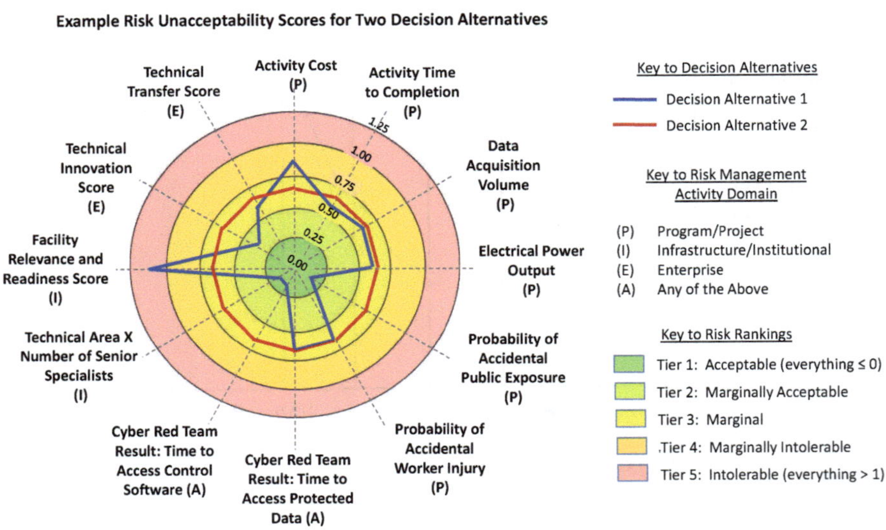

Fig. 4.5 Notional spider chart display comparing risk undesirability scores across P, I, and E risk management domains for each of two hypothetical decision alternatives

and enterprise. These are merely example performance measures that are not intended to be generic across all enterprises, but rather specific to the enterprise that is the subject of the analysis. The performance measures in the figure apply to a specific kind of high-tech organization in which exploration, data acquisition, power output, technical innovation, and technical transfer are important attributes.

Also, in Fig. 4.5, results are shown for two decision alternatives. In this example, Alternative 1 shows very low risk scores in several performance measures but very high risk scores in others. Alternative 2, on the other hand, shows a set of risk scores that are neither very low nor very high but are balanced across the spectrum of performance measures. In terms of satisfying the risk tolerance / risk acceptance postures elicited from the stakeholders, Alternative 2 is superior to Alternative 1 and would therefore be recommended to the decision makers as the preferable choice. Of course, if another alternative (Alternative 3, not shown) was found that provided uniformly lower risk undesirability scores than Alternative 2, it would be the preferred choice.

4.4 Determination of Risk Drivers and Identification of Mitigation and Control Options

A risk driver is a significant source of risk to one or more organizational objectives or mandated requirements. Contrary to common interpretation, a risk driver is not synonymous with a risk scenario, although risk scenarios can be risk drivers. However, identifying risk scenarios that contribute significantly to the aggregate risk does not necessarily identify the root causes of the risk concerns, and therefore may not point the way to identifying effective control or mitigation options. At a more basic and therefore more useful level, a risk driver might be a single performance parameter, a single event in a risk scenario, a single leading indicator, a faulty model or assumption, a set of performance parameters collectively, a set of events collectively, a set of leading indicators collectively, or some other combination of the above that, when varied over their range of uncertainty, causes the aggregate risk to change from acceptable or marginal to a higher level of unacceptability.

Risk drivers focus risk management attention on those potentially controllable situations that present the greatest opportunity for risk reduction. Often, risk drivers affect more than one individual risk and cut across more than one organizational unit. Risk drivers are determined after the integrated performance models have been created and executed by performing sensitivity analyses within the calculation of performance measures.

Following is an example list of potential risk drivers that might come forward while an analysis of aggregate risks and determination of their undesirability scores is being performed, especially when the risk management purview cuts across the program/project, infrastructure/institutional, and enterprise risk management activity domains:

1. Inadequate support for or excessive restrictions on needed acquisitions
2. Cross-cutting supply chain problems
3. Unexpected economic conditions
4. Excessive growth in process or operational complexity
5. Increase in time pressures due to changing requirements
6. Lack of management commitment to risk management, cross-cutting several projects
7. Model shortcomings or limitations in understanding
8. An externally or internally initiated cyberattack
9. Lack of specific components or subsystems needed to adequately address mission execution objectives
10. Lack of provisions in the design to address high-priority enterprise objectives such as technical innovation or extensibility
11. Unreliability of specific components, subsystems, or other provisions in the design leading to unacceptable failure rates
12. Lack of sufficient workforce capacity to address design or operational challenges in a timely manner
13. Insufficient provisions to address risks that cut across organizational boundaries
14. Excessive hardware or software complexity
15. Excessive integration complexity, particularly at subsystem interfaces
16. Excessive testing complexity given the state of the organization's test facilities
17. Lack of provisions for positive human intervention to manage unexpected challenges during operation
18. Insufficient diagnostics
19. Uncertainties in the human reliability models
20. Uncertainties in the load capacity, extent of deformation, or thermal properties of certain materials due to environmental conditions
21. Combinations of the above

The identification of risk drivers may sometimes need to be performed in two steps or more. The first step looks at each parameter, event, leading indicator, model limitation, or limitation in understanding individually to determine whether it is a driver by itself. If no drivers are identified by this process, then combinations of parameters, events, leading indicators, modeling limitations, and/or limitations in understanding are considered.

If the aggregate risks to objectives become excessive or unbalanced with respect to the organization's risk posture, internal controls or risk mitigation actions directed at the risk drivers may be attempted. Specific actions can take various forms, including changes in the design of a system that is in development, retrofits to existing systems, better quality control, additional testing, development of better analysis models, changes in manufacturing processes, changes in operating procedures, changes in management, formation of partnerships, proactive actions to inform and influence governing agencies, improved public relations, and cost sharing arrangements, to name a few.

Options for mitigating aggregate risks to objectives can be evaluated by assessing how the aggregate risks for the top organizational objectives would change as a result of incorporating the mitigation action. The process for performing this assessment includes the need to consider not only the positive effects that such options might have on some parts of a system or operation but also the possible unintended negative effects on other parts of the system or operation. The overall process of evaluation should rely on a combination of quantitative and qualitative analysis approaches. Examples will be provided in Sects. 10.3.1 through 10.3.3.

References

Bailey, T., et al. (2012). *Playing war games to prepare for a cyberattack* (Vol. 26). McKinsey on Business Technology.

Chegg. (2024). *Studies show that the length of time required for someone to solve a Rubik's cube puzzle for the first time is lognormally distributed.* www.chegg.com/homework-help/questions-and-answers/b-studies-show-length-time-required-someone-solve-rubik-s-cube-puzzle-first-time-lognormal-q154831128

GeeksforGeeks. (2023, November). *Lognormal distributions in business statistics.* www.geeksforgeeks.org/lognormal-distribution-in-business-statistics

LogRhythm. (2017, July). *NotPetya technical analysis.* LogRhythm Labs. www.logrhythm.com

McQuade. (2018, August). *The untold story of NotPetya, the most devastating cyberattack in history.* www.wired.com/story/notpetya-cyberattack-ukraine-russia-code-crashed-the-world

Mitnick. (2024). *Know your enemy: Top tips from Kevin Mitnick.* Business and Tech, Digital Security. www.futureofbusinessandtech.com/digital-security/know-your-enemy-top-tips-from-kevin-mitnic

Rosencrance, L. (2011, September). *Did 9/11 really improve cybersecurity?* www.nbcnews.com/id/wbna44432062

Temple-Raston, A. (2021, April). *A "worst nightmare" cyberattack: The untold story of the solarwinds hack.* www.npr.org/2021/04/16/985439655/a-worst-nightmare-cyberattack-the-untold-story-of-the-solarwinds-hack

Chapter 5
Adjusting the Predicted Aggregate Risks to Account for Unknown and Underappreciated Risks, Part 1: General Considerations, Cost, and Schedule

This chapter provides guidance relative to the lower right graphic in chart A of Fig. 4.1 and the top graphic in chart B of that figure. These graphics pertain to the development of correlations for the adjustments needed to account for U/U risk, based on historical data, and for the uncertainty in the correlations themselves. The particular purposes of this chapter are as follows:

- To outline the fundamentals of accounting for U/U risk as a contributor to the total aggregate risk;
- To summarize the principal leading indicators that have been found through many years of experience to correlate with the potential magnitude of the U/U risk;
- To present correlations of historical data that provide insight into the potential contribution from U/U risk to the total aggregate cost of a program or project; and
- To provide a table of adjustments to the calculated cost of a program or project to account for U/U risk, as a function of composite leading indicators.

5.1 Introduction

It is well known that scenario-based risk models are vulnerable to incompleteness, particularly for new systems with limited operational experience that may have unknown and/or underappreciated (U/U) sources of risk (Stamatelatos & Dezfuli, 2011; Benjamin et al., 2016). The incompleteness manifests itself when trying to compute the aggregate risk of not achieving an objective or performance measure by considering only known scenarios. The total aggregate risk, rather, emanates from two sources: the cumulative effect from known individual risk scenarios, and the cumulative effect from U/U risks. This additive relationship is illustrated schematically in Fig. 5.1.

A. S. Benjamin, *Integration of Project, Infrastructure, and Enterprise Risk Management*, Risk, Governance and Society 21,
https://doi.org/10.1007/978-3-031-85070-7_5

The cumulative effect from U/U risks may be estimated using leading indicators together with knowledge from historical experience and expert judgment about how the leading indicators correlate with undesired effects on the performance measures (Leveson, 2015). These correlations do not assume specific knowledge of the chain(s) of events leading from initiating event to end state. Rather, they recognize that the scenarios that result from U/U risk are hidden until such time as they may manifest themselves as a result of unexpected occurrences such as human errors of commission, phenomenological abnormalities, unknown failure modes, or arcane occurrences that cause unanticipated delays or cost overruns. Often, the correlations may involve a composite of individual leading indicators, each of which in itself may not lead to significant U/U risk but the combination produces a reinforcing effect.

This chapter identifies several leading indicators that correlate strongly with the potential magnitude of U/U risk in the various mission execution domains cited in Chap. 1. Chapters 5 and 6 then illustrate how to identify leading indicators and how to develop quantitative correlations that allow an estimation to be made, based on the leading indicators, for the potential magnitude of the effect of U/U risks on performance measure values. This provides the information needed to determine realistic adjustments to the calculated aggregate risk distributions. Guidance on how to implement these adjustments will be provided in Sects. 5.4, 6.2, and 8.3.5.

At the outset, the reader should appreciate that it is not the intent of this chapter to present prescriptive numerical guidelines for specifying U/U risk adjustments to be applied for any and all risk management activities. Rather, the chapter aims to provide an illustration of a process that will lead to useful and defensible adjustments that support the overall goals of risk management in service of the overall goals of risk leadership. Furthermore, it illustrates how data from a variety of

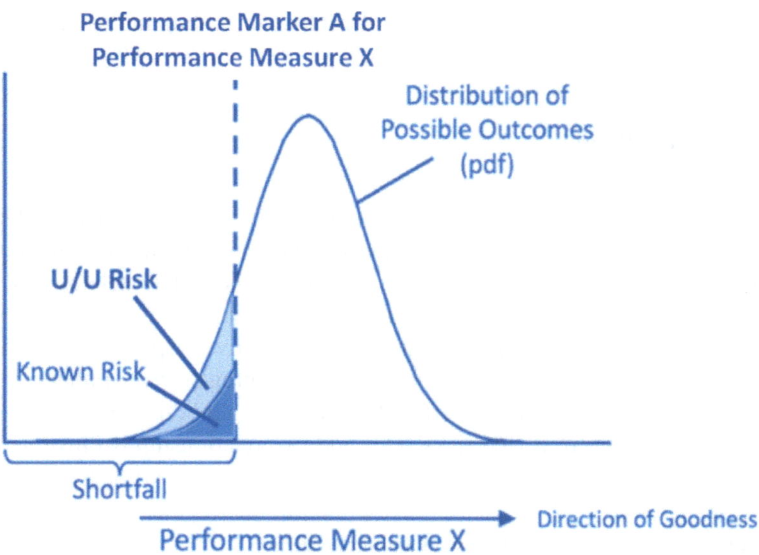

Fig. 5.1 Schematic representation of the results from an aggregation of known risk contributors and U/U risks

projects that are quite different from the project under consideration can be used to shed insight useful to the subject project.

5.2 Identification and Categorization of Leading Indicators of U/U Risk

There have been a number of attempts in the literature to equate the frequency of occurrence of disasters of various types with leading indicators of performance risk (Leveson, 2015; COSO, 2010; NASA, 2016; Benjamin, 2017). While the most pertinent leading indicators may vary somewhat according to the type of disaster (e.g., loss of lives vs. deleterious adversarial acts vs. acute cost overruns), many of them recurrently apply over all types of disasters. These more universal leading indicators tend to fall into four categories: general design factors, organizational factors, work environment factors, and external factors (Freaner et al., 2008; Benjamin et al., 2016; Benjamin, 2017).

5.2.1 General Design Factors

- *Complexity involving the interfaces between different elements of a system or process.* The concept of complexity is a term used by Charles Perrow to mean "baffling, hidden interactions" not anticipated in the original design that have the potential to "jump" from one subsystem to another (Perrow, 1999). For Perrow, technical systems more prone to failure are complex, tightly coupled systems that make the chain of events leading to a disaster incomprehensible to the operators. While normally being associated with physical systems, complexity is also pertinent to the interfaces between tightly interacting processes and to the protocols for communication between participating persons or groups.
- *Scaling beyond the domain of knowledge.* Barry Turner discusses three classes of technical design failures (Turner, 1984). The first involves designs that extend beyond the knowledge or experience of the designer and that stretch the limits of the previous design, either by scaling up an existing satisfactory design or scaling it down (see also Starbuck & Milliken, 1988). The second arises when designs are forced to operate under conditions that will ultimately lead to a much wider range of unknown variations and fluctuations of stress. The third pertains to inadequacies in the proper testing and/or prototyping of technological products or processes. Note again that scaling beyond the domain of knowledge is applicable not only to the operation of physical systems but also to the execution of technical or operational processes.
- *Fundamentally new technology or fundamentally new application of an existing technology.* Although most references do not cite new technology as a-priori a source of high risk, it is clear from many sources that systems developed from heritage technology tend to have a lower initial risk of catastrophic failure than similar systems that are fundamentally derived from new technology.

5.2.2 Organizational Factors

- *Priorities not focused toward safety and reliability.* Admiral Hyman Rickover established the principal characteristics of high-reliability organizations as (1) top management's commitment to safety as an organizational goal, (2) the need for personnel redundancy as well as engineering redundancy, (3) the development of a culture of reliability, and (4) the valuation of organizational learning (Sagan, 1993). When these principles are implemented, they have the effect of countering the potentially catastrophic consequences of interactive complexity and tight coupling that Perrow's theory predicts.
- *Hierarchical management style.* According to William Evan and Mark Manion, "[Avoidance of failures requires] a nonhierarchical and consultative relationship, at least in the planning stages and general operational processes. Two-way flows of information are especially essential in technological systems to maximize the sharing of information among all personnel regardless of position in the organizational hierarchy. … However, when a crisis arises in the operations of a technological system, the command model—namely, a hierarchical and single-directional mode of communication—[should] supersede the nonhierarchical consultative model in an effort to contain the crisis and limit the damages (Evan & Manion, 2002)."
- *History of management oversight problems.* Interfaces between different elements of a system provided by different suppliers or a process executed by different providers require stringent oversight by the managing agency and by contractor management. Inadequate oversight resulted in a catastrophic failure, for example, when the *Mars Climate Orbiter* failed on September 23, 1999, because one organization had written the flight system software to calculate thruster performance using metric units, while another was entering course correction and thruster data using Imperial units (Stephenson et al., 1999).

5.2.3 Work Environment Factors

- *Pressures to meet schedule and budget constraints.* Predominance of cost and schedule constraints over quality and carefulness are primary causes of U/U risk. According to I-S. Chang (see Chang, 1996) "[m]any current major space launch systems are based on early ballistic-missile technology, which regarded launch costs and schedules a higher priority than launch quality and reliability. The design of these space launch systems left much room for improvement, as demonstrated by launch failures of the past." Pressures to meet schedules and budget constraints were also cited in the Challenger Accident Investigation Board (CAIB) and the Aerospace Safety Advisory Panel (ASAP) reports on the Challenger and Columbia accidents (Challenger, 1986; Columbia, 2003), and time pressures are cited as a fundamental reason for high human error rates in virtually every model that is currently used for human reliability analysis.

5.2.4 External Factors

- Changes of requirements or funding profiles. The potential for U/U risk in all areas of execution is exacerbated by continual changes in requirements or funding profiles after an activity has been initiated, which in turn are influenced by evolving economic conditions and changes in Government leadership, both at national and local levels. In the public sector, such directional shifts might emanate from shifting priorities of the funding authorities (e.g., Congress and/or the President), whereas in the private sector, they might emanate from changing customer priorities. As stated in a report by the US Government Accountability Office (GAO) in reference to major defense acquisition programs at DoD, "it is after a program has formally started development that the myriad lower-level, technical requirements needed to complete a weapon system's design are defined, [and] it is the definition of these requirements … that leads to the realization that much more time and resources are needed" (GAO, 2015).
- Supplier or contractor financial difficulties. Stability in the supply chain for equipment and materials and in the services provided by contractors are essential components for maintaining adherence to cost and schedule constraints and for avoiding damage to an organization's reputation. According to Risk Optics, a risk management consulting firm for commercial businesses (RiskOptics, 2022): "Your supply chain is the core of your business, and any business interruptions can be devastating to your day-to-day operations. One small error or delay can bring your entire company to a halt and cause lost profits and irreparable damage to your reputation".

5.3 Example U/U Risk Correlations for Project Cost and Schedule

5.3.1 Robotic Space Missions and the James Webb Space Telescope

During the first decade-or-so of 2000, scientists and cost experts from the Aerospace Corporation developed a method for estimating the costs of robotic space missions from a set of system design attributes, component counts, and operational characteristics (Freaner et al., 2008; Bearden, 2008). As a key element of their work, they combined these attributes into a composite leading indicator, which they referred to as a "complexity index." The specific metrics incorporated into the complexity index for satellite missions, for example, included: the satellite launch mass; the design life; the maximum orbit distance from earth; the beginning and end of life power; the solar array area, cell type, and array/antenna configuration; the battery type and capacity; the structural material; the Attitude Determination & Control (ADC) System type; the number of payload instruments; the pointing accuracy and knowledge; the number of thrusters, the propulsion type; the downlink communications band; and the maximum data rate, solid state recorder memory, and thermal type. Subsequently they developed a computer tool, named "Complexity Based Risk Assessment (CoBRA)," with the specific capability of normalizing projects so that the cost and expected cost growth can be compared for equivalent project complexities.

Figure 5.2 shows the data they used and the best-fit correlation they developed for the cost versus complexity index for robotic space missions under $3 billion that were successfully launched and operated. Added to this (by the present author) are the 5th and 95th percentile correlations and two additional data points. The two points that are included for comparison purposes are the original development cost estimate for the James Webb Space Telescope (JWST) and the final actual development cost (All costs have been standardized to 2008 dollars.). The complexity index for the JWST was provided by the Aerospace Corporation (JWST, 2010). A similar figure pertaining to the effects of complexity on schedule will be provided in Sect. 8.3.5.

The first thing to notice is that the correlation between cost and complexity index has a high coefficient of determination ($R^2 = 0.88$ in that figure), but it should also be noticed that the complexity index is only partially indicative of the sources of cost increase. To wit, there is still approximately a factor-of-5 difference between the 5th and 95th percentiles. This variability in excess of the complexity index is explainable, at least in part, by the other leading indicators that are known to affect U/U risk, notably those listed in Sect. 5.2. Some of the likely culprits can be deduced by considering the challenges that NASA experienced with the development of the JWST.

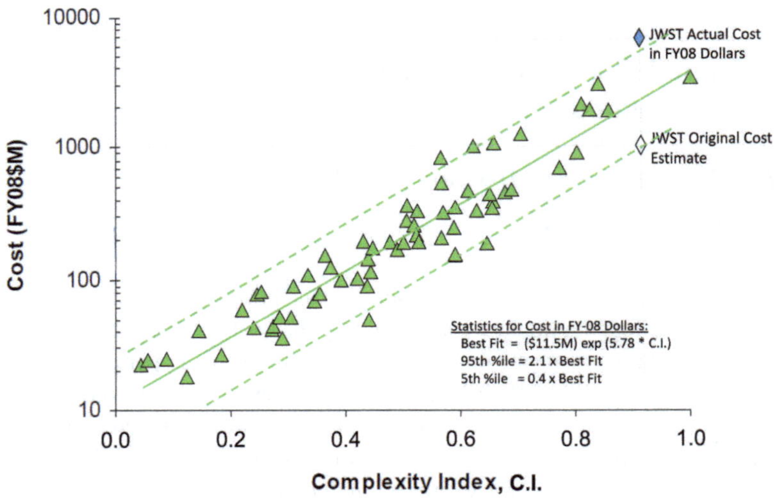

Fig. 5.2 Aerospace Corporation's correlation of project cost for satellite missions with a derived complexity index

The principal sources of information for this inquiry are Report GAO-15-100 on the JWST project, issued by the US Government Accountability Office in December 2014 to Congressional committees (GAO, 2014), and two online sources: "Manufacturing Issues Plague JWST," SpaceNews.com, November 2041 (SpaceNews, 2014), and "NASA Facing New Space Science Cuts," NationalGeographic.com, May 2014 (Foust, 2014). Also, the Jet Propulsion Laboratory report JPL D-67250 provides additional information on root causes of schedule and cost slippages, particularly those associated with the roles of NASA Headquarters and Goddard Space Flight Center in the 2010 timeframe (JWST, 2010). The problems associated with establishing realistic budgets were particularly emphasized. NASA management responded to the recommendations in the report in "NASA's Detailed Response to the James Webb Space Telescope Independent Comprehensive Review Panel Report," presently available on the web under that title.

5.3.1.1 Information Pertinent to JWST Schedule and Cost

- JWST is one of the most complex projects in NASA's history (GAO).
- In addition to the complex design, the scale of JWST's integration and test effort was more complex than most NASA projects. The cryocooler subsystem was particularly complex and challenging because of the relatively great distance between the cooling components and the need to overcome multiple sources of unwanted heat (GAO).
- The cryocooler subcontractor had experienced prior schedule delays and continued performance challenges (SpaceNews), and the schedule reserve for development of the cryocooler subsystem diminished in 2014 from 5 months to 0 months (GAO). The schedule reserve for the development of other subsystems had also diminished, but not as much as that for the cryocooler subsystem.
- The project entered fiscal year 2015 with approximately 40 percent of its cost reserves already committed, leaving fewer dollars available to mitigate other threats to the project schedule (GAO).
- The White House and Congress sparred about cancelling the JWST program and alternatively about cancelling other operating programs (e.g., SOFIA, Spitzer) to help fund JWST (National Geographic).

5.3.1.2 Corresponding Leading Indicators of U/U Risk

In addition to complexity of design, several other leading indicators of U/U risk identified in Sect. 5.2 are implied by the observations just listed. They include:

- Leading Indicator 1: Complexity involving the interfaces between different elements of a system or process.
- Leading Indicator 2: Scaling beyond the domain of knowledge.

- Leading Indicator 3: Fundamentally new technology or fundamentally new application of an existing technology.
- Leading Indicator 6: History of management oversight problems.
- Leading Indicator 8: Changes of requirements or funding profiles.

These additional indicators of U/U risk explain why the JWST final realized development cost shown in Fig. 5.2 was close to the 95th percentile of the cost uncertainty distribution for a design with a high complexity index. Based on Fig. 5.2, the combination of these additional leading indicators led to roughly a 100% increase in cost beyond what would be expected from a typical project with the same complexity index. Also based on Fig. 5.2, the original cost estimate for the JWST project was very optimistic.

The art of deriving composite leading indicators that incorporate all significant sources of U/U risk and of estimating the corresponding potential magnitude of the U/U risk will be taken up later in this chapter and the next, particularly in Sects. 5.4 and 6.2.

5.3.2 *Private Sector Projects and the Nelson Complexity Index*

Before their use for robotic spaceflight projects, a complexity index had been derived and applied successfully to the problem of estimating costs for the construction of oil refineries. The Nelson complexity index (NCI) was developed around 1960 (Nelson, 1960) and was based on an assessment of how each of about a dozen refining capabilities, if added to a basic refinery design, would add to the cost of construction.

For construction or development projects within the private sector, as well as in the public sector, it would be expected that the leading indicators listed in Sect. 5.2 should apply as contributors to U/U risk in addition to the system design complexity reflected in the complexity index. Depending on the nature of the enterprise, there may also be other significant leading indicators that are application-specific and that need to be deduced by analysis of data. Once they are deduced, correlations similar to Fig. 5.2 are applicable for determining an *overall* composite leading indicator that best incorporates the effects of all the significant leading indicators. Thereupon, the adjustments needed to accommodate the potential U/U risk can be estimated. This subject will be explored next.

5.4 Adjustments to Predicted Total Project or Activity Cost to Account for Unknown and Underappreciated Risks

Adjustments for total project or activity cost can be formulated using the type of data analysis and correlation processes described in Sect. 5.3.1. An example is presented in Table 5.1. The example includes costs for JWST as well as several other

NASA missions not included in Fig. 5.2 but reported in the open literature. Reporting for cost overruns incurred in private enterprises are not as readily available and so are not included in Table 5.1 under the Justification heading.

As mentioned in the preceding subsection, the example results are not intended to be prescriptive but rather to illustrate the process. Private companies wishing to develop realistic margins for their initial cost estimates could use a very similar process, but of course would rely more on data pertinent to their own experience.

Table 5.1 Example guidelines for estimating the mean value of the adjustment of the total project or activity cost to account for U/U risks

Condition Set Index	Applicable conditions	Mean value of adjustment	Justification
1	Least stressing conditions: Low integration and testing complexity; no use of fundamentally new or unproven technology; no scaling beyond the domain of knowledge; strong record of delivery on time and within budget for all participants; baseline cost estimate based on best-estimate assumptions rather than optimistic and consistent with experience; funding entity tolerant to budget overruns if unexpected conditions arise	~0	Results for projects included in Fig. 5.2 that experienced no or very low cost overruns
2	Closer to the least stressing conditions (row 1) than the most stressing conditions (row 5)	~0.3 times the mean value of the predicted total cost	NASA lunar trailblazer mission total cost was about 30% more than initial budget, as was the case for certain other NASA small satellite programs
3	Approximately equally divided between the least stressing conditions (row 1) and the most stressing conditions (row 5)	~1.0 times the mean value of the predicted total cost	The development cost for the ISS was twice the initial budget in inflation-corrected dollars
4	Closer to the most stressing conditions (row 5) than the least stressing conditions (row 1)	~2.5 times the mean value of the predicted total cost	The space shuttle actual cost per launch was about 3.1 times the original estimate in inflation-corrected dollars
5	Most stressing conditions: Very high integration and/or testing complexity; use of fundamentally new and unproven technology; history of contractor schedule delays and cost overruns; baseline cost estimate based on assumption that everything goes as planned; funding entity likely to be intolerant to budget overruns if unexpected conditions arise	~6.0 times the mean value of the predicted total cost	The development costs for JWST and the Hubble space telescope were 6 to 7 times the initial budget in inflation-corrected dollars. The fifth to ninety-fifth percentile variation in Fig. 5.2 is approximately the same

References

Bearden, D. (2008, June). Perspectives on NASA mission cost and schedule performance trends. In *NASA Goddard Space Flight Center System Engineering Symposium.*

Benjamin, A. (2017). *Enterprise risk and opportunity management: Concepts and step-by-step examples for pioneering scientific and technical organizations* (Finance series). Wiley.

Benjamin, A., et al. (2016, January). Developing probabilistic safety performance margins for unknown and underappreciated risks. *Journal of Reliability Engineering and System Safety, 145*, 329–340.

Challenger. (1986). *Report of the Presidential Commission on the space shuttle challenger accident.*

Chang, I.-S. (1996, March–April). Investigation of space launch vehicle catastrophic failures. *AIAA Journal of Spacecraft and Rockets, 33*(2).

Columbia. (2003). *NASA, Columbia Accident Investigation Board Report.*

COSO. (2010). *Developing key risk indicators to strengthen enterprise risk management.* Committee of Sponsoring Organizations of the Treadway Commission.

Evan, W., & Manion, M. (2002). *Minding the machines: Preventing technological disasters.* Prentice Hall.

Foust, J. (2014, May). *NASA facing new space science cuts.* National Geographic.

Freaner, C., et al. (2008, May). *An assessment of the inherent optimism in early conceptual designs and its effect on cost and schedule growth* European Aerospace Cost Engineering Working Group.

GAO. (2014, December). *James Webb space telescope project facing increased schedule risk with significant work remaining.* Government Accountability Office, GAO-15-100.

GAO. (2015, June). *Defense acquisition process: Military service chiefs' concerns reflect need to better define requirements before programs start.* Government Accountability Office, GAO-15-469.

JWST. (2010, October). *James Webb Space Telescope (JWST) independent Comprehensive Review Panel (ICRP) final report.* NASA Jet Propulsion Laboratory, JPL D-67250, Figure A.2.

Leveson, N. G. (2015, April). A systems approach to risk management through leading safety indicators. *Journal of Reliability Engineering and System Safety, 136*, 17–34.

NASA. (2016, November). *Organizational risk and opportunity management: Concepts and processes for NASA's consideration.* NASA/SP-2014-615.

Nelson. (1960). *Nelson Complexity Index.* https://en.wikipedia.org/wiki/Nelson_complexity_index, 2024, from original articles

Perrow, C. (1999). *Normal accidents: Living with high-risk technologies.* Princeton University Press.

RiskOptics. (2022, February). *What are the benefits of supply chain risk management?* RiskOptics. www.reciprocity.com

Sagan, S. (1993). *The limits of safety.* Princeton University Press.

SpaceNews. (2014, November). *Manufacturing issues plague JWST.* SpaceNews Article.

Stamatelatos, M., & Dezfuli, H. (2011, December). *Probabilistic risk assessment procedures guide for NASA managers and practitioners* (2nd ed.). NASA/SP-2011-3421.

Starbuck, W., & Milliken, F. (1988). Challenger: Fine tuning the odds until something breaks. *Journal of Management Studies, 25*(4), 319–340.

Stephenson, A., et al. (1999, November). *Mars climate orbiter mishap investigation board phase I report.* NASA.

Turner, B. (1984). *Man-made disasters.* Wykeham Press.

Chapter 6
Adjusting the Predicted Aggregate Risks to Account for Unknown and Underappreciated Risks, Part 2: Safety and Reliability

This chapter continues on from Chap. 5 and has the following purposes:

- To demonstrate correlations of historical data that provide insight into the potential contribution from U/U risk to the total aggregate frequency of life-threatening or mission-threatening accidents;
- To illustrate the synergism between and relevance of data from a variety of sources, including rocket launches, crewed space missions, nuclear reactor accidents, commercial and military system reliability performance, and human reliability performance; and
- To provide a table of adjustments to the calculated frequency of life-threatening or mission-threatening accidents to account for U/U risk, as a function of composite leading indicators.

The content of this chapter constitutes an update to my papers on the same subject in the Journal of Reliability Engineering and System Safety (Benjamin, 2016), the PSAM-12 Conference Proceedings (Benjamin et al., 2014), and in NASA's System Safety Handbook, Volume 2 (see Sect. 4.5 of NASA, 2014).

6.1 Case Studies

6.1.1 Launch Vehicle Failures

During the Cold War, there was an intense effort by both the United States and the Soviet Union to develop and test rocket launch vehicles capable of inserting payloads into orbit and sending men to the moon. As a result, there has been a long history of launch vehicle successes and failures for both US and USSR rocket launches since the 1950s. Between 1957 and 1999, for example, there were 390

A. S. Benjamin, *Integration of Project, Infrastructure, and Enterprise Risk Management*, Risk, Governance and Society 21,
https://doi.org/10.1007/978-3-031-85070-7_6

launch vehicle failures out of 4378 attempts throughout the world, most of them pertaining to American and Soviet rockets (Isakowitz et al., 1999). With such a large sampling of successes and failures, it becomes possible to perform meaningful statistical analyses of how the system failure rate has varied with time for a number of launch systems using a straightforward frequentist approach.[1] The results can help inform how leading indicators of U/U risk have contributed to the overall risk of failure. Examples of the results from this type of analysis are illustrated in Fig. 6.1 for three of the early launch systems.[2]

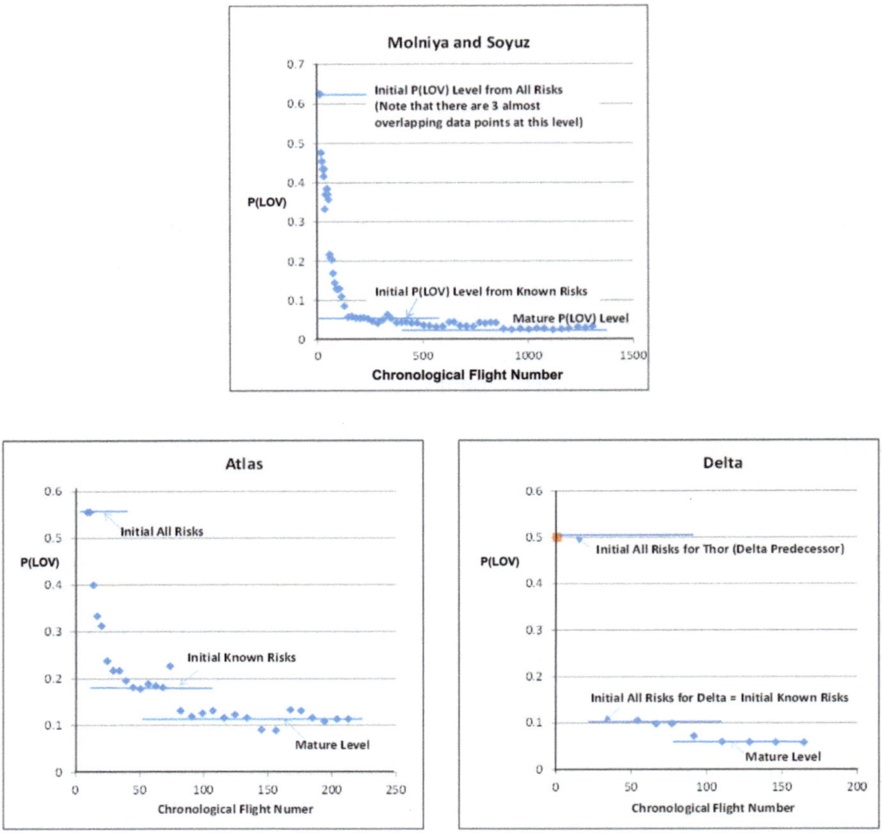

Fig. 6.1 Failure histories for the Molniya/Soyuz, Atlas, and Delta launch vehicles

[1] For comparison, Chang (1996) and Morse et al. (2010) used a Bayesian approach in examining the same data.

[2] In these case studies, I use the term "risk of failure" to mean the probability of failure during a single flight. This should be distinguished from the term "aggregate risk", which in this context refers to the risk that the probability of failure is greater than a specified constraint or target value. That is, "risk of failure" refers to a deterministic frequency obtained from actual data, and "aggregate risk" refers to the probabilistic uncertainty in that frequency.

The data for the Soviet launch vehicles in the top chart in Fig. 6.1, Molniya and Soyuz, are grouped together because they are of the same family and are very similar in design. Molniya/Soyuz was a launch system that was developed under extreme time constraints, and thus it is not surprising that the initial U/U risk contribution is very high. According to analysis of the data, the initial probability of loss of vehicle P(LOV) from all sources (known and U/U) was about 0.6, whereas the value of P(LOV) after the 100th launch was about 0.06 and remained so for another 300-or-so flights. Assuming that all important U/U risks had been wrung out by the 100th flight (a reasonable assumption), one can infer that the initial ratio of total risk (known plus U/U) to known risk alone was about a factor of 10 (i.e., 0.6 divided by 0.06). Subsequently, there was a steady slow decrease of P(LOV) to a value of about 0.03 after about 800 launches, from which one can postulate that improvements to the system after the 100th launch reduced the value of P(LOV) by another factor-of-two. Subsequently, P(LOV) remained more-or-less constant at 0.03 out through about 1300 flights.

Now looking at the lower-left chart, Atlas is a launch system that was developed by the US under moderately strong time constraints during the early phase of the Cold War. Using the same logic as described in the preceding paragraph, the ratio of the initial loss probability from all sources (known and U/U) to the initial loss probability from known sources was about 3, and the ratio of the initial risk from known sources to the mature-system risk was about 1.6.

Proceeding to the lower-right chart, Delta is a launch vehicle that was based on heritage technology. It was developed starting from the Thor vehicle with the objective of being more reliable. To accomplish this objective, components found to be unreliable in Thor were replaced by more reliable ones in Delta. A single point for Thor is included on the lower-right chart of Fig. 6.1 for references purposes. Its P(LOV) value of 0.5 is based on its average failure rate for its first year of operation (5 failures in 10 launches). By the time of Delta's first flight, the U/U risks associated with Thor's early failures were for the most case already shaken out. Thus, the initial loss probability for Delta from all sources was more-or-less equal to the initial loss probability from known sources. The ratio of the initial loss probability from known and U/U risks to the initial loss probability from just known risks was about 5, and the ratio of the initial loss probability from known sources to the mature-system loss probability was about 1.7.

Figure 6.2 focuses on the rate of burn-down of the U/U risks by considering only the portion of the data for which U/U risks significantly outweigh the known risks (i.e., the first 100-or-so launches). Also included in this comparison are data obtained from Space Shuttle experience, which will be more rigorously identified and analyzed in the next subsection. [It should be noted that loss-of-vehicle failures in the Space Shuttle program included not only launch vehicle failures (the Challenger accident) but also re-entry vehicle failures (the Columbia accident).] As shown, the rate of U/U risk burn-down (approximated by the burn-down rate for all risks) tends to be similar for all vehicles examined and can be characterized by an exponential relationship. For each launch vehicle, the total loss probability is reduced to about half of its initial value after about 40 flight and about one-sixth of its initial value

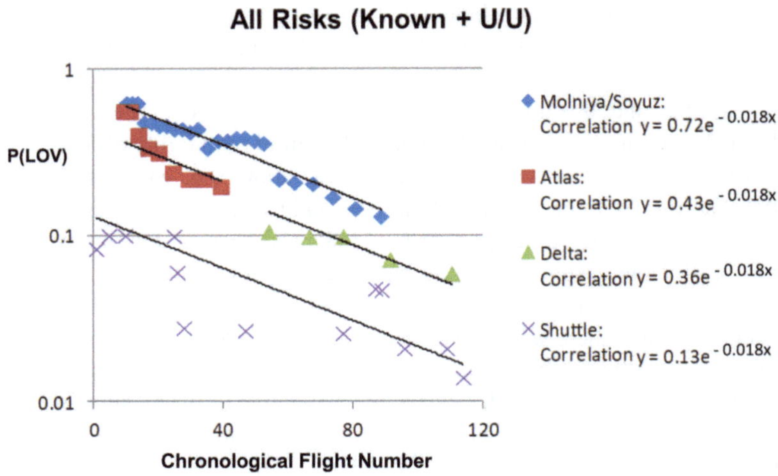

Fig. 6.2 Correlations of loss probability from all risks with chronological flight number

after about 100 flights. The reason the burn-down rate is more-or-less independent of flight program is because in all cases it has been the policy to eliminate each unknown and/or underappreciated risk through design or operational modifications as soon as the cause is manifested.

6.1.2 Space System Loss-of-Crew-and-Vehicle Accidents (the Space Shuttle)

A study published in 2011 by NASA scientist Teri Hamlin, et al., provides a basis for comparing the actual risk of loss of crew and vehicle, P(LOCV), prior to each flight with the risk that would have been calculated using known risks only (Hamlin et al., 2011). The calculations utilize the most recent Space-Shuttle full-scope PRA model (Thigpen, 2010) in a retrospective, or backward-looking, mode. The risk model, since it was created after the Columbia accident, includes the knowledge gained from the Challenger and Columbia accidents as well as from all the other flights that occurred during the Shuttle lifetime. Accordingly, the authors were able to use the risk model to estimate, in hindsight, what the total risk of LOCV was at the time of each launch. The result is shown in Fig. 6.3.

Also shown in Fig. 6.3 are results for P(LOCV) obtained from various risk assessments exercised in a predictive mode. The jagged nature of the retrospectively estimated total risks is caused by responses to unexpected events that resulted in changes to the design, fabrication, or operation of the system. For example, the first major change was the re-design after the Challenger accident, which resulted in a

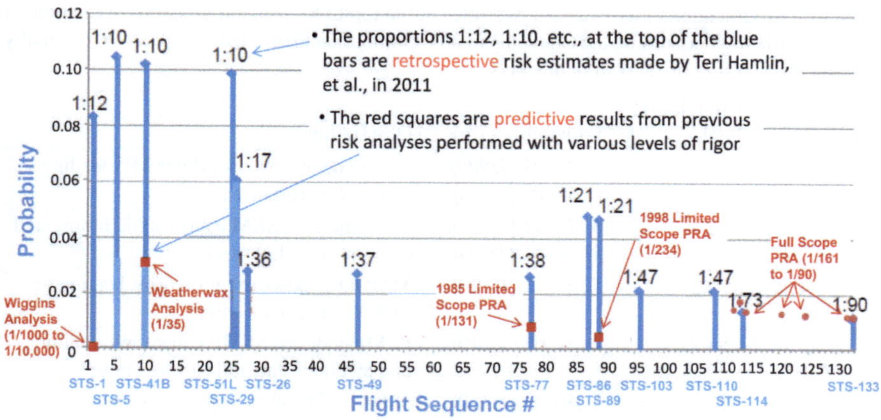

Fig. 6.3 Results of a retrospective analysis of P(LOCV) for the Space Shuttle compared to earlier PRA predictions

reduction of the total risk of LOCV by about 40%. Various other risk reductions occurred thereafter until STS-88, when NASA's compliance with an OSHA directive to discontinue the use of Freon in applying foam to the external tank unexpectedly caused a significant increase in the number of debris strikes on the Orbiter and raised the total risk of LOCV by about 80%. Return-to-flight changes after the Columbia accident during STS-107 resulted in a risk decrease of about 35% from its value before the accident.

The model used in the Hamlin analysis provided probabilities for all modeled accident scenarios that could lead to LOCV. A list of the top scenarios and their probabilities prior to the first flight, STS-1, is reproduced here in Table 6.1. Original values were calculated using the full-scale Shuttle probabilistic risk assessment (PRA) models modified to account for the design features at the time. Also shown in red are edited values based on assuming the Challenger and Columbia accidents had not occurred. For these values, the assessed values of P(LOCV) due to ascent debris strikes and solid-rocket-motor (SRM) catastrophic failure were changed to current day assessed values. The difference between the original and edited values is the effect of underappreciated risks based on the knowledge available at the time of STS-1. (Both the Challenger and Columbia accidents were caused by risks that were underappreciated rather than unknown.)

Using the process illustrated in Table 6.1, it is possible to infer the historical variation of known risks for the Shuttle. The result is shown in Fig. 6.4. The curve labeled "Backward-Look PRA Results Not Accounting for Revealed LOC Accidents," effectively deletes from the higher curve the information that was gleaned from the Challenger and Columbia accidents. The difference between the two curves provides an estimate of the relative contribution of risks that were unknown or underappreciated prior to each launch. As a point of reference, the actual risk before the 25th flight (STS-51L) was about a factor of 5 times the risk

Table 6.1 Modification of assessed probabilities of the top LOC accident scenarios at the time of the first shuttle flight assuming the Challenger and Columbia accidents had not occurred; originally assessed probabilities are shown in brackets

Rank	% of total	Cumulative total	Probability (1:n)	Description
1	53.5	53.5	***1.1E−03 (1:940)*** *[4.5E-02 (1:22)]*	Ascent debris strikes orbiter TPS leading to LOCV on orbit or entry
2	19.2	72.8	***6.5E−04 (1:1500)*** *[4.5E-02 (1:22)]*	SRM-induced SRM catastrophic failure and ejection seats fail to save crew
3	6.4	79.2	5.3E−03 (1:190)	MMOD strikes orbiter on orbit leading to LOCV on orbit or entry
4	5.0	84.2	4.2E−03 (1:240)	SSME-induced SSME catastrophic failure and ejection seats fail to save crew
5	3.7	87.9	3.1E−03 (1:320)	Orbiter APU shaft seal fracture entry and ejection seats fail to save crew
6	2.9	90.8	2.4E−03 (1:420)	APU external leak on entry and ejection seats fail to save crew
7	2.0	92.8	1.7E−03 (1:600)	Orbiter flight software error results in catastrophic failure during ascent and ejection seats fail to save crew
8	1.1	93.9	9.0E−04 (1:1100)	APU external leak on ascent and ejection seats fail to save crew
9	1.1	95.0	8.8E−04 (1:1100)	Orbiter APU shaft seal fracture ascent and ejection seats fail to save crew
10	0.8	95.7	6.3E−04 (1:1600)	SSME-induced safe shutdown of the SSME and ejection seats fail to save crew
Total		100.0	***2.4E−02 (1:42)*** *[8.3E-02 (1:12)]*	

Nomenclature for the Above Table: *TPS*, thermal protection system; *SRM*, solid rocket motor; *SSME*, space shuttle main engine; *LOCV*, loss of crew or vehicle; *MMOD*, micrometeoroids and orbital debris; *APU*, auxiliary power unit

that would have been predicted if a detailed PRA had been conducted at that time (i.e., 0.10 / 0.02 = 5). The difference between the two curves just before the 25th flight is principally attributable to risks that were later elucidated by the Challenger and Columbia accidents. Similarly, the actual risk before the 87th flight (STS-86) was about a factor of 3 times the risk that would have been predicted if a detailed PRA had been conducted at that time (i.e., 0.048 / 0.016 = 3 in Fig. 6.4).

6.1.3 Commercial Nuclear Reactor Fuel Melting Accidents

Although commercial nuclear reactors are entirely different from spacecraft in design, operation, and regulation, both industries are examples of high risk endeavors with a history of few catastrophic accidents.

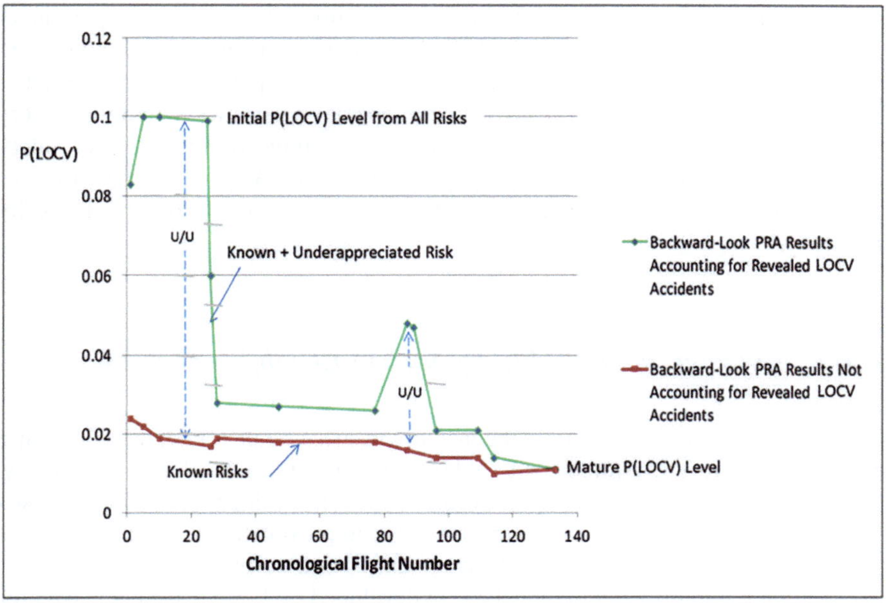

Fig. 6.4 Comparison of retrospective analyses of shuttle risks accounting for versus not accounting for revealed LOC accidents

World-wide, there have been three commercial nuclear reactor accidents resulting in core melting (Three-Mile-Island, Chernobyl, and Fukushima Daiichi) in about 15,000 reactor years of operation as of March 2011, the date of the last of these accidents, a rate of 1/5000. By comparison, the Reactor Safety Study, which was the first modern, full-scope, detailed PRA ever performed, predicted that the risk of a US commercial nuclear reactor accident resulting in core melting per reactor year was 1/20,000 (Rasmussen et al., 1975). Thus, the actual demonstrated reactor risk of core melting at that time was about 4 times as high as that predicted in the Reactor Safety Study (i.e., 1/5000 divided by 1/20,000). However, only one of the three accidents (Fukushima) can be categorized as emanating from a known risk.[3] TMI, on the other hand, progressed to a core melt accident mainly because of inadequate diagnostic equipment in the control room, a factor that was not included in the Reactor Safety Study assessment of the probability of not receiving emergency core cooling water. Chernobyl was precipitated by human errors of commission that were beyond the scope of existing risk analyses. Therefore, the rate of core melting from known risks has been about 1/15,000 reactor years, a number that is comparable to the Reactor Safety Study.

[3] Some would say that the Fukushima accident was an underappreciated risk, but since there has been only one accident of that type resulting in core melting, there is no way of disproving that it was not simply a random occurrence of an extremely rare event.

One could argue that the total-to-known risk ratio of 4 is an average over about 50 years of calendar time and that initially the ratio of unknown or underappreciated risks to known risks was considerably higher. For example, TMI and Chernobyl occurred within the first 4000 years of reactor operation worldwide, implying a core melt accident rate of 1/2000, or 10 times the value estimated in the Reactor Safety Study. Therefore, it seems prudent to say that the total risk at the time the Reactor Safety Study was performed was 4 to 10 times as high as the risk predicted by the study.

6.1.4 Commercial and Military System Reliability Growth

Reliability growth is a measure of the increase in success rate (or decrease in failure rate) from the time a system is first fielded to the time it has developed its maturity. As discussed earlier, the majority of the growth is usually due to the wringing down of U/U risks, but a lesser fraction may be due to improvements in design and fabrication that result from technology development and maturity.

The first reliability growth models were developed by J. T. Duane using data for electrical power and aircraft systems (Duane, 1964). As shown in Fig. 6.5 (e.g., the hydro-mechanical data in the figure), these data indicated that initial risks were as much as a factor of 12 times mature program risks. If a factor of 2 is attributable to improved technology (similar to the factor of 2 reduction in known risks for launch vehicles in Fig. 6.1 and the Space Shuttle in Fig. 6.4), the corresponding ratio of

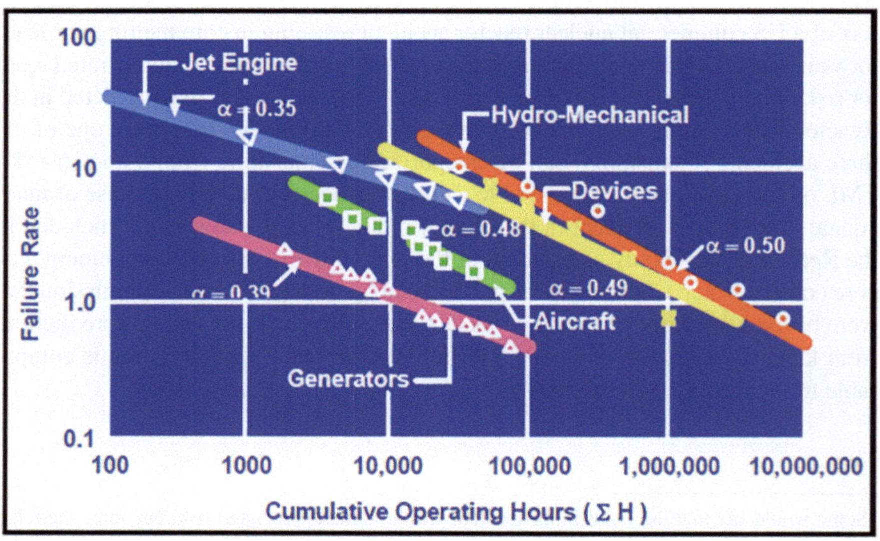

Fig. 6.5 Commercial and military system reliability growth data, from Duane (1964)

total to known risk for hydro-mechanical devices in Fig. 6.5 would be approximately 6.

Somewhat later in time, reliability growth models were developed as part of the Army Materiel Systems Analysis Activity, or AMSAA (Ellner & Trapnell, 1990) and published in detail in MIL-HDBK-139A. These were based on reliability growth data for Army systems including helicopters, missiles, navigation systems, and ground radar. The AMSAA data indicated that initial risks were as much as a factor of 6 times mature program risks. Assuming a factor of 2 for technology development, the corresponding ratio of total to known risk would be approximately 3.

6.1.5 Human Reliability and Performance Shaping Factors

Many of the catastrophic accidents and total operational system failures caused by unknown and/or underappreciated risks are the result of a combination of factors of which human error is a prime contributor. Two types of human error that can lead to catastrophic results are generally recognized in the literature: errors of commission and errors of omission. Errors of commission are defined by Swain (1983) as: "the incorrect performance of a system-required task/action given that a task/action is attempted, or the performance of some extraneous task/action that is not required by the system and that has the potential for contributing to a system failure (e.g., selection of a wrong control, sequence error, timing error)." As such, errors of commission can be interpreted as a class of causation mechanisms that are similar to unknown risks: they are not anticipated, therefore are not usually modeled in PRAs, and frequently lead to unpredictable results. On the other hand, errors of omission are defined in the same reference as: "the failure to initiate performance of a system-required task/action (e.g., skipping a procedural step or an entire task)." Prior to the development of performance shaping factors, these errors constituted a particular type of underappreciated risk: they were anticipated and could be modeled in PRAs but their probabilities of occurrence were not accurately estimated.

For example, performance shaping factors identified in the Cognitive Reliability and Error Analysis Method (CREAM) for Human Reliability Analysis (HRA) indicate that most of them concern organizational issues that if inadequately managed can produce stress or inadequate communication of information (Hollnagel, 1998). According to the CREAM report, available time is the most critical performance shaping factor. A continuously inadequate availability of time is assessed to result in a factor-of-5 increase in the human error probability for all four types of cognitive activities considered by CREAM: observation, interpretation, planning, and execution. This implies that the effect of inadequate time on the portion of U/U risks associated with human errors could be as high as a factor of 5. As noted earlier, many of the U/U risks that have occurred in the space and commercial nuclear reactor programs have involved human errors of one kind or another, and the same can be shown to be true in other sectors.

Performance shaping factors other than time availability were also found to have up to a factor-of-5 effect on the human error probability for certain cognitive activities. Inadequate training and preparation, too many simultaneous goals (over capacity), deficient crew collaboration quality, inappropriate man-machine interface (MMI) design, and deficiencies in operational support have each been shown to lead to excessive human error probabilities in various areas of activity including planning, execution, and observation.

6.2 Adjustments to Predicted Probability of a Life-Threatening Accident to Account for Unknown and Underappreciated Risks

When an accident or unexpected failure occurs, the activities undertaken to prevent further accidents or failures of that type involve identifying the causes and instituting design changes, operational changes, and/or administrative controls to prevent them from happening again. Most of the time, these changes and controls are formulated to affect a broader spectrum of accidents or failures than just the one that is promulgating the action. For example, after the Space Shuttle Columbia accident, one of the main corrective actions was to photographically scan the surface of the shuttle while in orbit to detect damage caused by foam debris so as to be able to initiate astronaut extra-vehicle activities to repair any damage that night be significant enough to endanger re-entry. This corrective action had the effect of protecting not only against foam debris impacts but also against damage caused by micrometeoroids and orbital debris (MMOD), which is considered to be one of the main sources of risk for orbiting space vehicles. In addition, the return-to-flight activities associated with Columbia included a restructuring of the management within NASA to address generic shortcomings identified in the Columbia Accident Investigation Board (CAIB) report (Columbia, 2003). Similarly, after the occurrence of the Three Mile Island (TMI) nuclear reactor accident, corrective action included redesigning the control room diagnostics to be more informative and user-friendly. These types of corrective action have a generic character that provides protection against many potential accident scenarios or causes of failure.

The implication is that the reduction of known risks also reduces U/U risks. Clearly, however, that reduction is only possible when the protection against the known risks has a generic character as was the case for Columbia and TMI. It would not be the case if the reduction of known risks was focused very narrowly on the specific events contained in a known scenario.

Based on the types of data analyses presented in the preceding sections, spanning multiple areas of execution, and accounting for the leading indicators identified in Sect. 5.2 and alluded to throughout the preceding subsections in this chapter, it is possible to derive guidelines for determining appropriate adjustments for loss probabilities that are derived by considering known risks. As an aid to risk practitioners

Table 6.2 Example guidelines for estimating the mean value of the adjustment of the loss probability, at the time of operational start-up, to account for U/U risks

Condition set index	Applicable conditions	Mean value of adjustment	Justification
1	Systems that can take credit for at least 125 actual cycles of operation of the same or equivalent systems with positive indication that the risk has leveled off to a mature system value	~0	Results for Shuttle, Atlas, Delta, and Molniya/Soyuz after 125 spaceflights
2	New systems that are developed and operated under at most mild time pressure, with reliability and safety having a higher priority than cost and schedule, with an inclusive management structure, and with a design philosophy that does not involve significantly new technology or new integration of an existing technology or scaling of an existing technology beyond the domain of knowledge or tight functional coupling	~1 times the mean value of the predicted loss probability	Results for Delta, first 75 flights
3	New systems that are developed or operated under at least moderate time pressure, with cost and schedule having at least an equal priority with reliability and safety, and with a tendency for the management structure to be hierarchical, but with a design philosophy that does involve significantly new technology or new integration of an existing technology or scaling of an existing technology beyond the domain of knowledge or tight functional coupling	~2 times the mean value of the predicted loss probability	Results for Atlas, first 75 flights.
4	New systems that are developed or operated under significant time pressure, and with a design philosophy that involves either new technology or new integration of an existing technology or scaling of an existing technology beyond the domain of knowledge or tight coupling, but with reliability and safety having a higher priority than cost and schedule, and with an inclusive management structure,	~2 times the mean value of the predicted loss probability	Results for shuttle retrospectively, first 75 flights, if safety had been the top priority with management

(continued)

Table 6.2 (continued)

Condition set index	Applicable conditions	Mean value of adjustment	Justification
5	New systems that are developed or operated under significant time pressure, with cost and/or schedule having at least an equal priority with reliability and safety, with a tendency for the management structure to be hierarchical, and with a design philosophy that involves either new technology or new integration of an existing technology or scaling of an existing technology beyond the domain of knowledge or tight coupling	~ 4 times the mean value of the predicted loss probability	Results for shuttle, first 75 flights. Also nuclear reactor experience, military and commercial system reliability experience, and human reliability experience.
6	New systems that are developed or operated under extreme time pressure, with cost and/or schedule having significantly higher priority than reliability and safety, with a highly hierarchical management structure, and involving either new technology or new integration of an existing technology or scaling of an existing technology well beyond the domain of knowledge	Up to 9 times the mean value of the predicted loss probability	Results for Molniya/ Soyuz first 75 flights

who need to determine adjustments and managers who need to understand them, Table 6.2 provides representative quantitative guidelines for performance adjustments that follow from the data analyses provided in this chapter. As mentioned at the beginning of this chapter, the reader should understand that what is presented here is not intended to be a set of prescriptive guidelines that apply to all execution activities, but rather an illustration of a process that will lead to useful and defensible results in support of the overall aims of risk management in service to the overall goals of risk leadership.

6.3 Closing Thought on U/U Risk Correlation Uncertainty

Table 6.2 provided examples that enable estimates of the effects of U/U risks on performance measures to be inferred at a mean, or average level, On the other hand, there is also the matter of uncertainties in the correlations themselves. This issue was previously brought to attention in Fig. 4.1 of Sect. 4.1 (see Chart A, lower right), where an uncertainty distribution for the U/U adjustment was added into the collection of other uncertainty distributions to be sampled, namely model uncertainty, model input uncertainty, event frequency uncertainty, and leading indicator uncertainty. Realistic estimation of the correlation uncertainty for the U/U adjustment can be inferred from the correlation coefficient, commonly referred to as the *r* value of the correlation. Information on the calculation and interpretation of *r* values may be found in many statistical publications (e.g., Moore, 2021; Weisstein, 2020).

The subject of U/U risk and its importance with respect to assessing risk acceptability at all levels of the enterprise will be visited again in each remaining chapter.

References

Benjamin, A. (2016, January). Developing probabilistic safety performance margins for unknown and underappreciated risks. *Journal of Reliability Engineering and System Safety, 145*, 329–340.

Benjamin, A., et al. (2014, June). Developing probabilistic safety performance margins for unknown and underappreciated risks. In *Proceedings of the Probabilistic Safety Assessment and Management Conference, PSAM-12*.

Chang, I.-S. (1996). Investigation of space launch vehicle catastrophic failures. *AIAA Journal of Spacecraft and Rockets, 33*(2).

Columbia. (2003). *NASA, Columbia Accident Investigation Board Report.*

Duane, J. (1964). Learning curve approach to reliability monitoring. *IEEE Transactions on Aerospace, 2*, 563–566.

Ellner, P., & Trapnell, B. (1990, June). *AMSAA reliability growth data study*. US Army Materiel Systems Analysis Activity, Interim Note IN-R-184.

Hamlin, T., et al. (2011). Shuttle risk progression: Use of the shuttle PRA to show reliability growth. In *AIAA SPACE Conference & Exposition*.

Hollnagel, E. (1998). *Cognitive reliability and error analysis method (CREAM)*. Elsevier.

Isakowitz, S., et al. (1999). *International reference guide to space launch systems* (3rd ed.). American Institute of Aeronautics and Astronautics.

Moore, D. S. (2021). *The basic practice of statistics* (9th ed.). W.H. Freeman and Company.

Morse, E., et al. (2010). Modeling launch vehicle reliability growth as defect elimination. In *AIAA SPACE 2010 Conference & Exposition*.

NASA. (2014, November). *NASA system safety handbook, Volume 2, System safety concepts, guidelines, and implementation examples*. NASA/SP-2014-612.

Rasmussen, N. C., et al. (1975, October). *Reactor safety study. An assessment of accident risks in U. S. commercial nuclear power plants*. U.S. Nuclear Regulatory Commission, WASH-1400.

Swain, A., et al. (1983). *Handbook of human reliability analysis with emphasis on nuclear power plant applications*. Sandia National Labs SAND80-0200, USNRC NUREG/CR-1278.

Thigpen, E. (2010, November). *Shuttle PRA iteration 3.3 changes notebook*. NASA Internal Document, Johnson Space Center.

Weisstein, E. W. (2020). *Statistical correlation*. Wolfram MathWorld. mathworld.wolfram.com/StatisticalCorrelation.html

References

Chapter 7
Processes for Optimally Balancing Risks Against Opportunities in Strategic Portfolio Planning

The purposes of this Chapter are as follows:

- To provide introductory perspective on how the risk modeling and analysis needs for strategic portfolio planning differ from those for system design, development, and operation, in terms of the relative degree of reliance on quantitative vs. qualitative techniques;
- To review the methodology used by NASA's Review of Human Spaceflight Committee (the so-called Augustine Committee) to assess the relative benefits and costs of alternative spacecraft programs for NASA;
- To extend the Committee's methodology to include risk posture, so as to risk-inform the selection of a comprehensive portfolio of programs rather than rely just on relative comparisons;
- To introduce the concept of benefit significance scores as measures of opportunity for aspirational enterprise objectives (e.g., community involvement, technology transfer, etc.), and to provide examples of how to conduct elicitations of high-level planning authorities to quantify the benefit significance scores and to determine associated risk tolerance levels and risk acceptance levels;
- To illustrate how the Monte Carlo analysis for assessing the aggregate risks in individual programs may be expanded to apply to enterprise-level program portfolios containing multiple program elements and to objectives that include both containment of aggregate risks and promotion of enterprise opportunities; and
- To demonstrate the use of spider charts to display the resulting risk and opportunity posture for each candidate strategic portfolio in a management friendly format

A. S. Benjamin, *Integration of Project, Infrastructure, and Enterprise Risk Management*, Risk, Governance and Society 21,
https://doi.org/10.1007/978-3-031-85070-7_7

7.1 The Similarities and Differences Between Risk Analyses Needed for Strategic Portfolio Planning vs. Design, Development, and Operation of a System

Just as the design, development, and operation of a complex system requires an analysis of risks across all risk management activity domains and the consideration of all risk types within each domain, so does the selection of a strategic portfolio of programs from among a variety of portfolio alternatives. The main differences between managing risk for a complex system versus designing a strategic program portfolio come down to the specification of performance measures and the selection of analysis methods. For system design, development, and operation, the analyses tend to be almost exclusively quantitative because of the quantitative nature of the performance measures: e.g., weights, capacities, technical capabilities, safety criteria, schedule, and cost. For portfolio design, many of the performance measures are more qualitative in nature: e.g., adherence to stakeholder preferences and subjective rankings of the long-term benefits provided by one concept versus those provided by another. Thus, the optimal balance of risks versus benefits for one portfolio concept versus another requires quantitative methods combined with the judgment and deliberation of technical experts, financial experts, and management authorities, who together bring the requisite knowledge and experience to make the best decisions. The next two sections and their subsections illustrate and elaborate upon this point.

7.2 The Augustine Committee Assessment of Alternative Human Spacecraft Programs for NASA

In 2009, a blue-ribbon committee headed by Norman Augustine, former Chairman and CEO of Lockheed Martin Company and Chairman of the National Academy of Engineering, performed and published a study (Augustine et al., 2009), requested by the White House Office of Science and Technology Policy and entitled "Seeking a Human Spacecraft Program Worthy of a Great Nation." According to the preface, the committee was charged with conducting an independent review of the current program of record and providing alternatives to that program that would ensure that "the nation is pursuing the best trajectory for the future of human spaceflight—one that is safe, innovative, affordable and sustainable."

The committee considered a number of proposed near-term to mid-term (10-year) future directions for NASA, which included:

- (Option 1) Program of Record—Constrained to the 2010 budget with minor modifications and founded upon the Constellation program
- (Option 2) ISS + Lunar—Would extend the ISS until 2020 and begin a program of lunar exploration using a derivative of the Ares V launch vehicle

- (Option 3) Program of Record—Less constrained to the 2010 budget in order to allow for extension of the Space Shuttle program into 2011 and de-orbiting of the ISS in 2016.
- (Option 4A) Moon First—Ares—Similar to Option 2 but raises the priority of lunar exploration as a training ground for eventual missions to Mars
- (Option 4B) Moon First—Extend Shuttle—Similar to Option 4A but extends the Space Shuttle to 2014 and includes the development of a heavy-lift launch vehicle
- (Option 5A) Flexible Path—Ares—Visits a series of locations and objects in the inner solar system as preparation for missions to Mars, and uses the derivative of the Ares V launch vehicle
- (Option 5B) Flexible Path—EELV—Same as Option 5A but uses the Evolved Expendable Launch Vehicle (EELV) as heritage for a commercial heavy-lift launch vehicle
- (Option 5C) Flexible Path—Shuttle Derived—Similar to Option 5A but uses a Shuttle-derived heavy-lift launch vehicle

For each, they considered 12 evaluation criteria consisting of:

1. Exploration Preparedness—Does the program provide the opportunity to demonstrate technology, systems, and operations that will be important in future exploration, most particularly missions to Mars?
2. Technology Innovation—Does the program enable technology maturation, foster the development of new modes of operation, and create new technologies and new engineering knowledge that will enhance exploration, and will it be of use to stakeholders beyond NASA?
3. Science Knowledge—Does the program address research areas critical to the scientific community as defined by the National Academies' decadal survey priorities?
4. Expanding and Protecting Human Civilization—Does the program lead to the possibility of a sustained off-planet human presence, and does it support research for (a) physiological effects associated with radiation and zero-g or low-g and (b) psychological effects associated with long-duration remote exploration?
5. Economic Expansion—Does the program encourage and stimulate a growing, profitable industrial base, provide an opportunity for sustained commercial engagement, and help the U.S. development and production capabilities?
6. Global Partnerships—Does the program provide the opportunity to strengthen and expand international partnerships in the human spaceflight program?
7. Public Engagement—Does the program have the potential to inspire current and future generations, educate the public about the opportunities and societal benefits gained from space missions, and motivate young people to pursue an education in science, technology, engineering, and mathematics?
8. Schedule and Programmatic Risk—Is the program likely to deliver a stated exploration capability on schedule by exploiting a technical design that is robust and technologies that are reasonably mature, with sufficient schedule and technical margins to support risk mitigation?

9. Mission Safety Challenges—Does the program produce mission scenarios that have high risk and complexity with high potential impact on crew safety and mission reliability?
10. Workforce Impact—Does the program impact the status of critical skills across the nation and the ability to retain or develop the needed critical skills both nationally and within NASA?
11. Programmatic Unsustainability—Does the program not have a broad base of support for ongoing future funding, have an unmanageable impact on pre-existing contracts, or not enable a smooth transition from current human space-flight operations?
12. Life-Cycle Cost—Does the program not stay within or close to the FY 2010 budget.

Of these, the last five basically concerned agency-level *programmatic* objectives, focused on *minimizing aggregate risk* to program schedule (Number 8), safety and mission reliability (Number 9), workforce skills and availability (Number 10), funding support and program sustainability (Number 11), and life-cycle cost (Number 12). The first seven, however, mostly emphasized agency-level *aspirational* objectives, focused on *promoting opportunities* to develop and demonstrate new technology that will be needed in the future (Numbers 1 and 2), perform scientific research of national priority (Number 3), support a long-term human presence on celestial bodies far from Earth (Number 4), stimulate the national economy (Number 5), promote partnerships with commercial and global entities (Numbers 5 and 6), and stimulate the public's imagination (Number 7).

Quoting from the report, "the committee deliberated at length in public meetings about the advantages and disadvantages of each option with respect to these 12 points. Wherever possible, quantitative analytical assessments were utilized to inform the ratings. In the end, however, it was usually necessary to interpret the available information through the considered judgments of the 10 members of the committee, based on their experience in space matters. The results were captured using a score of −2 (least benefit), −1, 0, 1, or 2 (most benefit) for each attribute of each integrated option."

The results of the committee's deliberations were presented via spider charts, some of which are shown in Fig. 7.1. It is important to note that their results were based on a ranking of the relative benefit of each program option compared to the others, without explicit consideration for the absolute benefit, which would require the specification of performance measure constraints and/or targets. Nor did it explicitly consider risk for most of the performance measures, or define what would constitute acceptable, marginal, or intolerable risk, which would require specification of risk tolerance and acceptance levels. Rather, the five levels of benefit were founded on a non-risk-based ranking scheme that relied on arguments about whether one program option, when compared with another, would be more, or less, conducive to producing notable achievements in the rather broad evaluation areas being considered. The subject of introducing performance measures, constraint and target values, aggregate risk, risk tolerance levels, and risk acceptance levels into strategic analyses of the type pursued by the Augustine committee will be taken up in the next section.

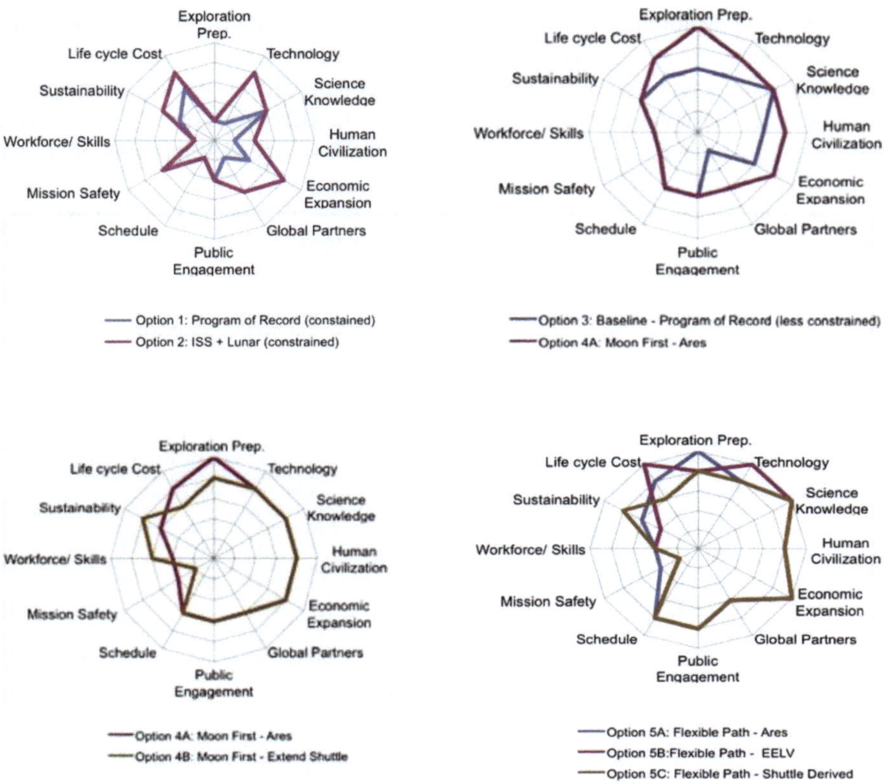

Fig. 7.1 Spider charts showing results obtained by the Augustine committee and reported in "Seeking a Human Spaceflight Program Worthy of a Great Nation"

7.3 Going Beyond the Augustine Committee Assessment of Relative Benefits to Risk-Inform the Selection of a Comprehensive Portfolio of Programs

7.3.1 Introduction

As mentioned in Sect. 7.1, a main difference between designing a risk-informed strategic program portfolio versus managing risk for a complex system involves the need to deal not only with performance measures that apply to enterprise-level or agency-level programmatic objectives, which tend to be quantitative in nature, but also with performance measures that apply to enterprise/agency-level aspirational objectives, which tend to be more qualitative in nature.

For the *programmatic objectives*, which deal largely with cost, schedule, safety and security, workforce alignment, and technical performance, a significant challenge exists in formulating and implementing reliable quantitative models before detailed program plans and design concepts are available. The problem is akin to the challenge of developing estimates of the aggregate risks when unknowns dominate the risk landscape. As shown in the previous two chapters, insights gained from analogous situations, and the informed use of such insights, is the key to success.

Figure 7.2 illustrates the types of models needed to address one of the programmatic performance measures, namely lifecycle cost, prior to the development of design

AFFORDABILITY METHODOLOGY EMPLOYED BY THE AEROSPACE CORPORATION

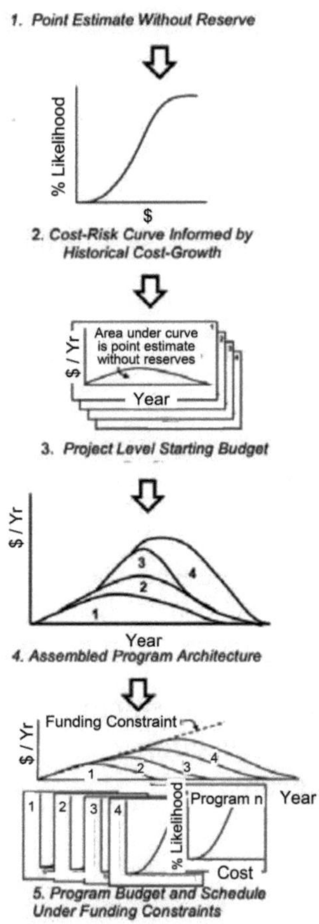

1. A process for comparing in-development programs with conceptual programs is applied. Point estimates for each project element in a program are collected and reserves are removed. Point estimates are informed by the Program of Record (POR), other related programs, prior NASA studies, and HSF Committee briefings.

2. Cost growth data from 77 previously completed NASA programs, including human spaceflight, robotic spaceflight, and ground element development programs are used to model future cost growth. These data show 51% cost growth on average from the start of Phase B to the end of development. Program of Record project elements that are past the start o phase B are adjusted for cost growth already realized and a factor less than 51% is applied to "cost to go" only. This results in a reduced factor, typically on the order of 20-30%, which represents potential future cost growth. For less mature project elements, assumed to be pre-phase B, the full 51% factor is applied. These data are used to develop a cost-risk cumulative probability distribution function (so-called "S-curve").

3. Starting budget profiles ($ over time) for each project element are developed using the point estimate. Profiles for Program of Record elements use current program schedules and milestones. Profiles for other elements are informed by historical program budget levels and duration.

4. Project elements are assembled into a program. Starting budget profiles are phased in time so that program level schedule interdependencies between the individual projects are maintained. Project element and program schedules are unaffected by funding availability. Once the input assumptions of element linkages and cost-risk statistics are established for each of the Project elements that comprise an option, an affordability (or so-called "Sand Chart") analysis is performed.

5. A budgetary constraint is applied. Monte-Carlo analysis, using the project S-curves, simulates cost growth. Using algorithms derived from the historical behavior of past projects, the portfolio is forced to fit the available budget. Schedule interdependencies combined with individual project cost growth, determine the final adjusted schedule add to the final cost. Cost and schedule outputs are probabilistic and reported at the 65% confidence level.

- All costs and schedules are specified at 65 percent confidence level
- Impact of interdependence of individual program element schedules on overall schedule and cost are included
- Cost growth factors are derived from 77 actual NASA programs (Note: Subset of human spaceflight programs experience approximately double the factor used herein; hence, "present analysis" may underestimate cost growth)
- Impact of schedule slippage on cost is included in model
- Cost growth factors specific to operations (*vis a vis* development) are used where appropriate
- Cost growth factors are applied only to "to go" costs
- Prior cost growth and reserves are "credited" against program total cost
- Program interdependencies included via Monte Carlo analysis

Above approach permits comparison of programs having various degrees of maturity.

Fig. 7.2 Aerospace Corporation Methodology Used for Estimating Cost Uncertainty Distributions for the Program Options Evaluated by the U.S. Human Spaceflight Plans (Augustine) Committee

concepts. This figure was prepared by the Aerospace Corporation for the Augustine Committee report, and appears in that report as Fig. 6.2.3.2. It serves as an example of the types of models needed to address programmatic performance measures in general. More information on the Aerospace Corp. approach may be found in Skratt (2010).

Evaluation of the *aspirational objectives*, which deal with benefits to the nation economically and technically, long-term exploration advances, and the fostering of partnerships, rely more on a committee-based scoring approach similar to the approach that led to Fig. 7.1. However, the approach should be expanded from that in Sect. 7.2 to incorporate consideration of performance constraints, performance targets, risk tolerance levels, risk acceptance levels, and performance uncertainty, in the manner previously described in Sect. 4.3.1 and illustrated in Fig. 4.4. The next subsection will provide my recommendations on how to treat these considerations.

7.3.2 Defining Benefit Significance Scores as Performance Measures for the Enterprise-Level Aspirational Objectives

To evaluate the aspirational objectives in the process of deciding between enterprise-level or agency-level program portfolio options, a process which requires significant subjective judgment, I recommend working with a type of measure that I will refer to as a *benefit significance score*. I think of it as being an *achievement measure*, that is to say a type of performance measure that relates to pursuit of an opportunity rather than prevention or mitigation of a failure or loss. There are three basic steps for defining the benefit significance score for each aspirational objective, as summarized below:

Step 1: Establish the number of benefit significance levels. The significance scale for a particular aspirational objective measures the amount of benefit that could conceivably be gained for that objective by pursuing the opportunities that are available in the portfolio being considered. The number of significance levels would normally be large for objectives that have the potential for benefit far above the status-quo, and small for objectives that have only a minimal potential for added benefit. For example, the objective for technology innovation might have, say, 10 benefit significance levels, if there is a potential for groundbreaking achievement, with the scores defined in qualitative terms as follows:

- Level 1: No or very low benefit significance
- Levels 2–9: Equally ascending levels of benefit significance between Levels 1 and 10
- Level 10: Benefit significance as high as imaginable for the objective in question

On the other hand, the objective for public engagement might have, say, 3 benefit significance levels if public engagement is already quite satisfactory.

Included in the definition of each level should be a specification of corresponding achievements or non-achievements. For example, a score at the highest level would normally be possible only if the portfolio of programs covered all the bases needed for such a high score and all the programmatic and aspirational objectives were comprehensively addressed by the portfolio. A score at the lowest level would be appropriate if the important bases were not covered by the portfolio or if many of the programmatic or aspirational objectives were left unaddressed due to program shortcomings.

Step 2: Elicit the benefit significance level assuming that the portfolio is executed successfully in all areas, by polling one or more committees of experts. The Augustine-led committee was selected to evaluate program alternatives for a specific mission: namely, establishing a human presence first on the moon and then on Mars. In the present context, the scope is defined more broadly to include not just the mission of colonizing Mars, but also all other missions that NASA wishes to include in their portfolio. At NASA, there is a precedent for choosing different committees to evaluate different elements of a portfolio, namely a committee for heliophysics, one for astrophysics, another for planetary science, and yet another for earth science. The results of their assessments are reported in the annual NASA Volume of Integrated Performance (see, for example, VOIP, 2024). In the present context, the analysis would hinge on an assessment of potential future benefit that can be expected to be gained for each program option under consideration, rather than on past benefit already gained from ongoing programs (the focus of the VOIP). Uncertainty distributions for the benefit significance level would be assigned based on the divergence of responses obtained from the individual members of the advisory committee. Step 2 involves eliciting a benefit significance score for each aspirational objective assuming all the programs in the portfolio succeed as planned. The details of the elicitation will be discussed in Sect. 7.3.4.

Step 3: Elicit the benefit significance levels from the committee(s) for various instances of portfolio degradation. Separate specifications should be requested from the expert committee for different portfolio success or failure statuses. For example, the benefit significance score would be different from the values specified in Step 2 if Program A succeeded and one project in Program B failed due to a mishap, or different still if Program A succeeded and Program B was cancelled due to a funding shortage and/or failure to meet milestones. If either of those were the case, or some other negative situation arose, some of the experts might judge that their original benefit scores should be reduced by one or more levels (say from score 9 to score 8, 7, or 6). Enough variations in the portfolio success status should be considered in this step to enable the risk management team to equate other states of degradation that arise during the Monte Carlo analysis to those considered during the elicitation. Again, the details of the elicitation will be discussed in Sect. 7.3.4.

7.3.3 Expanding the Monte Carlo Analysis for Individual Programs to Apply to Program Portfolios Containing Multiple Program Elements

The overall modeling and simulation approach that combines consideration of enterprise-level or agency-level programmatic objectives and aspirational objectives is similar to the one that was presented in Sect. 4.1 leading to Fig. 4.1, but that approach has to be extended to simultaneously consider entire portfolios of programs rather than just single projects, and to incorporate new metrics that involve the ranking of the benefits of each candidate portfolio with respect to each of the aspirational objectives. The needed extensions to Fig. 4.1 are illustrated in Fig. 7.3, and the additions made to the predecessor figure to produce the successor figure are summarized in the following paragraphs.

First, as indicated in Charts A and B of Fig. 7.3, evaluations of the performance measures for the *programmatic objectives* are performed for each program element of the portfolio using Monte Carlo sampling techniques. As before, inputs to the evaluation include weighting factors for different performance models; uncertainty distributions for parameter inputs, event occurrence probabilities, and leading indicators; and uncertainty distributions for the U/U risk adjustment. These results are then *aggregated* to obtain results for the portfolio as a whole. During the aggregation process, care is taken to ensure that double counting is avoided and that other dependencies are accounted for. The aggregation processes described in earlier chapters are applicable here as well.

Second, as indicated in Chart E, evaluations of the achievement measures for the *aspirational objectives* are performed, also within the Monte-Carlo shell, using a combination of quantitative results and expert judgment. The quantitative results from the evaluation of the programmatic objectives serve as inputs to the evaluation of the aspirational objectives. For example, as explained in the preceding subsection, if a particular Monte Carlo sampling results in a success for Program A but a failure to complete Program B successfully, that may result in a loss of some of the benefit that the portfolio provides relative to one or more aspirational objectives. The use of expert judgment is based on an elicitation of experts that enters into the determination of benefit significance scores, as described in Sect. 7.3.2.

7.3.4 Strategic Portfolio Planning Elicitations (and Felicitations)

In order to provide the inputs needed to perform the Monte Carlo analysis in Fig. 7.3 and evaluate the risk undesirability score for each performance measure and achievement measure as in Fig. 4.4, it is necessary to elicit information from the members of the expert committee(s). The dialogues below, based on the prototype in Sect. 3.2.2, provide an example of how an interview might proceed. By virtue of the much larger scope that is inherent in deciding between alternative portfolios containing many programs and projects and including both programmatic and aspirational objectives, compared to the more limited scope of decisions pertaining to whether or not to proceed with an individual project according to the project plan, the example dialogues in this section cover more bases and are more complex than the example dialogues in Sect. 3.2.2. The first dialogue clarifies the purpose of each individual project or program within the portfolio under consideration, defines the

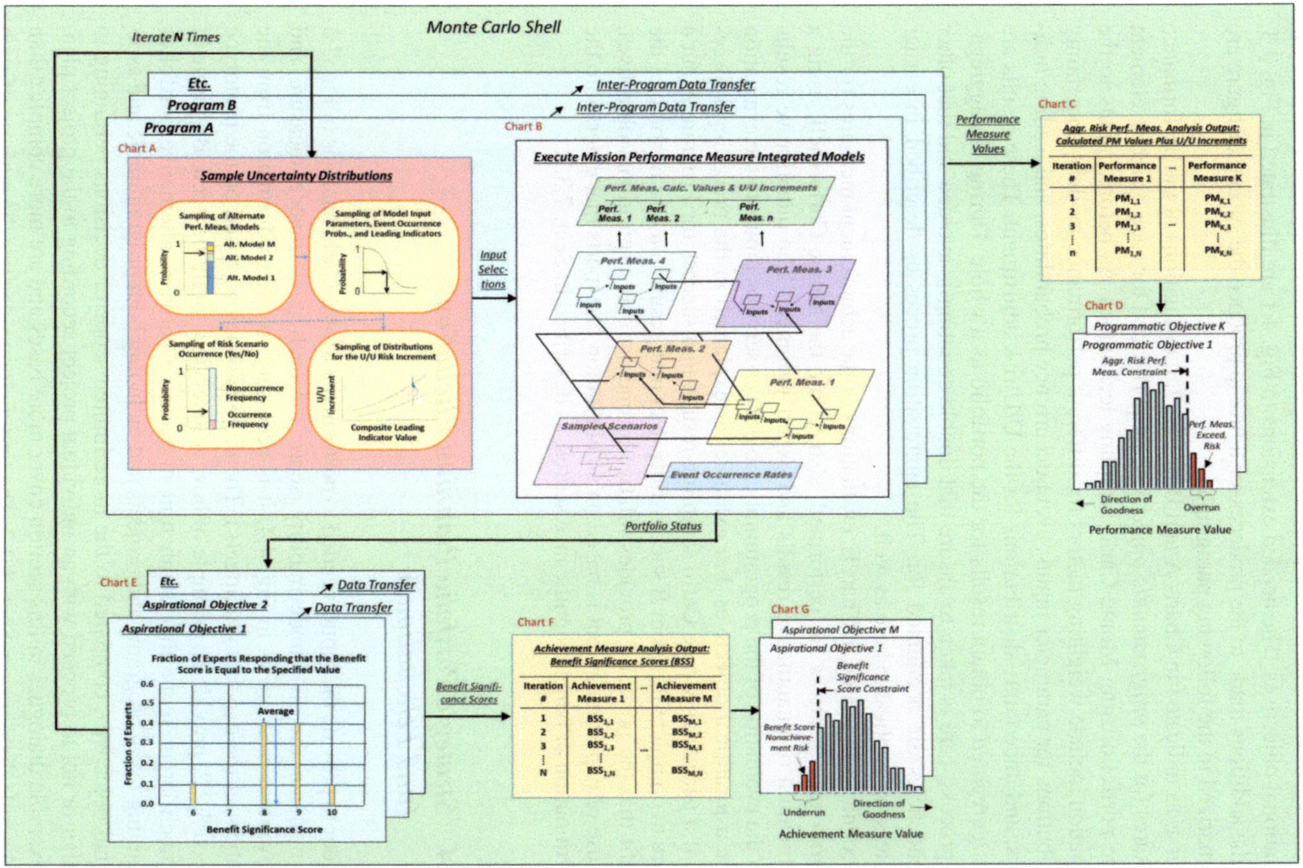

Fig. 7.3 Determination of histograms for aggregate risk performance measures and benefit significance opportunity measures using integrated model simulation and expert input within a Monte Carlo sampling procedure

benefit significance levels with respect to the aspirational objective that is being investigated, and clarifies the criteria that constitute each benefit significance level.

Analyst: Let's talk about Aspirational Objective 2, which is to enable technology maturation, foster the development of new modes of operation, and create new technologies and new engineering knowledge that will enhance exploration and be of use to stakeholders outside the Agency. One of the new technologies that your committee considered to be essential to achieve the objective was to develop more powerful propulsion systems for the spacecraft, so that they could reach one of the outer planets in a timeframe that is measured in months rather than years. Could you elaborate on this? Committee Member: Well, for example, a fusion-based nuclear electric or nuclear thermal spacecraft propulsion system would likely accomplish this. So would other propulsion ideas. Analyst: Could you name some? Committee Member: Yes. Ion propulsion, hall effect thrusters, and antimatter propulsion. Analyst: And what kind of thrust and total energy capacity would it take for you to say that the new propulsion system satisfies your wildest dreams? Committee Member: Oh, enough to get us to Alpha Centauri in a year. Analyst: Yes, but be reasonable since that would require travel much faster than the speed of light. Committee Member: Okay, enough thrust to get us to Alpha Centauri in five years, and enough capacity to get us back in another five years. Alpha Centauri is about 4.4 light years from Earth. Analyst: Fine. So would you say that is a 10 in terms of benefit on a scale of 1 to 10? Committee Member: Yes, I would. Analyst: And how much would you back off from that to say that the new propulsion system provides a 9 on a scale of 1 to 10? Committee Member: Hmm. I would say the ability to get to Alpha Centauri in ten years and get us back in another ten years. Analyst: And if you didn't have enough capacity to get us back to Earth, would you rate that an 8 out of 10? Committee Member: No, I'd give that a 7. Analyst: And finally, what capability would you rate as a 1 on a scale of 1 to 10, or in other words, what capability would provide a small but still useful benefit compared to today's propulsion systems? Committee Member: Oh, perhaps the ability to get to Saturn's moon Titan in a year and back in another year. Saturn is about 800 million miles from Earth. Analyst: Very good.

The dialogue follows on to clarify the goals of other projects and programs in the portfolio and to establish corresponding benefit significance levels with associated criteria.

Analyst: Now let's go on to other new technologies that are needed to greatly expand our exploration capability. Your committee stated that the ability to send a much larger amount of real-time data from distant planets to Earth on a continuous basis, including high-definition images and video feeds, is a priority. So is the development of spacesuits that are more lightweight, flexible, and functional than today's spacesuits over a larger range of space and planetary environmental conditions. And also the development of new technologies to save space on the transport spacecraft and landing vehicle. Can you elaborate on these? Committee

Member: Yes. The use of laser communication would be one promising means for achieving reliable high-resolution communication, regardless of interference from clouds on Earth or at the destination. Also, we are planning a program to develop an exploration extravehicular mobility unit to address the need for better spacesuits. And the saving of space during transit would be enhanced by developing inflatable heat shields that would be compressed during flight but inflate prior to entry to a planet or moon that has a significant atmosphere. Analyst: That's impressive. Now let's take a break and then consider each of those items one at a time, with my asking the same sort of questions I asked in reference to the development of a more powerful propulsion system. Committee Member: Okay, but do I get extra pay for overtime? …

The next dialog establishing weighting factors for the individual projects and programs relative to the aspirational objective being considered, so that an aggregate benefit significance score can be calculated through weighted addition for the aspirational objective under consideration. (Other benefit aggregation processes beside weighted addition could, of course, be used instead, as will be noted in the dialog.)

Analyst: Welcome back. Now we are going to try to get a handle on your prioritization of the various technology developments we discussed. I've brought some gumdrops for you to chew on while we wrap our brains around this one. Committee Member: Yummy. Analyst: I'm going to ask you how you would rate each technology advancement in terms of priority on a scale of 1 to 10, 1 being the lowest and 10 the highest. We could use the Analytical Hierarchy Procedure or Multi-Attribute Utility Theory to do this, but instead I'll try to keep it simple by just asking for your direct inputs. How would you rate the priority of propulsion technology advancement, planet to earth communication technology advancement, spacesuit technology development, and space saving technology development, in that order. Committee Member: 10 for propulsion and 5 each for communications, spacesuits, and space saving. Analyst: So on a scale of 0 to 1, propulsion gets a weighting factor of 0.40, communications 0.20, spacesuits 0.20, and space savings 0.20. This seems to imply that if you rated the benefit significance level of the proposed new propulsion technology at 10 out of 10 and the others respectively at 8, 7, and 5, the benefit significance level for the combination of all those advancements in technology would be $(0.40 \times 10) + (0.20 \times 8) + (0.20 \times 7) + (0.20 \times 5) = 8$ out of 10. Does that sound right to you? Committee Member: Pretty much. Analyst: It also implies that if the space saving technology development failed, the combination benefit significance level would be $(0.40 \times 10) + (0.20 \times 8) + (0.20 \times 7) + (0.00 \times 5) = 7$ out of 10, and if the propulsion technology development failed but the others succeeded, the combination benefit significance level would be $(0.00 \times 10) + (0.20 \times 8) + (0.20 \times 7) + (0.20 \times 5) = 4$ out of 10. Does all that sound right to you? Committee Member: I think so, but I need some more gumdrops. Analyst: Let's go with it then, and here are some more gum drops.

The final dialogue concerns elicitation of the committee member's definition of constraint values, risk tolerance levels and risk acceptance levels for each benefit significance score.

Analyst: Welcome back again. Lastly, we are going to try to deduce your risk tolerance level and risk acceptance level for each benefit significance score. Like before, this elicitation pertains to the objective of enabling technology maturation, fostering the development of new modes of operation, and creating new technologies and new engineering knowledge that will enhance exploration and be of use to stakeholders outside the Agency. I've brought some doughnuts for you to munch on while we ponder this one. Committee Member: Hmm. I'd rather have the gumdrops. Analyst: Okay. I have some left over. Now for this purpose, we take a benefit significance score of 10 out of 10 as being the target, and a lower benefit significance score as being the constraint. The first thing we need to do is establish the benefit significance score for the technology development objective that qualifies as a constraint. Would you say that a score of 6 out of 10 should be the minimum tolerable score for each portfolio alternative under consideration? That would imply that the constraint is slightly better than halfway between exceptional accomplishment (a score of 10) and barely perceptible accomplishment (a score of 1). Committee Member: I'll accept that, at least for the time being. Analyst. Okay, then. So how much risk would you be willing to accept for the chance to achieve a benefit significance score of 10 out of 10 for technology development? Committee Member: I'd say that I'd accept a 20% risk as barely tolerable and a 10% risk as acceptable. Analyst: So your risk tolerance level for a 10 out of 10 benefit significance score is 20%, or 0.2, and your risk acceptance level is 10%, or 0.1. Now how much risk would you be willing to accept for the benefit significance score being less than the constraint value of 6 out of 10. Committee Member: I'd accept much less risk in that case, perhaps 5% as barely tolerable and 2% as acceptable. Analyst: So your risk tolerance level for a 6 out of 10 benefit significance score is 5%, or 0.05, and your risk acceptance level is 2%, or 0.02. Now let's figure out your risk tolerance and acceptance levels for benefit significance scores of 7, 8, and 9. When we're done, I'll open up a bottle of champagne for both of us. Committee Member: I don't think we can do that in this office, but I'm willing to accept cranberry apple juice. ...

The elicitation of information for aspirational objective number 2 is now complete, and the same elicitation process can be reiterated for each of the other aspirational enterprise or agency objectives.

7.3.5 Displays Comparing the Risk Postures of Different Portfolio Alternatives

Once the histograms of performance measure values have been determined for the programmatic objectives, the steps described in Sect. 4.3.1 and illustrated in Fig. 4.4 can be performed to determine risk undesirability scores for each programmatic objective. A similar process can be used to calculate risk undesirability scores for the aspirational objectives, using the histograms of achievement measure value. Figure 7.4 illustrates the comparative processes and provides example results for each calculation.

Lastly, Fig. 7.5 presents an example spider chart showing how the results may compare for two different program portfolio alternatives. In this comparison, Portfolio 2 fares slightly better than Portfolio 1 because the highest risk undesirability score over all objectives is lower for Portfolio 2. However, the lack of balance in the risk undesirability results for both alternatives suggests that there may be another one that achieves better overall results. The chart suggests that some combination of the program elements in the two portfolios might offer a better alternative.

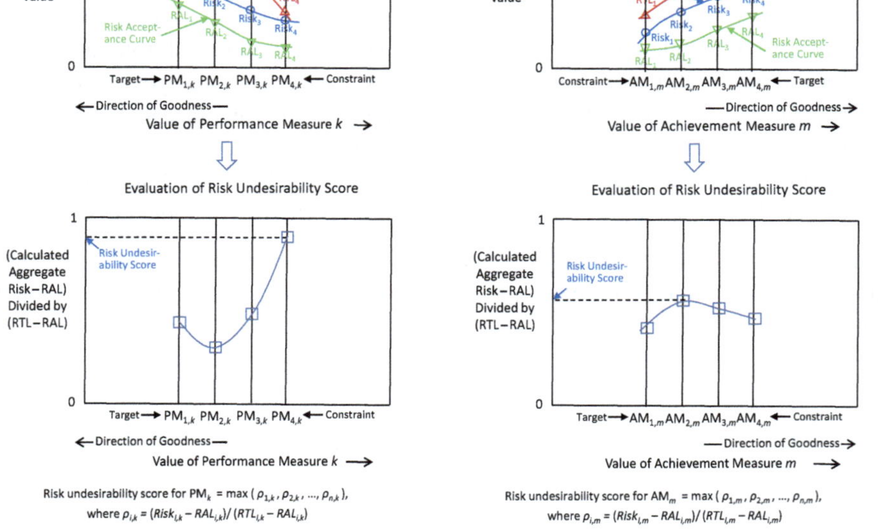

Fig. 7.4 Illustration of the method for calculating risk undesirability scores when there are both programmatic objectives and aspirational objectives

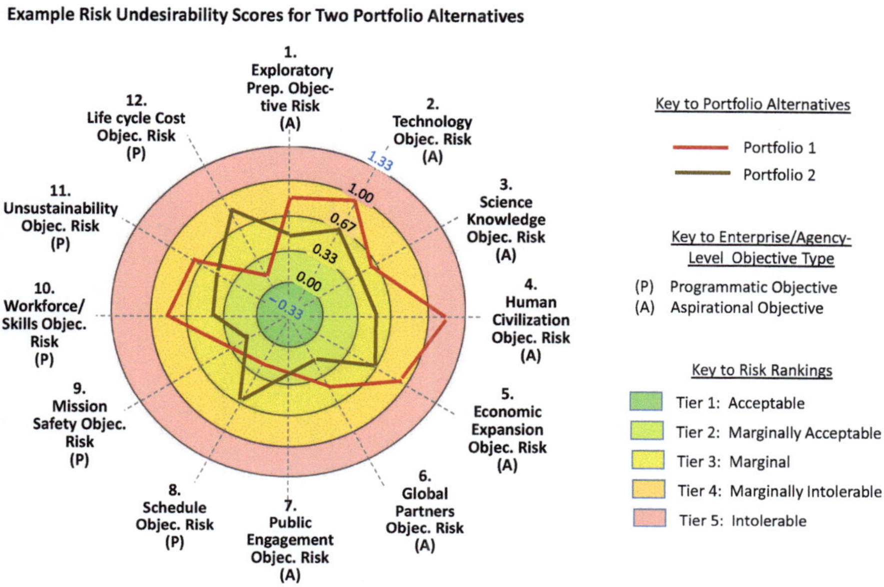

Fig. 7.5 Notional spider chart display comparing risk undesirability scores for programmatic and aspirational objectives at enterprise or agency level for each of two hypothetical portfolio alternatives

References

Augustine, N., et al. (2009, October). *Seeking a human spaceflight program worthy of a great nation*. Review of Human Spaceflight Committee.

Skratt, J. P. (2010, March). Independent assessment of alternative launch vehicles for the augustine committee. In *2010 IEEE Aerospace Conference*, Big Sky, MT, pp. 1–11.

VOIP. (2024, March 11). *FY2025 volume of integrated performance*. NASA, Office of the Chief Financial Officer.

Chapter 8
Continuous Risk Management, Part 1: Models and Simulation Processes

The principal purposes of this chapter are:

- To emphasize the idea that CRM concerns the continuous management of both individual and aggregate risks, as opposed to just individual risks, and to accordingly frame the five sequential steps of CRM (Identify, Analyze, Plan, Track, and Control) in terms of both individual and aggregate risks;
- To highlight and explain some of the principal analytical models used in CRM, including risk scenario diagrams, performance analysis models (and their usefulness for different phases within the lifecycle of programs, projects, and other activities), fault-tree-based risk aggregation models, and leading-indicator-based correlations of schedule risk;
- To demonstrate by example the importance of accounting for event dependencies and risk scenario dependencies during risk aggregation; and
- To reference other risk analysis tools that are commonly used within the CRM process

8.1 The Fundamentals of Continuous Risk Management (CRM)

8.1.1 CRM in the Traditional Sense

Continuous Risk Management can be defined as a systematic and iterative process that identifies, analyzes, plans, tracks, controls, communicates, and documents risks associated with the implementation of designs, plans, and processes (NASA, 2022).

The concept of CRM was originally formulated and explained in a foundational report published in 1996 by the Carnegie Mellon University Software Engineering Institute (SEI), which defined it as a "practice with processes, methods, and tools for managing risks in a project (CMU, 1996)." The SEI report was instigated by the need to manage risks in software development and implementation, but its usefulness was recognized to apply to all risk management activity domains and it became a standard for CRM in general. The basic principles and methods expounded by SEI

A. S. Benjamin, *Integration of Project, Infrastructure, and Enterprise Risk Management*, Risk, Governance and Society 21,
https://doi.org/10.1007/978-3-031-85070-7_8

remain the principal basis for CRM application in most operational enterprises to this day.

The SEI guidebook recognized the need for risk to be considered in unison with opportunity: "Risk and opportunity go hand in hand. Many development projects strive to advance current capabilities and achieve something that hasn't been done before. The opportunity for advancement cannot be achieved without taking risk." The guidebook also quoted from another SEI report in supporting this viewpoint: "Risk in itself is not bad; risk is essential to progress, and failure is often a key part of learning. But we must learn to balance the possible negative consequences of risk against the potential benefits of its associated opportunity (Van Scoy, 1992)."

The CRM process starts from the five cyclical functions of *Identify*, *Analyze*, *Plan*, *Track*, and *Control*, supported by comprehensive *Communicate* and *Document* functions. This process is shown graphically in Fig. 8.1.

In the SEI set of functions, and in the majority of its applications undertaken subsequently, the emphasis has been on individual risks (NASA, 2011; COSO, 2004; ENISA, 2022). According to SEI (in CMU, 1996): "[CRM] provides a disciplined environment for proactive decision-making to assess continuously what could go wrong (risks), determine which risks are important to deal with, and implement strategies to deal with those risks."

Furthermore, it is common in a majority of CRM applications up to the present for the emphasis to be on minimizing the risk to explicitly stated requirements rather than to broadly stated objectives. This book, however, attempts to distinguish between requirements and objectives and to place different priorities upon them.

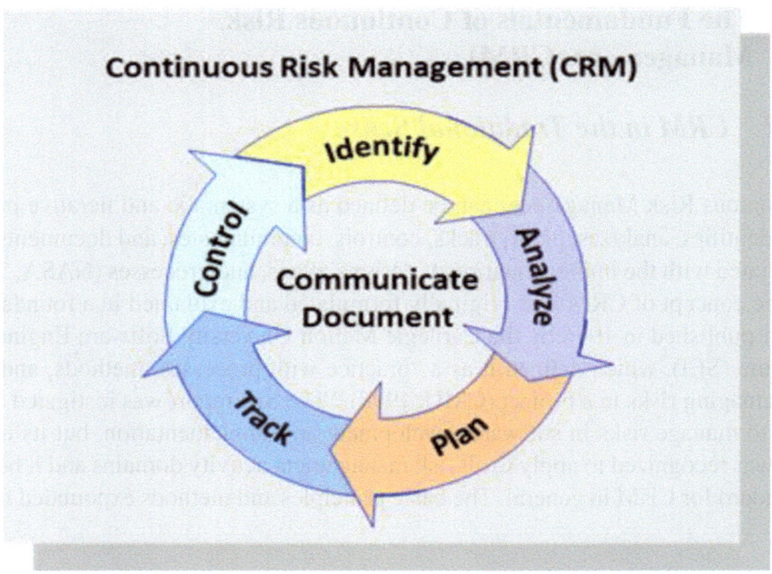

Fig. 8.1 Schematic of the CRM process

8.1.2 CRM in an Expanded Sense

In an expanded sense, CRM should go well beyond the initial goal of managing individual risk scenarios (and opportunity scenarios) to the ultimate goal of managing aggregate risks, the cumulative effect of individual risks on the performance metrics that measure organizational performance against objectives.

Because CRM can be applied both within the realm of individual risks and opportunities and within the realm of aggregate risks to organizational objectives, it is useful to present the step-wise description for each realm side-by-side. This is done in Table 8.1, below. The implement/track and control steps do not require a distinction between realms, and so none is shown in Table 8.1 for those steps.

8.2 The Distinction Between Mandated Requirements and Objectives in CRM

In the practice of CRM, a distinction is often made between "requirements" and "objectives," but the distinction is sometimes nebulous. Because the difference between them is important for prioritizing actions that respond to risks, I purport to offer my own clear distinction between them in this section.

As stated earlier in Sect. 3.1.1, explicitly stated requirements, which I refer to as "mandated requirements," are not necessarily objectives-based. Mandated requirements could include specific design requirements (e.g., mandated use of particular components), technical requirements (e.g., ability to record a specified amount of data), acquisition requirements (e.g., specification of a particular government or commercial partner), process requirements (e.g., compliance with policies and procedures used by other government agencies), and/or tradition-based requirements (e.g., adherence to historically accepted best practices such as mandatory redundancy). In this book, the role of CRM during activity execution includes evaluation of both the objectives-based performance requirements and the mandated requirements that are formulated prior to the initiation of activity execution.

In many references, some "requirements" are defined as having a continuous risk profile while others are defined as binary. For example, a requirement to achieve a specified orbit around a celestial object within a specified degree of resolution may be subject to gravitational or atmospheric uncertainties, such that the risk of not satisfying the requirement is probabilistic. Other requirements, however, are checklist items. For example, a subsystem either has the required redundancy or does not (i.e., its risk profile is binary). For requirements that are checklist items, the default risk tolerance is zero; that is, the checklist requirement must be satisfied unless there is a waiver.

In this book, I include only binary requirements under the umbrella of "mandated requirements" and include the continuous requirements under the umbrella of objectives. For example, reaching a specified orbit is considered to be a "technical

Table 8.1 The steps of CRM relative to individual and aggregate risks

Step	Management of individual risks and opportunities	Management of aggregate risks to organizational objectives and mandated requirements
1. Identify	Identify the risk and opportunity scenarios that need to be considered, the resulting potential impacts or benefits from each, and the affected assets. Prepare corresponding risk and opportunity statements and associated narratives.	Identify the organizational objectives and mandated requirements that are affected by each risk or opportunity scenario and specify how they are affected. Identify associated performance measures, constraint and target values, and risk tolerances. Identify the leading indicators that may be harbingers of U/U risk.
2. Analyze	Select and justify analysis models for individual risks and opportunities. Analyze the likelihood, potential impact or benefit, and timeframe for each scenario. Rank and record results.	Select and justify integrated analysis models for calculating aggregate risks. If practical, calculate or estimate a probability distribution for each performance measure; otherwise, use more simplified models to estimate ranges of probability. Estimate values for the leading indicators of U/U risk, and draw upon historical experience and expert judgment to determine associated margins/reserves for the risk tolerances. By comparing risks to risk tolerances, determine the acceptability of each aggregate risk. Deduce corresponding risk and opportunity drivers.
3. Plan based on AoA	Determine whether each scenario needs to be watched, researched, mitigated, elevated, or closed out. If a mitigation response is needed, conduct an analysis of alternatives (AoA) using quantitative methods where feasible, qualitative methods where not. Then select and justify an alternative for implementation. Modify the baseline plan to accommodate the decision and prepare a control plan.	Determine whether the risk to each performance measure needs to be watched, researched, responded to or elevated. If a mitigation response is needed, either (1) select the mitigation response outright or, if needed, (2) conduct a risk-informed analysis of alternatives (AoA) using a graded RIDM approach that includes both quantitative and qualitative analysis. Then select and justify an alternative for implementation. Modify the baseline plan to accommodate the decision and prepare a control plan.
4. Implement, track	Implement the plan by assisting management in setting up the organizational roles, responsibilities, and interfaces, making the necessary acquisitions and partnerships if needed, and putting the necessary processes into effect. Monitor risk indicators and response actions.	
5. Control	Correct for deviations from the control plan. Determine whether the CRM cycle needs to be reinitiated.	

objective" whose associated performance measure is the degree of resolution. I make this distinction for the sake of definitional clarity, analytical consistency, and ease of decision-making .

The difference between objectives and mandated requirements during CRM, then, enters into the deliberations on what should be done to manage aggregate risks if the specified risk tolerance posture, defined in terms of objectives, is no longer satisfied. If it is found that some of the mandated requirements are contributing to unresolvable difficulty in being able to achieve the specified objectives to within their specified risk tolerances, the possibility of waiving or deviating from one or more of the mandated requirements needs to be considered. For example, it may be deemed beneficial to reduce a mandated level of redundancy for a particular subsystem from a higher level of fault tolerance to a lower level if doing so results in the program safety, technical, security, cost, and schedule objectives all being met within their respective risk tolerances, whereas not doing so causes one of them (say the risk of not meeting the cost constraint) to exceed its risk tolerance. Ultimately, of course, the decision to waive or deviate from a mandated requirement must emanate from a careful deliberation by the decision authorities to ensure that factors that may be known to them but unknown to the risk management team are taken into account.

8.3 Summary of CRM Models for Analyzing Risks Initiated by Random Events

Sequences of events initiated by accidental occurrences, random failures, unplanned delays, and unexpected costs are examples of unintended scenarios that can lead to undesirable consequences. These scenarios are characterized by defined sequences of events, starting from an initiating event or perturbation, and leading after some set of pivotal events to an end state that results in an undesired loss. As discussed in the preceding chapters, the evaluation of aggregate risks to objectives takes into account not only the cumulative effects of the known risk scenarios that contribute to the aggregate risks, but also the potential magnitude of unknown and/or underappreciated (U/U) risk that can be estimated through the use of leading indicators. The following subsections focus mainly on the characteristics of the quantitative methods that may be used to evaluate the portion of the aggregate risks that is attributable to known accident scenarios.

8.3.1 Risk Scenario Diagrams

A risk scenario diagram is a flowchart with paths that start from a unique initial condition and lead to different end states. Along each path, pivotal events are identified as either occurring or not occurring. Each end state reflects, either qualitatively or quantitatively, the effects of the scenario on the ability to satisfy one or more organizational objectives. The RSD is a particular instantiation of an event tree (ET) or event sequence diagram (ESD), in which the end states are directly referenced to performance objectives (see Fig. 8.2).

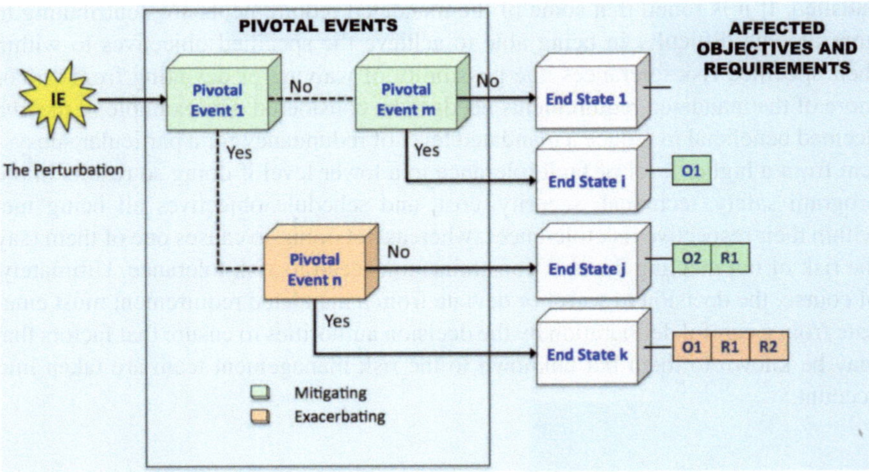

Fig. 8.2 An example RSD showing the effects of each pathway on the organizational unit's objectives

The objectives affected by any scenario in an RSD may span different RM activity domains, and within a particular activity domain, may span different risk types (see Fig. 8.3).

RSDs are primarily intended to be communications aids to facilitate inter-organizational discussions of the risks. They do not necessarily translate exactly to the more detailed risk analysis modeling, but they do serve as a tool for helping ensure that the models cover all the important elements of the risk. At this stage of analysis, the intent of the RSDs is to identify the possible pathways that can lead to positive or negative effects on the successful achievement of organizational objectives, but not yet to quantify them. Furthermore, they do not yet contain any reference to mitigation or research options that are not part of the present plan.

When several organizational units have risks that emanate from the same condition and depend, at least in part, on the same departure event, it is important for these organizational units to be aware of this commonality. With respect to the RSDs produced by the different organizations, the ultimate goal is for them to be consistent and unified in the areas where they are cross-cutting. In this way, the collection of RSDs produced within the project or activity forms an integrated and consistent representation of how each cross-cutting risk affects each organizational unit. This concept is illustrated schematically in Fig. 8.4. The events within the circles in this example and their relationship to one another are copied from one RSD to another to ensure that the representation is consistent.

More explicitly, organizational unit "Blue" identifies an individual risk and constructs an RSD consisting of a condition, several pivotal events, and several consequences. All of these elements first identified by "Blue" are denoted in blue. Organizational unit "Green," on the same level as "Blue," determines that it also has an individual risk with the same condition and some of the same pivotal events as "Blue," but its consequences are different from "Blue's," so some of the pivotal events leading to them are also different. The unique elements for "Green" are

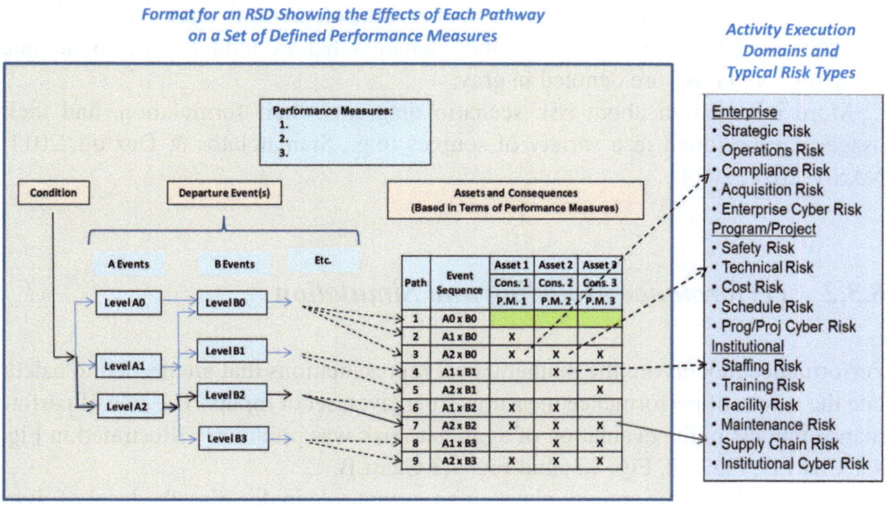

Fig. 8.3 An expanded RSD showing the consequences for each pathway, with each consequence related to a performance measure, an RM activity domain, and a risk type

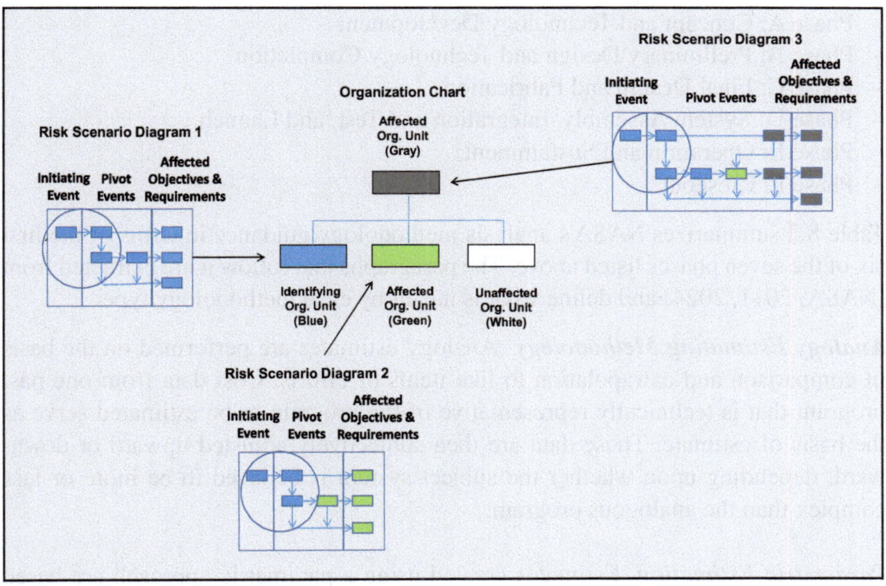

Fig. 8.4 Interfacing of risk scenario diagrams for different organizational units

denoted in green. Organizational unit "Gray" resides above both units in the organizational structure, and its consequences are influenced by both "Blue" and "Green" who are suppliers to "Gray". Thus, there is an individual risk pertinent to "Gray" that derives from the same condition that "Blue" has identified and has some of the same pivotal events as "Blue" and "Green." Its consequences, however, are different from both "Blue's" and "Green's," and so "Gray" has some unique pivotal events that apply specifically to it. Its RSD contains some elements that appear in "Blue's" and "Green's" RSDs, but contains other elements that are unique to it. The unique elements for "Gray" are denoted in gray.

More information about risk scenario diagrams, their formulation, and their usage may be found in a variety of sources (e.g., Stamatelatos & Dezfuli, 2011; NASA, 2011, 2024).

8.3.2 Performance Modeling and Simulation

Performance models are the mathematical representations that are needed to calculate the values of performance measures for a given set of inputs. The role of performance models in the evaluation of aggregate risk was previously illustrated in Fig. 4.1 Chart B, Fig. 4.2, Fig. 4.3, and Fig. 7.3 Chart B.

The maturity of the activity plays an important role in deciding the level of rigor needed in the models used to calculate performance. NASA, for example, defines seven phases of a program or project, as follows (NASA, 2020):

- Pre-Phase A: Concept Studies
- Phase A: Concept and Technology Development
- Phase B: Preliminary Design and Technology Completion
- Phase C: Final Design and Fabrication
- Phase D: System Assembly, Integration and Test, and Launch
- Phase E: Operation and Sustainment
- Phase F: Closeout

Table 8.2 summarizes NASA's analysis methodology guidance in terms of the first six of the seven phases listed above. The paragraphs that follow it are extracted from (NASA, 2011, 2024) and define what is meant by each methodology type.

Analogy Estimating Methodology Analogy estimates are performed on the basis of comparison and extrapolation to like items or efforts. Cost data from one past program that is technically representative of the program to be estimated serve as the basis of estimate. These data are then subjectively adjusted upward or downward, depending upon whether the subject system is believed to be more or less complex than the analogous program.

Parametric Estimating Estimates created using a parametric approach are based on historical data and mathematical expressions relating cost as the dependent variable to selected, independent, cost-driving variables through regression analysis. Generally, an estimator selects parametric estimating when only a few key pieces of data are known, such as weight and volume. The implicit assumption of parametric estimating is that the same forces that affected cost in the past will affect cost in the future.

Table 8.2 Analysis methodology guidance chart

	Pre-Phase A	Phase A	Phase B	Phase C/D	Phase E
	(a) Cost estimating methodology				
Analogy	Primary	*Applicable*	*Applicable*	*Applicable*	Inapplicable
Parametric	Primary	Primary	*Applicable*	*Applicable*	Inapplicable
Engineering build-up	*Applicable*	*Applicable*	Primary	Primary	Primary
	(b) Technical estimating methodology				
First-order	Primary	Primary	*Applicable*	Inapplicable	Inapplicable
Detailed simulation	Inapplicable	Primary	Primary	Primary	*Applicable*
Testing	Inapplicable	Inapplicable	*Applicable*	Primary	Primary
Operating experience	Inapplicable	Inapplicable	Inapplicable	Inapplicable	Primary
	(c) Safety, reliability, and operations estimating methodology				
Similarity	Primary	*Applicable*	*Applicable*	Inapplicable	Inapplicable
First-order parametric	Primary	Primary	*Applicable*	*Applicable*	Inapplicable
Detailed logic modeling	Inapplicable	Inapplicable	Primary	Primary	Primary
Statistical methods	Inapplicable	Inapplicable	Inapplicable	*Applicable*	Primary

Engineering Build Up Methodology Sometimes referred to as "grass roots" or "bottom-up" estimating, the engineering build up methodology rolls up individual estimates for each element into the overall estimate. This methodology involves the computation of the cost of a work breakdown structure (WBS) element by estimating at the lowest level of detail (often referred to as the "work package" level) wherein the resources to accomplish the work effort are readily distinguishable and discernable. Often the labor requirements are estimated separately from material requirements. Overhead factors for cost elements such as Other Direct Costs (ODCs), General and Administrative (G&A) expenses, materials burden, and fees are generally applied to the labor and materials costs to complete the estimate.

First-Order Estimating Methodology First-order estimates involve the use of closed-form or simple differential equations which can be solved given appropriate bounding conditions and/or a desired outcome without the need for control-volume based computational methods. The equations may be standard physics equations of state or empirically-derived relationships from operation of similar systems or components.

Detailed Simulation Estimating Methodology Estimates using a detailed simulation require the construction of a model that represents the physical states of interest in a virtual manner using control-volume based computational methods or methods of a similar nature. These simulations typically require systems and conditions to be modeled to a high-level of fidelity and the use of "meshes" or network diagrams to represent the system, its environment (either internal, external, or both), and/or processes acting on the system or environment. Examples are computational fluid dynamics (CFD) and finite-element modeling.

Testing Methodology Testing can encompass the use of table-top experiments all the way up to full-scale prototypes operated under real-world conditions. The objective of the test is to measure how the system or its constituent components may perform within actual mission conditions. Testing could be used for assessing the expected performance of competing concepts or for evaluating that the system or components will meet flight specifications.

Operating Experience Methodology Once the system is deployed, data gathered during operation can be analyzed to provide empirically accurate representations of how the system will respond to different conditions and how it will operate throughout its lifetime. This information can serve as the basis for applicable changes, such as software uploads or procedural changes, that may improve the overall performance of the system. Testing and detailed simulation may be combined with operating experience to extrapolate from known operating conditions.

Similarity Estimating Methodology Similarity estimates are performed on the basis of comparison and extrapolation to like items or efforts. Reliability and operational data from one past program that is technically representative of the program to be estimated serves as the basis of estimate. Reliability and operational data are then subjectively adjusted upward or downward, depending upon whether the subject system is believed to be more or less complex than the analogous program.

First-Order Parametric Estimation Estimates created using a parametric approach are based on historical data and mathematical expressions relating safety, reliability, and/or operational estimates as the dependent variable to selected, independent, driving variables through either regression analysis or first-order technical equations (e.g., higher pressures increase the likelihood of tank rupture). Generally, an estimator selects parametric estimating when the system and its concept of operation are at the conceptual stage. The implicit assumption of parametric estimating is that the same factors that shaped the safety, reliability, and operability in the past will affect the system/components being assessed.

Detailed Logic Modeling Estimation Detailed logic modeling estimation involves "top-down" developed but "bottom-up" quantified scenario-based or discrete-event logic models that segregate the system or processes to be evaluated into discrete segments that are then quantified and mathematically integrated through Boolean logic to produce the top-level safety, reliability, or operational estimate. Detailed technical simulation and/or testing, as well as operational data, can be used to assist in developing probability density functions for quantification of the model. Typical methods for developing such models may include the use of fault trees, influence diagrams, and/or event trees.

Statistical Methods Statistical methods can applied to data collected during system/component testing or from system operation during an actual mission. This is useful for characterizing the demonstrated safety, reliability, or operability of the system. In addition, patterns in the data may be modeled in a way that accounts for randomness and uncertainty in the observations, and then serve as the basis for design or procedural changes that may improve the overall safety, reliability, or operability of the system. These methods are useful for answering yes/no questions about the data (hypothesis testing), describing associations within the data (correlation), modeling relationships within the data (regression), extrapolation, interpolation, or simply for data mining activities.

8.3.3 Fault-Tree-Based Risk Aggregation Models

As defined in Appendix A Sect. A.4, an aggregate risk is the cumulative effect of individual risk scenarios (which characterize known risk) and leading indicators (which characterize U/U risk) on a higher-level objective, or more specifically on a performance measure that has been defined to characterize the objective. Individual risk scenarios tend to feed into lower-level objectives in the objectives hierarchy because of the high degree of specificity in the scenario definitions. Leading indicators of U/U risk, on the other hand, tend to feed into higher-level objectives because they are not associated with specified scenarios.

The risk aggregation schematic shown in the form of an objectives logic tree in Fig. 8.5 provides an example. The high-level objective in the example is to ensure that there is sufficient technical support for completing Project X successfully. The mid-level objectives divide the high-level objective into various technical disciplines needing support, and the lowest-level objectives consider the various means by which technical support may be provided. In essence, the project can retain a sufficient number of senior-level technical personnel to satisfy the staffing need, or if that is not possible, can alternatively hire a sufficient number of recent college graduates to make up the difference and provide the training they need to bring them up to the task.

Figure 8.5 also shows the "And" and "Or" operators that define the relationship of lower-level objectives to higher-level objectives. Note that in more general cases where the combinational logic is more complex, other types of logic gates (such as *M* of *N* combination gates) could also be included in the objectives decomposition.

The aggregation of failure probabilities from risk scenarios to lower-level objectives and from lower-level objectives to higher-level objectives can be formulated by converting the success pathway logic shown in Fig. 8.5 into failure pathway logic as in Fig. 8.6, using a fault tree format. Figure 8.6 extends upward beyond Fig. 8.5 by including higher level objectives O8 through O10, culminating in failure to complete the subject project X successfully within the not-to-exceed time constraint, along with including associated leading indicator I2 and showing the involvement of an expert review committee at that level. The probabilities of failure for each objective in the fault tree can be quantified using Boolean algebra and standard fault-tree quantification algorithms. The process will be discussed further in the remainder of this chapter and in Chap. 12.

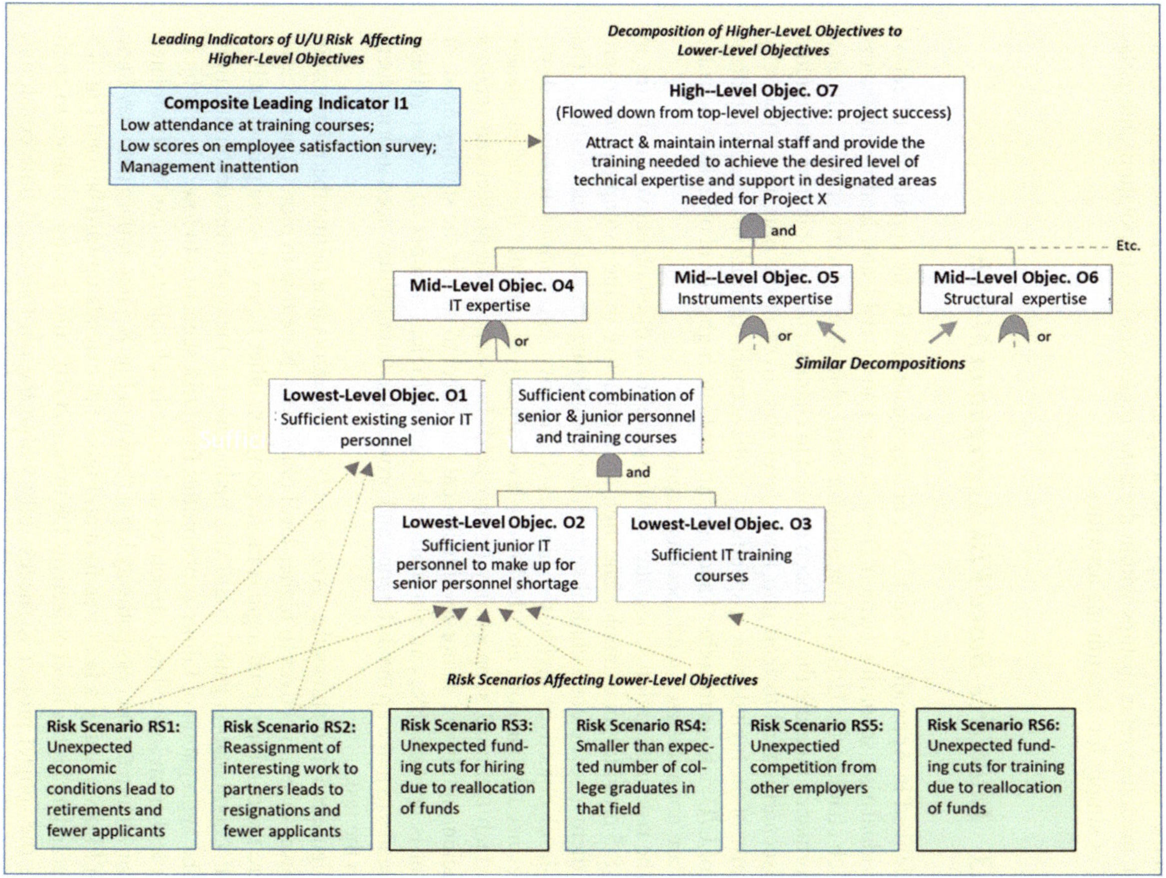

Fig. 8.5 An example objectives logical decomposition diagram, showing where individual risk scenarios and leading indicators of U/U risk interface with the objectives

Also, additional information and guidance concerning fault tree analysis may be found in many publications on probabilistic risk assessment (e.g., Rasmussen et al., 1975; NRC, 1981; Stamatelatos & Dezfuli, 2011).

8.3.4 The Importance of Accounting for Dependencies During Risk Aggregation

Accounting for dependencies in the quantification of aggregate risk is extremely important and often overlooked, leading to incorrect results.

Consider the base objectives O1, O2, and O3 and the next higher objective, O4 in Fig. 8.6. Objective O1 concerns the ability of the organizational unit to maintain a sufficient number of senior IT specialists to support Project X; objective O2 concerns its ability to hire a sufficient number of junior IT specialists fresh from college if objective O1 is not met; and objective O3 concerns its ability to provide in-house courses on the organizational unit's IT networks and processes for the newly hired junior IT specialists. If objective O1 is unsuccessful and either objective O2 or O3 is unsuccessful, then objective O4, concerning the overall level of IT expertise needed for Project X, is considered to be unsatisfied. As shown in Fig. 8.6, the failure to achieve objective O1 is mediated by the combined effects of risk scenarios *RS*1 and *RS*2, objective O2 by scenarios *RS*1 through *RS*5, and objective O3 by scenario *RS*6. Scenarios *RS*1, *RS*3, and *RS*6 are not independent, because they each originate from unexpected economic conditions. A major national recession could simultaneously lead to early retirements (*RS*1), funding cuts for hiring (*RS*3), and funding cuts for training (*RS*6), which means that if *RS*1 actualizes, it is more likely that *RS*3 and *RS*6 will actualize. Since the aggregate risk of not meeting Objective O4 is dependent upon combinations of scenarios occurring, and some of those combinations involve dependent events, the quantification of that aggregate risk has to account for the synergisms between the scenarios that contribute to it.

The importance of accounting for dependencies during risk aggregation will be highlighted in Chap. 12, which will expand upon this example to provide guidance on what needs to be done to account for dependent events and dependent risk scenarios. As will be demonstrated in that chapter, the problem of dependencies can be made more tractable through the use of common cause methodology.

Common cause analysis identifies the modes of failure that have the potential of being triggered by a single, more basic root cause, and incorporates the root cause as the initiating event for all risk scenarios that are affected by it. For the example being addressed here and in Chap. 12, it would involve decomposing scenarios *RS*1, *RS*3, and *RS*6 into event sequences with the common initiating event being the occurrence of a major recession. In addition to that initiating event, however, it would be necessary to consider other common cause initiating events that could lead to similar results. For example, in addition to economic causes, common cause sources of dependent failures sometimes include political causes, broadly-felt

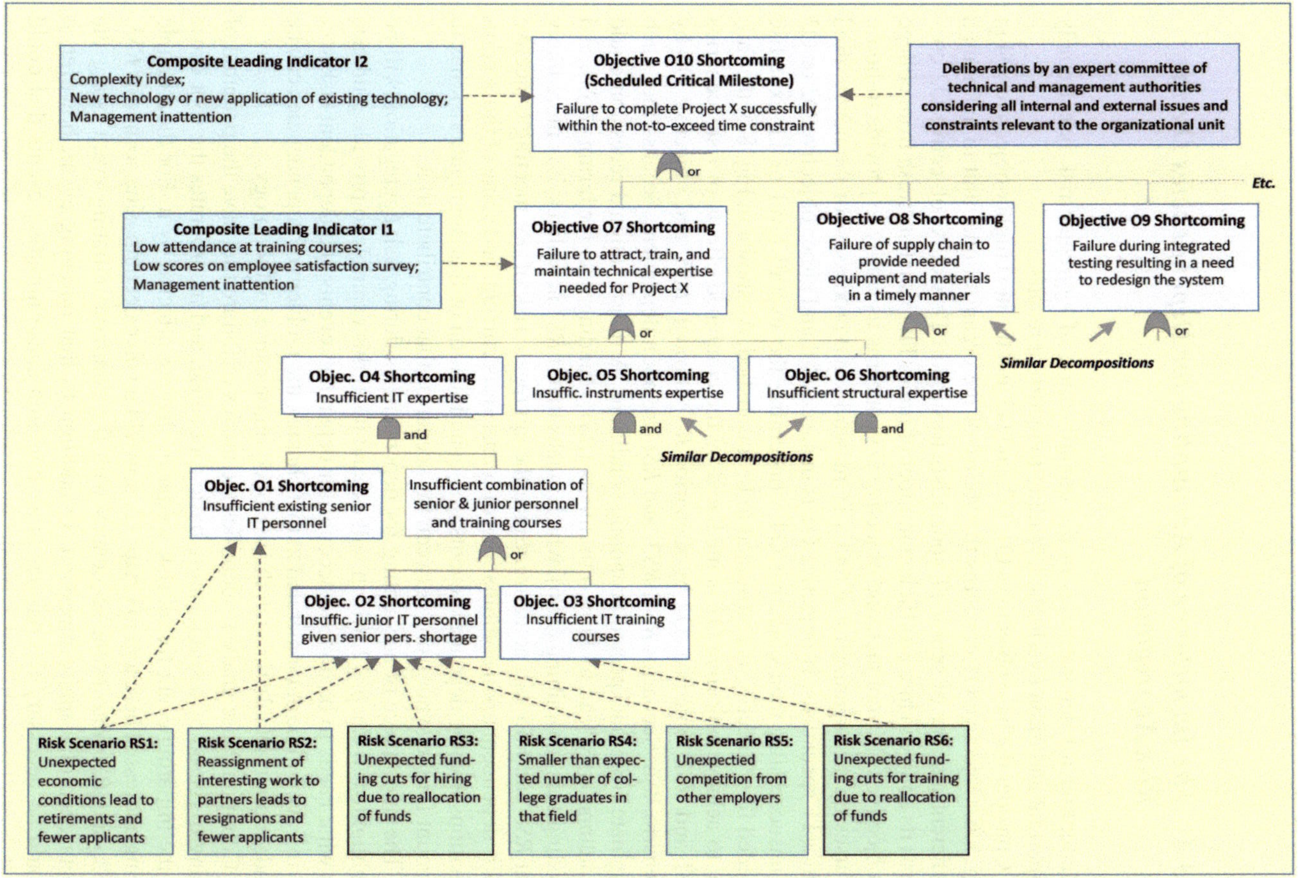

Fig. 8.6 Fault tree counterpart of the example objectives logical decomposition diagram, including additional higher-level objectives

technology failures, operational failures, inappropriate procedures, poor design, poor maintenance, lack of clearly defined standard operating procedures, poor working conditions, use of substandard materials, quality control deficiencies, environmental causes, material aging, operator error, and "acts of God," to name a few. Not all of these would apply for the present example.

Insights and guidance on how to use common-cause techniques to account for dependencies within fault-tree analysis may be found in various sources (e.g., Worrell & Stack, 1977; NRC, 1981, 2007; Rasmuson & Mosleh, 2007; Stamatelatos & Dezfuli, 2011; Jones, 2012). Most of these references focus on common causes of hardware or software failure in physical systems, rather than common causes that pertain to processes and operations, human interfaces with a system, institutional or infrastructure risks, or enterprise risks. However, the general means for addressing them within a fault-tree or other logic-diagram methodological approach remain broadly applicable in all of these usages.

8.3.5 Making Adjustments for U/U Risk

The two composite leading indicators of U/U risk in Fig. 8.6 are:

I1: Low attendance at training courses and low scores on employee satisfaction surveys, combined with management inattention. These conditions taken together indicate that it will be harder to attract, train, and maintain people with the technical expertise needed to accomplish the project, denoted as Objective O7 Shortcoming in Fig. 8.6.

I2: Highly complex systems and/or operations, and the use of fundamentally new technology or existing technology in a fundamentally new application, again combined with management inattention. These indicators in composite portend difficulties in completing the project within its not-to-exceed time constraint, denoted as Objective O10 Shortcoming in Fig. 8.6, or possibly completing it on time but emphatically not within its mandated budget.

As pertains to leading indicator I1, there is a large supply of data from other programs and projects of various types, with various purposes, and under various managers that provide data capable of establishing correlations between leading indicators of dissatisfaction and the likelihood of job abandonment (one of the main contributors to failure of Objectives O7 in Fig. 8.6). For example, in an article for Harvard Business Review, Professors Brooks Holtom of Georgetown University and David Allen of Texas Christian University described how they used "big data and machine-learning algorithms" to develop a "turnover propensity index (TPI)," and how they correlated that index with employee turnover (Holtom & Allen, 2019). Their analysis relied upon publicly available data and the sampling of 500,000 individuals.

Regarding leading indicator I2, correlations between cost overruns, complexity, and other factors were described in Sects. 5.3 and 5.4 and the results were summarized in Table 5.1 in the form of a table of performance measure adjustments as a composite function of the leading indicators. The basis for the table was an analysis by James Bearden et al., at Aerospace Corporation (Bearden, 2008), combined with observable results of cost overruns experienced during development of the James Webb Space Telescope (JWST), the Lunar Trailblazer, and the International Space Station (ISS). In addition to the effect of complexity on development cost, which was shown earlier in Fig. 5.2, Bearden analyzed the effect of complexity on the time to completion of development (the performance measure of interest in Objective O10 of Fig. 8.6). His results for development time are illustrated in Fig. 8.7. Again, I've added two points representing the initial development time estimate and the final actual development time for the JWST.

8.4 Putting It Together

Risk scenario diagrams, math-based performance models, fault trees, correlations to account for U/U risk, and red-team simulations are tools used in the overall risk aggregation process. Other related processes include hazard analysis (HA), failure modes and effects analysis (FMEA), failure modes, effects, and criticality analysis (FMECA), accident precursor analysis (APA), event tree analysis (ETA), Petri net analysis (PNA), binary decision analysis (BDA), dynamic and dependent tree theory (D^2T^2), system-theoretic process analysis (STPA), and probabilistic risk assessment (PRA), to name a few. (The latter processes are mentioned here only in passing but are explained and demonstrated in many references that are readily available.)

These individual processes, however, do not constitute the totality of the approach. Rather, they appear as parts of the larger Monte Carlo simulation methodology that was depicted in Fig. 4.1, for individual organizational entities, and in Fig. 7.3, for the enterprise as a whole, and as parts of a risk scoring methodology

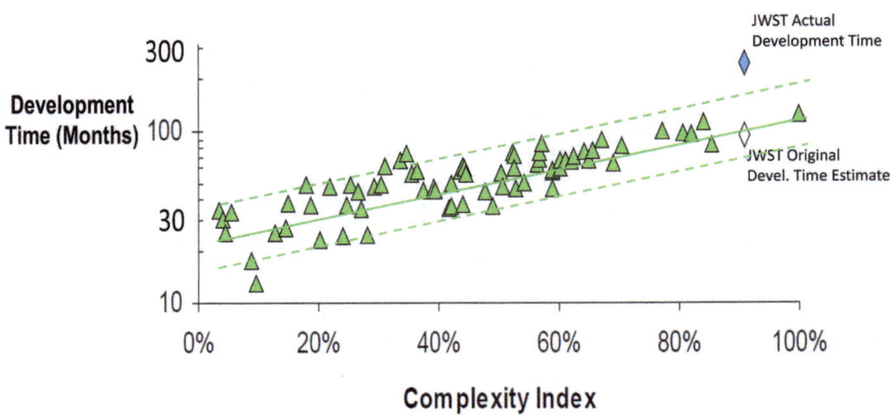

Fig. 8.7 Aerospace Corporation's correlation of project development time for satellite missions with a derived complexity index

such as the one depicted in Fig. 4.4. An example keyed to the implementation of these approaches will be provided in Chap. 14.

The topic of Continuous Risk Management will continue in Chap. 10, where the focus will shift from modeling and simulation to internal control, risk mitigation, and actions to avail mission-advancing opportunities.

References

Bearden, D. (2008, June). Perspectives on NASA mission cost and schedule performance trends. In *NASA Goddard Space Flight Center System Engineering Symposium*.

COSO. (2004). *Enterprise risk management – Integrated framework*. Committee of Sponsoring Organizations of the Treadway Commission, 2004 (updated in 2017).

Dorofee, A., et al. (1996, January). *Continuous risk management guidebook*. Carnegie Mellon University, Software Engineering Institute, Rept. No. 19970108 045.

Holtom, B., & Allen, D. (2019, August). Better ways to predict who's going to quit. *Harvard Business Review*.

Jones, H. W. (2012, November). *Common cause failures and ultra reliability*. American Institute of Aeronautics and Astronautics, AIAA 2012-3602.

Lambrinoudakis, C., et al. (2022, January). *Compendium of risk management frameworks with potential interoperability: Supplemental to the interoperable EU risk management framework report*. European Union Agency for Cybersecurity (ENISA).

NASA. (2011, November). *NASA risk management handbook (Version 1)*. NASA/SP-2011-3422.

NASA. (2020, January). *NASA systems engineering handbook*. NASA/SP-2016-6105 Rev2.

NASA. (2022, April). *Agency risk management procedural requirements*. NASA NPR 8000.4C.

NASA. (2024, November). *NASA risk management handbook (Version 2, Part 1)*. NASA/SP-2024-3422.

NRC. (1981, January). *Fault tree handbook*. Nuclear Regulatory Commission, NUREG-0492.

NRC. (2007, September). *Common-cause failure database and analysis system: Event data collection, classification, and coding*. Nuclear Regulatory Commission, NUREG/CR-6268, Rev. 1.

Rasmuson, D. M., & Mosleh, A. (2007, June). *A brief history of common-cause failure analysis*. IAEA Technical Meeting on CCF in Digitial Instrumentation and Control Systems for Nuclear Power Plants.

Rasmussen, N. C., et al. (1975, October). *Reactor safety study. An assessment of accident risks in U. S. commercial nuclear power plants*. US Nuclear Regulatory Commission, WASH-1400.

Stamatelatos, M., & Dezfuli, H. (2011, December). *Probabilistic risk assessment procedures guide for NASA managers and practitioners* (2nd edn), NASA/SP-2011-3421.

Van Scoy, R. (1992). *Software development risk: Opportunity, not problem*. Carnegie Mellon University, Software Engineering Institute, CMU/SEI-92-TR-30.

Worrell, R. B., & Stack, D. W. (1977). *Common cause analysis using SETS*. Sandia National Laboratories, SAN 77-1832.

Chapter 9
Special Considerations for Risks Associated with Cyberattacks

The purposes of this chapter are as follows:

- To elaborate upon Sect. 4.2 by addressing, in more detail, some of the essential differences between analyzing risks associated with cyberattacks and other intentional acts, versus risks associated with accidents and other random occurrences;
- To propose the use of conditional probabilities and measures of performance that are based on the time it takes for an adversary to find a way to breach the system and inflict harm without being detected;
- To discuss the relevance of lessons learned from a previously perpetrated large-scale cyberattack (SolarWinds);
- To advocate for red teams consisting of both government and private cybersecurity experts to take a war-game approach for uncovering the fastest ways of penetrating existing distributed cyber networks without being detected; and
- To describe a process for developing probability distributions for such performance measures using results obtained from the red-teams

9.1 Use of Conditional Probabilities

Given the variety of attack scenarios that an adversary can choose from and the fact that most adversaries favor attacks that are unexpected and thus more likely to succeed, the main difficulty faced by the risk analyst is predicting the absolute likelihood of occurrence for each scenario type (i.e., the threat likelihood). For this reason, the aggregate risks for various performance measures are often best framed, for intentional scenarios, as conditional probabilities rather than absolute probabilities.

By dealing with conditional probabilities, the analyst presumes that an attack has been initiated aimed at a particular threat-consequence type under consideration, and focuses on the likelihood that the assailant is successful achieving their desired consequence within their desired timeframe. Pursuing the risk aggregation in terms of conditional probabilities, of course, does not preclude the possibility of also

A. S. Benjamin, *Integration of Project, Infrastructure, and Enterprise Risk Management*, Risk, Governance and Society 21,
https://doi.org/10.1007/978-3-031-85070-7_9

pursuing the problem in terms of absolute probabilities, if and when a reasonable amount of information becomes available about the likelihood and nature of the threat (e.g., from intelligence sources).

9.2 Performance Measure Markers and Risk Tolerance Levels for Cybersecurity Aggregate Conditional Risk

As discussed in Sect. 4.2, there are various types of cybersecurity breaches that an organization might be concerned with. In order of complexity, from least to most, the following three types of breach might be of interest to any enterprise:

1. An attempt to steal sensitive data from an IT storage system
2. An attempt to defeat the functioning of an IT network in a way that creates a major interruption of work flow
3. An attempt to add malicious commands into critical control software just before it is implemented into a critical system.

Examples of the third type of breach might be an adversary trying to infect the control system that will be used on a NASA heavy-launch assent vehicle, a DoD weapon system or system-of-systems, or a commercial nuclear reactor power modulation system so as to cause catastrophic failure of a mission or operation.

It seems reasonable to take as a given that intelligent, determined adversaries will find a way to breach cybersecurity protections in an IT network if given enough time, per the discussion in Sect. 4.2 and the supporting evidence (e.g., in Rosencrance, 2011, Mitnick, 2024, and others). Thus, I posit that the most effective performance measure for gaging the strength of cybersecurity protection is the amount of time it would take for an adversary, once the attempt has been initiated, to (a) succeed in finding a way into the portion of the IT network that is applicable to the adversary's intent and (b) inflict harm, all without being detected. This position is also strongly supported in the online literature (e.g., Tunggal, 2024; SecurityScorecard, 2024).

As an example, assume that for one of the breach types listed above, a constraint on the time it would take an adversary time to breach and infect a given critical system has been specified as 15 months, the risk tolerance level as 0.20, and the risk acceptance level as 0.10. That means that (for this example) the aggregate conditional risk would be intolerable if the probability of being able to perpetrate the damage in less than or equal to 15 months was greater than or equal to 0.20, marginal if the probability was between 0.10 and 0.20 (with various degrees of marginality specified within that range), and acceptable if the probability was less than 0.10. These numbers correspond to a process of specifying risk posture that is in accordance with Appendix A Sects. A.2 and A.5.

9.3 Performance Measure Probability Distribution and Level of Acceptability

Section 4.2 also provided an argument, citing evidence (e.g., Miller, 2024; Bailey et al., 2012), that the most effective way for determining the amount of time it would take a capable adversary to breach the cybersecurity protections of a distributed IT network and compromise the system is to form a select number of red teams and have them perform war-game type exercises. As mentioned in that section, the red teams would ideally include not only IT and cybersecurity personnel from the organization that is trying to protect itself against cyberattacks, but also personnel from Federal agencies charged with identifying and assessing cyber threats, acting in a supporting manner.

As opposed to a Monte Carlo analysis procedure, which uses iterative sampling of uncertainty distributions for input parameters followed by execution of integrated analysis models, the derivation of performance measure probability distributions for intentional acts relies on the results obtained from multiple red teams. For example, suppose three red-teams have been formed, and that each operates without the actual IT team within the organization being aware of their attempts to foil the system. Each red team independently tries to identify a vulnerable pathway and defeat the system within the shortest amount of time. It they are detected and stopped before they can succeed, they shift gears and try another pathway. The amount of time it takes each team to eventually succeed constitutes a distribution of the time it takes for an adversary to succeed.

Example results are shown in Fig. 9.1, in which it is assumed that three independent trials result in times-to-succeed of 16.2 months, 13.7 months, and 25.8 months and that the distribution is lognormal. As discussed in Sect. 4.2, the literature provides evidence that the time to solve a difficult puzzle (which is certainly what the red teams are trying to do) tends to be lognormally distributed (GeeksforGeeks, 2023; Chegg, 2024), but any other type of distribution that has three or fewer quantifiable parameters and is supported by experience would suffice as well.

The parameters μ and σ of the distribution are evaluated from the sample data as follows (Pavlovic, 2022):

$$\mu = \frac{\ln(16.2) + \ln(13.7) + \ln(25.8)}{3} = 2.88$$

$$\sigma = \sqrt{\frac{\left[\ln(16.2) - 2.88\right]^2 + \left[\ln(13.7) - 2.88\right]^2 + \left[\ln(25.8) - 2.88\right]^2}{(3-1)}} = 0.38$$

where the denominator inside the square root sign for σ has been set to one less than the number of trails, as is commonly done in order to eliminate statistical bias (see, for example Taboga, 2017).

Fig. 9.1 Example results for three red-team simulations

TABULATED RED-TEAM RESULTS

Team Number	Number of Months
1	16.2
2	13.7
3	25.8

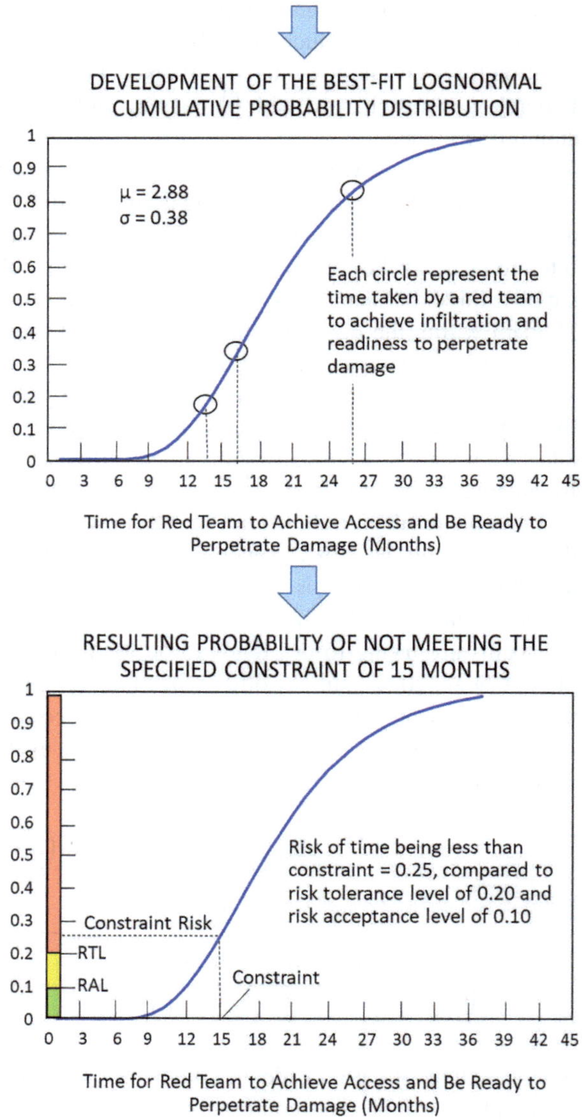

As stated on the bottom chart of the figure, the resultant risk of not achieving a minimum time of 15 hours (the constraint) is 0.25, whereas the risk tolerance level was set at 0.20 and the risk acceptance level at 0.10 in Sect. 9.2. This means that the aggregate risk of not meeting the objective would be rated as intolerable, and something would have to be done to fix it.

9.4 Societal Integration Approach for Scenarios Initiated by Cyberattacks

Vulnerability to cyberattacks is a societal problem because of the interconnectedness of today's broadly dispersed cyber systems. That characteristic of the cyber landscape permits communications among a multitude of parties to occur almost instantaneously, allowing business to be conducted and advances to be made at unprecedented speeds. At the same time, it invites potential attackers to select from among many potential ports of entry, spanning many agencies, companies, and other organizations or individuals that have access to the interconnected system, and to perpetrate damage that can compromise many of them, as well as society as a whole. Their reach extends to health systems, banking systems, supply chains, and power grids (as evidenced by the Russian NotPetya attack, see McQuade, 2018; LogRhythm, 2017).

Many lessons were learned, for example, from the SolarWinds attack in 2020, where a sophisticated adversary (believed to have been masterminded by the Russian intelligence service, the SVR (Temple-Raston, 2021) exploited the "soft underbelly of our digital lives". Eighteen thousand customers are believed to have downloaded malicious code that was implanted into network management software distributed by the Texas-based company SolarWinds. As a result, the Biden administration announced sanctions against Russia for what it characterized as the "seen and unseen" response to the SolarWinds breach.

As explained by Temple-Raston, none of the tripwires put in place by private companies or the government seemed to have seen the attack coming. In early July of 2020, the founder of a cybersecurity company called Volexity saw some suspicious activity on a client's computers, traced it back, thought it might be related to a bad update with SolarWinds, made sure no one was in their customers' systems, and left it at that. They did not feel they had enough detail to report the problem to SolarWinds or the U.S. government. Then three months later, another cybersecurity company called Palo Alto Networks discovered a malicious backdoor that seemed to emanate from the SolarWinds software but could not pinpoint a supply chain attack, so the ticket got closed. Finally, It was the cybersecurity firm FireEye that diagnosed the intrusion. The company's CEO used to be in the U.S. Air Force Office of Special Investigations, so he recognized the patterns.

As a result of the SolarWinds attack, an idea started to gain traction for creating something analogous to a National Transportation Safety Board, or NTSB, to investigate cyberattacks in a more formal way. When there is a major airplane crash, the NTSB gathers the facts, comes up with a theory of what needs to be fixed, and oversees the fixes. The idea for cybersecurity is to institute the same kind of function in the U.S. government (perhaps through the FBI) to investigate, learn from, and oversee controls against cyberattacks. The rationale is that any conflict is cyberspace is going to involve both the government and the private sector, so that both need to be involved in a cooperative arrangement.

A natural extension of this rationale is to initiate a more proactive rather than reactive coordination between the public and private sectors. In a proactive approach, red teams consisting of both government and private cybersecurity experts would take a war game approach to uncover the fastest ways of penetrating existing distributed cyber networks without being detected. The process would be similar to that discussed in Sect. 4.2 concerning the use of red-teaming applied within an individual enterprise, but would have a nation-wide span rather than just an enterprise-wide span.

There are clearly risks to such an approach. Competitive enterprises would be concerned about protecting their proprietary information from competitors, so safeguards to ensure that protection would be necessary. Additionally, there would be a potential for abuse by individuals having access to that level of information about national vulnerabilities, either for purposes of financial gain or for accession of political advantages. Institution of a special black-level category of classification might be necessary to combat that risk.

References

Bailey, T., et al. (2012). *Playing war games to prepare for a cyberattack* (Vol. 26). McKinsey on Business Technology.

Chegg. (2024). *Studies show that the length of time required for someone to solve a Rubik's cube puzzle for the first time is lognormally distributed.* www.chegg.com/homework-help/questions-and-answers/b-studies-show-length-time-required-someone-solve-rubik-s-cube-puzzle-first-time-lognormal-q154831128

GeeksforGeeks. (2023, November). *Lognormal distributions in business statistics.* www.geeksforgeeks.org/lognormal-distribution-in-business-statistics

LogRhythm. (2017, July). *NotPetya technical analysis.* LogRhythm Labs. www.logrhythm.com

McQuade, M. (2018, August). *The untold story of NotPetya, the most devastating cyberattack in history.* www.wired.com/story/notpetya-cyberattack-ukraine-russia-code-crashed-the-world

Miller, M. (2024). *Advantages and disadvantages of red team engagements.* Triaxion Security. www.triaxiomsecurity.com/advantages-and-disadvantages-of-red-team-engagements

Mitnick. (2024). *Know your enemy: Top tips from Kevin Mitnick.* Business and Tech, Digital Security. www.futureofbusinessandtech.com/digital-security/know-your-enemy-top-tips-from-kevin-mitnic

Pavlovic, M. (2022, February). *Log-normal distribution – A simple explanation.* www.towardsdatascience.com/log-normal-distribution-a-simple-explanation-7605864fb67

Rosencrance, L. (2011, September). *Did 9/11 really improve cybersecurity?* www.nbcnews.com/id/wbna44432062

SecurityScorecard. (2024, January 2). *22 cybersecurity metrics & KPIs to track in 2024*. www.securityscorecard.com/blog/9-cybersecurity-metrics-kpis-to-track/

Taboga, M. (2017, December). *Lectures on probability theory and mathematical statistics* (3rd edn). StatLect Book.

Temple-Raston, D. (2021, April). *A 'worst nightmare" cyberattack: The untold story of the solarwinds hack*. www.npr.org/2021/04/16/985439655/a-worst-nightmare-cyberattack-the-untold-story-of-the-solarwinds-hack

Tunggal, A. (2024, January 22). *14 cybersecurity metrics + KPIs you must track in 2024*. www.upguard.com/blog/cybersecurity-metrics

Chapter 10
Continuous Risk Management, Part 2: Internal Controls, Risk Mitigations, and Mission-Advancing Opportunities

This chapter continues on from Chap. 8 and has the following purposes:

- To provide definition and guidance relevant to the tracking and control steps of CRM;
- To discuss the nature and purpose of hierarchical internal controls with respect to risk management;
- To elaborate upon the summaries provided in Sect. 4.4 on the use of risk drivers to inform the identification of internal controls and risk mitigations;
- To identify information that should be provided to decision makers in order to facilitate their deliberations on whether to select or reject candidate risk mitigation options;
- To highlight the difference between tactical opportunities and strategic opportunities with respect to advancing the organization's mission;
- To provide a demonstration pertinent to the evaluation of strategic opportunities through the lens of risk drivers and the balancing of aggregate risks.

10.1 Introductory Remarks

The principal differences between risk-informed internal controls, risk mitigations, and mission-advancing opportunities, as means for achieving organizational objectives and goals and minimizing aggregate risks, can be characterized as follows:

- Risk-informed internal controls focus on the formulation and implementation of processes and provisions to ensure that aggregate risks that are deemed to be acceptable or at worst marginally acceptable remain so.
- Risk mitigations involve the identification and implementation of responsive actions, such as retrofits or add-ons, that are deemed to be needed if the aggregate risks have become intolerable or at least marginally intolerable.
- Mission-advancing opportunities concern the identification and implementation of forward-looking actions, such as introducing previously unavailable new technology or forming previously infeasible new partnerships, when the advantage of

A. S. Benjamin, *Integration of Project, Infrastructure, and Enterprise Risk Management*, Risk, Governance and Society 21,
https://doi.org/10.1007/978-3-031-85070-7_10

pursuing the opportunity can be shown to be worth the competing risks introduced by that pursuit.

To be most effective, internal controls, risk mitigations, and mission-advancing opportunities focus on the root causes of the aggregate risks, which are referred to as the risk drivers. These are determined from the results of sensitivity studies that are executed after the risk models have been developed and simulations have been completed for the baseline design and mode of operation. As discussed in Sect. 4.4, individual risk scenarios may be among the risk drivers, but the full set may also include individual performance parameters, individual events that appear in risk scenarios, individual leading indicators, faulty models or assumptions, uncertainties in input parameters, or combinations of the above that, when varied over their range of uncertainty, cause the aggregate risk to change from acceptable or marginally acceptable to intolerable or marginally intolerable. Section 4.4 also provided a list of twenty-one potential risk drivers, which can serve as a starting point for identifying other potential risk drivers.

10.2 CRM and Risk-Informed Internal Controls

In Sect. 1.3, a high-level view of the relationship between internal control, risk management, and governance was provided, and the concept of deriving hierarchical control loops to ensure that assumptions are protected and weaknesses are corrected was introduced. This section elaborates upon that earlier discussion to demonstrate the processes involved in developing hierarchical control loops.

10.2.1 Hierarchical Control Loops

Each control loop in a set of hierarchical control loops may be viewed as having the basic form shown in Fig. 10.1, which is based on a model presented by Nancy Leveson (in Leveson, 2012). The terminology in that figure was originally formulated to apply to control loops for mechanical systems, but it applies in a more general sense to control loops intended for any application. Some of the control loops act at the enterprise level, others at infrastructure/institutional levels, and still others at program/project levels.

An example form of a control loop hierarchy is shown in Fig. 10.2. The important features are as follows:

- The primary control loop derives from a strategic or top-level objective of the organization and follows the format of Fig. 10.1.
- Each monitoring and control mechanism in the primary control loop is considered to be an activity that may in itself need to be controlled via a secondary control loop. A secondary control loop would be necessary if there are risky

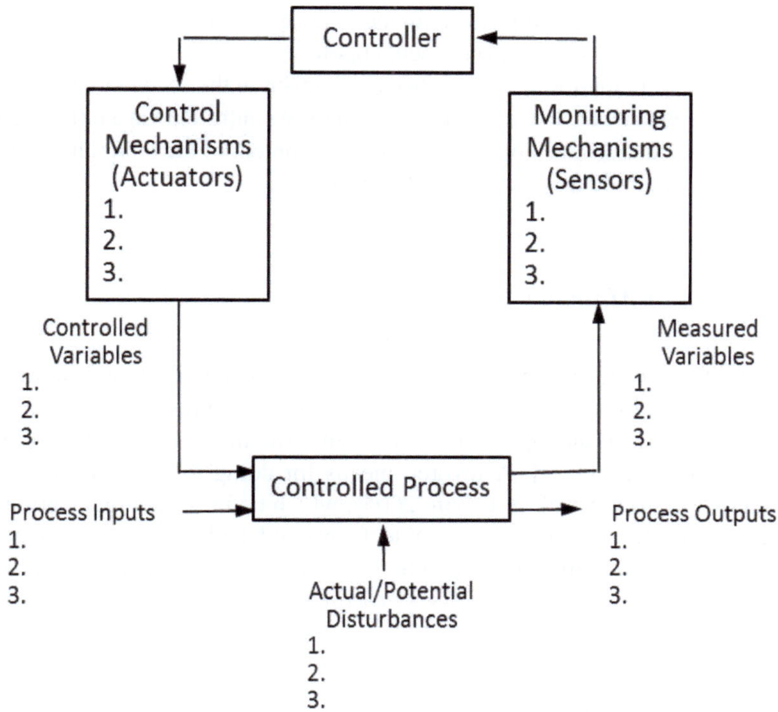

Fig. 10.1 Standard control loop form

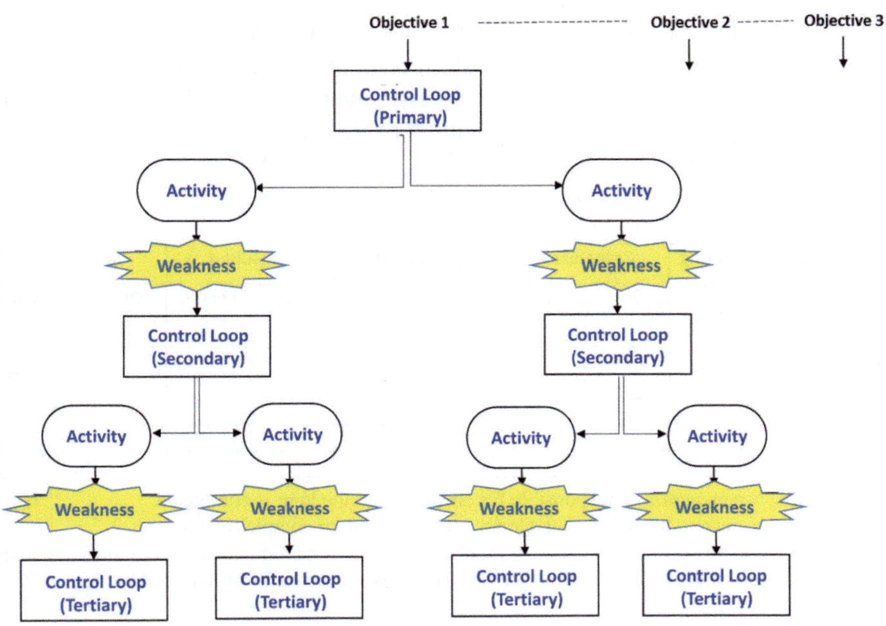

Fig. 10.2 Example form of a hierarchical system of internal control loops

elements of the activity (referred to in the figure as "weaknesses") that need to be monitored and, when appropriate, acted upon.

- Likewise, each monitoring and control mechanism in the secondary control loop is considered to be an activity that may need to be controlled via a tertiary control loop, based on risks that apply to it. The development of the hierarchy of control loops may continue to lower levels if needed.

10.2.2 RACI Matrices

Each activity in the hierarchy that spawns a lower-level control loop is assigned to an appropriate entity in the organization, has appropriate management oversight, and is communicated among other entities that have an interest or obligation that interfaces with that activity. A favored means for doing this is to develop a so-called RACI matrix (Smith & Erwin, 2005), which defines the organizations and people who are Responsible, Accountable, Consulted, and Informed on each activity (hence the acronym). An example form for a RACI matrix is shown in Table 10.1.

10.2.3 An Example

A detailed example demonstrating the processes described in the preceding two subsections may be found in my earlier book on risk management (Benjamin, 2017). The example concerns the identification of internal controls in an area that is pertinent to institutional/ infrastructure risk management (IRM): namely, the enterprise-wide institutional responsibility for safety and mission assurance.

Table 10.1 Example form of a RACI matrix

Control Loop	Monitoring or Control Activity	Responsible		Accountable		Consulted		Informed	
		Org.	Person	Org.	Person	Org.	Person	Org.	Person

Responsible = person or role responsible for ensuring that the item is completed
Accountable = person or role responsible for actually doing or completing the item
Consulted = person or role whose subject matter expertise is required in order to complete the item
Informed = person or role that needs to be kept informed of the status of item completion

10.3 CRM and Risk-Balancing Mitigations

10.3.1 Introduction to Risk Mitigation

During the lifecycle of a program, project, or other activity, conditions may arise that cause the aggregate risk to one or more organizational objectives to approach or exceed its risk tolerance level. If an aggregate risk is assessed to be intolerable, or at best marginally intolerable, it becomes important (perhaps essential) to consider mitigation options that have the potential to bring it back to acceptable, or at worst marginally acceptable. Mitigation options typically address one or more risk drivers, and are focused on reducing the performance risk where it is most in need of reduction, without producing too large a collateral increase of performance risk in other areas (e.g., cost and schedule). Because mitigation options can address one or more risk drivers, and because a single risk driver can be present in a number of individual risks, a single mitigation option can potentially be responsive to a substantial number of individual risks.

Mitigation can be classified into two broad categories. The first involves a reduction in the probability of conditions that have caused the risk to become intolerable, or in some cases an elimination of those conditions (as, for example, when an unreliable component that can cause an undesired event to occur is removed from a system). The second is a reduction of the severity of the consequence if the event or condition occurs.

Sometimes, successful mitigation (i.e., mitigation that brings all the aggregate risks to an acceptable or at least marginally acceptable level) can be accomplished easily, but in other cases, it may not be possible to do so unless one or more performance measure constraints, targets, risk tolerance levels, or risk acceptance levels are relaxed. This topic was discussed in Sect. 2.3, and the means for considering waivers and deviations was illustrated in Fig. 2.4. Figure 10.3 presents another graphical rendering of the deliberations involved in adjudicating requests for waivers and deviations, addressing it from management's point of view. These management decisions are within the purview of risk management but outside the purview of the risk analysts.

10.3.2 Identifying Mitigation Alternatives that Address Risk Drivers

The formulation of risk mitigations can take many forms, including (as mentioned in Sect. 4.4) changes in the design of a system that is in development, retrofits to existing systems, changes in manufacturing processes, changes in operating procedures, changes in management, formation of partnerships, proactive actions to inform and influence governing agencies, improved public relations, and cost sharing arrangements, to name a few.

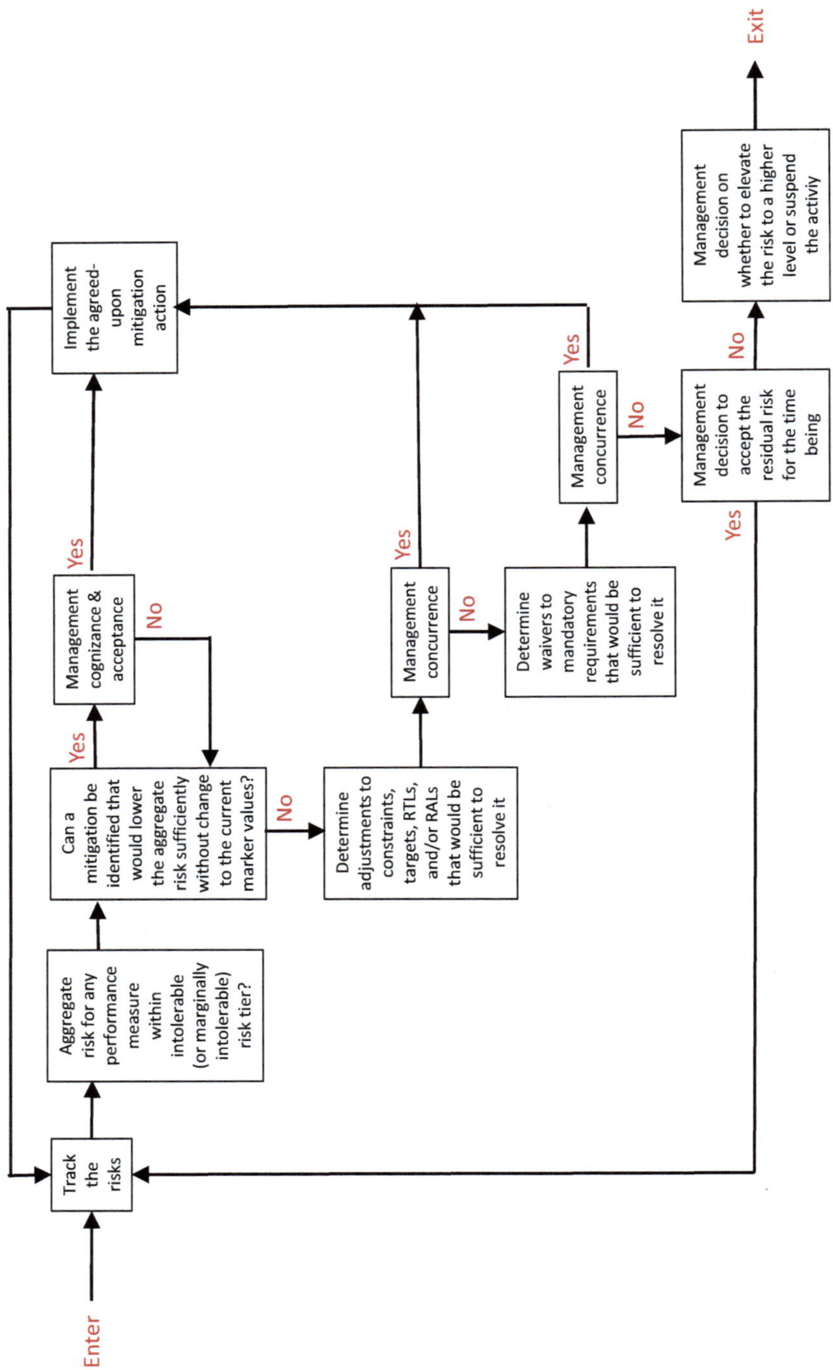

Fig. 10.3 Flow diagram of CRM aggregate risk result deliberations and management decisions regarding their acceptance or mitigation

Also as mentioned, the identification of risk mitigation options is directed at finding viable ways to reduce aggregate risks when they become intolerable or close to intolerable by acting on risk drivers. There is, however, an obvious limitation on the ability of an agency or business to influence risk drivers, in that not all drivers are actionable. When a driver is not actionable, the fallback is to identify other risk drivers that are actionable and that can exert an influence on the aggregate risk. For example, it is not within the province of a large high-tech organization to influence whom the voters choose to elect to Federal office, but it is within their province to track public sentiment and plan for alternative scenarios.

Table 10.2 provides a hypothetical set of seven risk drivers, and for each driver, two hypothetical risk mitigation options. It is not intended for the list to be at all comprehensive but rather to be illustrative of how mitigation options might be matched to risk drivers. Given the fact that the mitigation options differ for different risk drivers, it might well be necessary to propose that several mitigation options be investigated as part of a package so as to address all the important risk drivers that need addressing. I use the term "mitigation alternative" to refer to a package of mitigations options that addresses all important risk drivers.

Table 10.2 A set of example risk drivers and corresponding example mitigation options

Risk driver (root cause)	Mitigation options
1. Inadequate support for or excessive restrictions on needed acquisitions	• Develop an in-house capability in specified areas to replace the need for acquisitions
	• Establish partnerships on a quid-pro-quo basis
2. Model shortcoming or limitations in a particular subject area	• Additional directed or integrated testing to verify/validate the models
	• Retrofits or operational provisions that provide extra margin or defense-in-depth
3. An externally or internally initiated cyberattack	• Upgrades to cybersecurity software to detect and flag intrusions
	• Entry to sensitive areas allowed only with a security guard escort
4. Unreliability of specific components, subsystems, or other provisions in the design leading to unacceptable failure rates	• Replacement of unreliable components with more reliable ones
	• Retrofits or operational provisions that provide more fault tolerance
5. Workforce resignations due to dissatisfaction, reducing the capacity to address design or operational challenges in a timely manner	• Funding of incentives that increase employee satisfaction and therefore employee retention
	• More usage of qualified contractor personnel
6. Lack of provisions for positive human intervention to manage unexpected challenges during operation	• Better diagnostics to assist operator awareness of system status
	• More interactive usage of robotic systems including artificial intelligence
7. Uncertainties in the load capacity, extent of deformation, or thermal properties of certain materials due to environmental conditions during operation	• Redesign to provide shielding against environmental conditions such as radiation
	• Replacement of existing materials with hardened materials

10.3.3 Evaluating Mitigation Alternatives and Making the Case for a Particular One

Once a set of mitigation alternatives has been devised and defined in enough detail to support the analysis of individual and aggregate risks, the methods described in Sects. 4.1, 4.3.1, and 7.3.3 and illustrated in Figs. 4.1, 4.4, and 7.3 may be used to perform the analyses. Normally, if the mitigations comprising a mitigation alternative are relatively straightforward, it will be possible to carry over the models and simulation processes developed for the original risk analyses and risk undesirability scoring evaluation with minimal modification to account for the mitigations. This rule of thumb may not apply if the proposed mitigations are far reaching and complicated, however, and a new set of models may need to be developed. Once the models are in place, the analyses proceed as previously described in the earlier chapters. When done in that manner, the results will be displayable in the form of spider charts, as illustrated schematically in Fig. 10.4.

From the hypothetical results in Fig. 10.4, the decision maker would be led to conclude that Mitigation Alternative 2 should be selected over Alternative 1 because the highest risk undesirability score over all the performance measures is lower for Alternative 2 than for Alternative 1 or for the base case (unmitigated) alternative. However, for the decision to be well-informed and capable of being defended, other considerations should be included in the deliberation beside a comparison of risk undesirability scores.

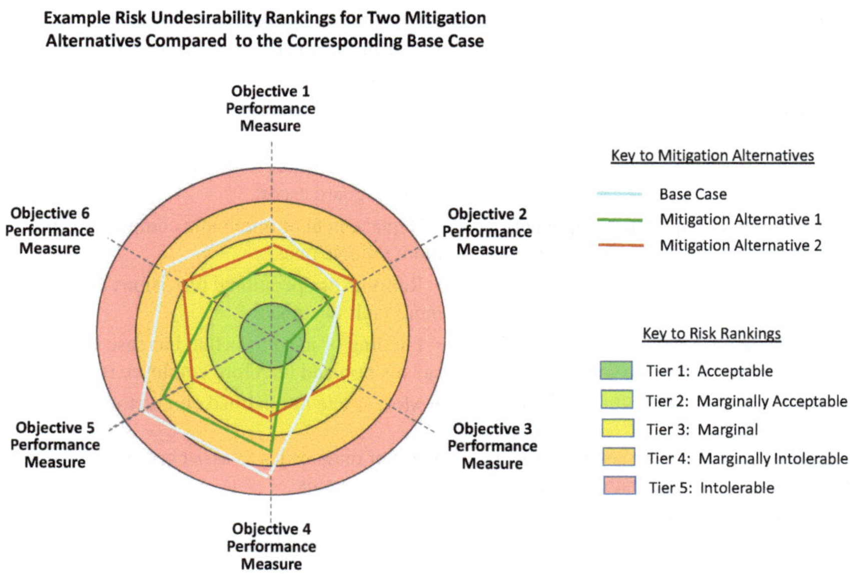

Fig. 10.4 Notional spider chart display for six organizational objectives comparing risk undesirability scores for two hypothetical mitigation alternatives and the corresponding base case

Toward this purpose, the following information and data should also be provided:

- A list of the most important risk drivers before and after the mitigation: Since the mitigation of aggregate risks is accomplished by attacking the root causes of these risks, it is important to provide perspective on the risk drivers that led to the set of mitigation alternatives being considered, and to highlight the potential risk drivers that remain after a mitigation alternative has been implemented and need to be monitored.
- The pros and cons of each alternative: An itemized table of all the pros and cons of each alternative is recommended because it enables conflicting opinions to be documented and captures elements of subjective value to the deliberators.
- Competing risks introduced by each alternative: Mitigation alternatives can potentially generate new risk scenarios or new U/U risk potentialities as the cost of addressing existing risk drivers. These should be identified and communicated to the decision-maker so that he or she understands not just the benefit but also the downside of each alternative.
- Cost-benefit tradeoff for each alternative: The cost and completion date for implementing and executing each alternative, along with their complete uncertainty distributions, should be made available to the decision maker so that the decision can be made with full knowledge of the issues that could affect funding and scheduling.
- The subjective opinions of technical authorities and subject matter experts: During the course of the deliberation, it is important for technical authorities and subject-matter experts to be present as participants in the discussion so that potential differences of opinion can be fully aired and understood.

10.3.4 Re-baselining the Program, Project, or Activity Plan When Necessary

In the course of CRM, a situation may arise where the aggregate risks have grown over time due to changes in conditions and it is not possible to reduce them to acceptable values that are in balance according to the risk tolerance and risk acceptance posture, even after considering relaxation of imposed restrictions such as constraints, risk tolerance and acceptance levels, and non-objectives based requirements. If that situation were to arise, the remaining option is to scope down some of the organizational objectives and consider adding new ones that offer a better promise for success. For example, if it is no longer feasible to accomplish Mission A within the acceptable risk posture, consider scoping it down to achievable proportions and adding Mission B. This alternative might necessitate a re-baselining of the portfolio of programs, including the de-scoping of some old ones and inclusion of some new ones. The re-baselining would constitute, in effect, a re-start.

A more constructive and more direct means for accomplishing the same thing, however, might be to find and take advantage of emerging strategic opportunities. This will be the subject of the next section.

10.4 CRM and Mission-Advancing Opportunities

10.4.1 Introduction to Tactical and Strategic Opportunities

As highlighted in Sect. 1.1.5, risk management in an opportunity-seeking culture involves finding a balance between seeking opportunity and accommodating risk within an acceptable risk posture. In a very basic sense, acting upon an opportunity occurs when the stakeholders' sense of gain from implementing it exceeds their sense of pain from the aggregate of the risks that are introduced by implementing it. (This statement constitutes a high-level definition of risk posture.)

Within the context of risk management, two types of opportunity may be distinguished: tactical and strategic (NASA, 2024):

1. Tactical opportunities provide a potential for reducing the risk to one or more of an entity's *existing* objectives. For example, a government agency that has begun execution on a project may be presented with an unexpected chance to involve a commercial partner that has specialized expertise not currently present in the organization unit, resulting in the task being performed more expeditiously and at lower cost, as well as promoting the generic goal of transferring technology to the private sector.
2. Strategic opportunities provide an opening for the organization to promote *new* objectives that advance the organization's overall mission. For example, the emergence of a new technology may open up possibilities for a government agency like NASA to explore further into the universe than was previously possible, or for a business enterprise to open up new avenues of revenue.

Both types of opportunity require an action to be performed in order for the opportunity to be realized: e.g., establishment of a contractual working relationship with the partnering organization or maturation and implementation of the new technology.

For both tactical and strategic opportunities, estimation of the magnitude of the benefit of an opportunity action requires consideration of both its positive effects and its negative effects. For example, a tactical action to involve a partnering organization with specialized skills and experience in an existing project may *reduce the risk* of exceeding the schedule and cost targets (its positive effect), but may also *increase the risk* from cyberattack by ceding control of part of the cybersecurity function to an organization outside the acquiring organization's direct control (its negative effect). Similarly, a strategic action to initiate a new program for purposes of exploiting a new technology breakthrough may allow the enterprise to pursue new objectives that align with its fundamental mission, which would likely provide a *potential for great benefit* (its positive effect), but at the same time would likely provide a *potential for high risk in the areas of cost and schedule* (its negative effect). Two potential sources of higher risk that go beyond cost and schedule include: (1) the fact that implementing fundamentally new technologies increases the potential for incurring unknown and underappreciated (U/U) risks, and (2) the possibility that manpower might have to be diverted from other programs to the new program, thereby inhibiting the enterprise from accomplishing all of its present objectives.

Tactical opportunities are treated in terms of risk tradeoffs, in the same way that an analysis of mitigation alternatives involves trading off risks to various objectives until the residual risks are as low as reasonably achievable (ALARA), while being balanced across objectives so as to satisfy the risk tolerance and acceptance posture. For example, the decision about whether or not to involve a partnering organization may hinge on whether the reduction in cost and schedule risk are needed to achieve the ALARA state and improve the risk balance when other risks, including reliability, safety, and cybersecurity, are considered together. Thus, the analysis of tactical opportunities and subsequent deliberation is no different from risk-informed decision making, which is a part of many organizations' current risk management practices.

Strategic opportunities, on the other hand, involve considerations of whether or not the program portfolio needs to be re-examined and re-baselined, and therefore employs the kinds of analyses described in Sect. 7.3.3 (Fig. 7.3, also Fig. 4.3 in Sect. 4.1). The last subsection in this chapter will explore in more detail the aspects of analysis and deliberation needed to help decision makers determine whether or not to implement a new strategic opportunity that requires adjustments to the enterprise's portfolio of programs and activities.

10.4.2 Demonstration of the Analysis of Alternative Portfolio Re-Baselining Options to Take Advantage of Emerging Strategic Opportunities

In this demonstration, a breakthrough spacecraft propulsion technology is assumed to occur (e.g., nuclear fusion propulsion), which enables NASA to contemplate conducting robotic spaceflights to reach orbit around and study planetary bodies in a neighboring solar system. This objective is not currently within the mission objectives listed in NASA's strategic plan because of the distance that must be traversed.

For this demonstration, I consider the following set of Agency-level objectives which are abstracted from NASA's, 2022 Strategic Plan and its FY23 Volume of Integrated Performance:

A. <u>Human Exploration of Moon & Mars</u>—Set up human colonies on the Moon and on Mars
B. <u>Robotic Exploration of Solar System</u>—Explore the Sun and other non-terrestrial bodies in the solar system through robotic system visits

C. Telescope Exploration of Universe—Learn more about other solar systems and galaxies in the universe using powerful telescopes
D. Weather Research from Space—Research weather dynamics on Earth from Space
E. Biological Research in Space—Prepare humans to survive in space environments
F. Aeronautical Systems Development—Develop high-tech aeronautical systems
G. Testing Facilities Development—Develop and maintain testing facilities
H. Staff & Supervisor Training—Train staff members and managers
I. Public Education & Engagement—Educate the public and build positive engagement

These are by no means intended to be a complete set of NASA's strategic objectives, but are rather selected to illustrate a process.

Given these objectives, the new technology breakthrough enables the following additional objective to be considered by NASA:

J. (New) Robotic Exploration of a Neighboring Solar System—Explore the star, planets, and moons of another solar system by sending a robotic mission to that solar system using propulsive power from a newly available technology (e.g., nuclear fusion propulsion)

To develop the demonstration further, the following two candidate portfolios are considered:

- Portfolio Option 1: No change to the present portfolio, which addresses Objectives A through I.
- Portfolio Option 2: Add a program to the portfolio to send a robotic spacecraft to a neighboring solar system to orbit some of the planets and moons of that solar system and return scientific data to Earth (thereby addressing New Objective J)

For portfolio option 2, it is immediately apparent to the risk analysts and to management that some scoping-down of programs in the original portfolio is necessary in order to compensate for the extra cost, manpower requirements, and facility usage that are required by the new program. The decision is made to apply the down-scoping across the set of existing programs in a manner that minimizes the amount of "pain" to the stakeholders; i.e., by conforming with the stakeholders' prioritization of the mission objectives as implied by their respective risk tolerance and acceptance levels. As a result, some amount of down-scoping is applied to all the existing programs, but in a way that does not incur an inordinate penalty to any one of them.

As mentioned above, the analysis to be performed for each portfolio option follows the methods and processes laid out previously in Sect. 7.3.3 and illustrated in Figs. 7.3 and 4.3. When it is completed, the resulting risk undesirability scores are plotted for each portfolio alternative on spider charts, as in Figs. 10.5 and 10.6.

In this demonstration, the original program portfolio, Option 1, succeeds in achieving an optimal balancing of the aggregate risks to Objectives A through I (Fig. 10.5), but since it does not address New Objective J, its risk score for that

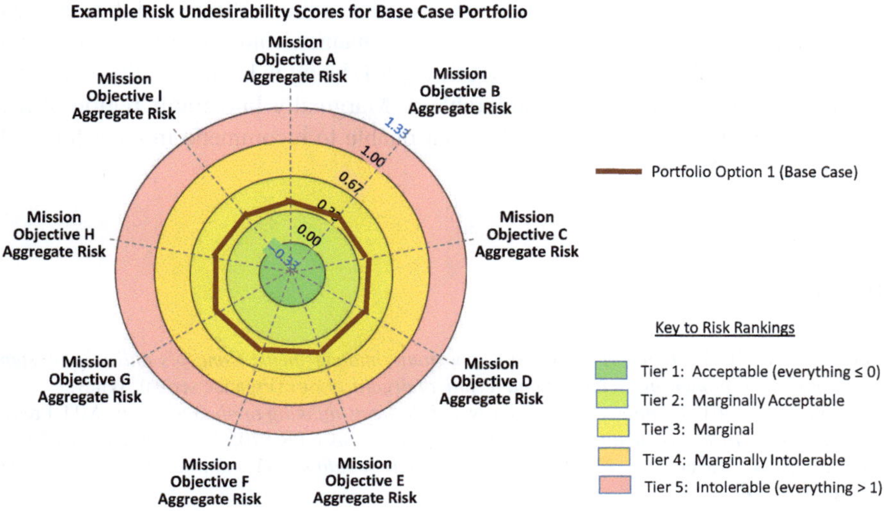

Fig. 10.5 Notional spider chart showing risk acceptability results for each original mission objective, for the baseline portfolio

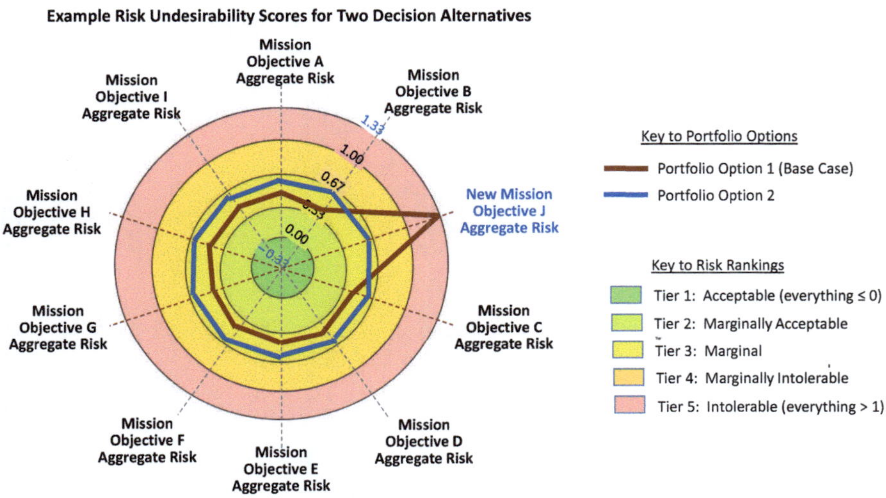

Fig. 10.6 Notional spider chart showing risk acceptability results for each original mission objective and the new objective, for the baseline portfolio and the re-baselined portfolio

objective is at the extreme end of "Intolerable" (Fig. 10.6). To be more precise, the risk undesirability score for New Objective J using Portfolio Option 1 is infinite, when calculated via the equation in Fig. 4.4, because the risk of program failure is 1.0 (since there is no program), while the risk tolerance and acceptance levels are both 0.0 (since there is no benefit).

In any event, the inclusion of the new program in the portfolio and the decision to divert the needed funding in a proportionate manner from each of the other programs results in all of the objectives (A through J) being in balance in this example, and none of them being in the Intolerable or Marginally Intolerable region of the chart. That being the case, it would be reasonable to recommend moving forward with Portfolio Option 2.

References

Benjamin, A. (2017). *Enterprise risk and opportunity management: Concepts and step-by-step examples for pioneering scientific and technical organizations* (Finance series). Wiley.

Leveson, N. G. (2012). *Engineering a safer world: Systems thinking applied to safety*. MIT Press.

NASA. (2022). *Risk classification for NASA payloads*. NASA NPR 8705.4C, Updated April 2022.

NASA. (2024, November). *NASA risk management handbook (Version 2, Part 1)*. NASA/SP-2024-3422.

Smith, M. L., & Erwin, J. (2005). *Role & Responsibility Charting (RACI)*. PMForum.org.

Chapter 11
Graded Analysis and Screening Analysis Approaches

The purposes of this Chapter are as follows:

- To provide guidance on how the level of comprehensiveness needed in the determination of aggregate risks and risk undesirability scores is governed by the importance of the activity, the time available to make a decision, and a number of other factors;
- To define different levels of comprehensiveness applicable to various situations, where the level of comprehensiveness is defined in terms of the diversity and completeness of the scenarios, leading indicators, and performance measures that are covered in the analysis;
- To identify and characterize simplified screening approaches that can be used to weed out inferior decision alternatives; and
- To introduce a set of equations that may be used in place of more complicated computational models when performing a screening analysis

11.1 Graded Analysis Approaches

11.1.1 Introduction

The purpose of applying a graded approach in the implementation of risk management is to maintain a level of detail and rigor that adds value without incurring unnecessary expenditure of unit resources. The resources and depth of analysis are commensurate with the stakes and the complexity of the decision situations being addressed.

The application of a graded approach has two dimensions:

- Dimension 1: Completeness of Coverage. The first dimension concerns the scope of the risk management purview, including the diversity and completeness of the objectives, performance measures, scenarios, leading indicators, input parameters, and sources of uncertainty that are covered.

A. S. Benjamin, *Integration of Project, Infrastructure, and Enterprise Risk Management*, Risk, Governance and Society 21,
https://doi.org/10.1007/978-3-031-85070-7_11

- Dimension 2: Model Rigor. The second dimension has to do with the nature of the models that are developed to evaluate the aggregated risks to performance associated with various concepts, designs, solutions, or mitigation responses. The models may be quantitative or qualitative, probabilistic or deterministic, first-order or highly detailed, applicable directly or by analogy, focused on individual scenarios or on aggregate risks, etc.

The second dimension was covered in Sect. 8.3.2, and so this subsection and the next focuses on the first dimension.

The nature of the graded approach in the breadth dimension (completeness of coverage) depends on a variety of factors, among which are:

- The importance of the activity. Importance has several sub-dimensions including (1) the activity's priority within the enterprise, (2) the activity's significance in the public domain, and (3) and the total cost of the activity (NASA, 2022, 2024). Generally speaking, activities of high importance demand rigor in modeling and completeness in coverage, while for activities with lower importance, a lower level of modeling rigor and coverage may be sufficient.
- The complexity of the activity. Complexity also has several sub-dimensions, including (1) complexity of design, (2) operational complexity, and (3) programmatic complexity. Within the dimension of design complexity, systems that have complex interactions between and among hardware elements, software elements, and/or human elements generally require a more rigorous level of analysis and testing than those that do not (see Perrow, 1999). These interactions may involve interfaces between hardware elements, between hardware and software elements, or between hardware/software and human elements.
- The novelty of the solution. Activities that rely on new technology or new processes are subject to many uncertainties regarding operational feasibility, technical performance, safety, security, and/or schedule and cost. For such activities, particular attention has to be paid, in each of these areas, to how the uncertainties are modeled, the completeness of coverage of all sources of uncertainty, and the applicability of the data used to populate the parameters of the uncertainty distributions. Such activities also require a risk management approach that emphasizes careful tracking of progress, midcourse corrections when needed, and analysis flexibility to enable adjustment to new findings along the way.
- The time available for response to risks. This factor affects the level of analysis coverage that can be exercised within the time available for responding to risks that have been newly uncovered, or to changing conditions that affect previously identified risks. It is sometimes true that less coverage may be necessary in order to obtain preliminary results that can be used for rapid-response decision making, with the understanding that more complete coverage will be exercised after the rapid response is completed. During the rapid response period, the issues, scenarios, leading indicators, and performance measures included in the analysis may be limited to those that are known from experience to be likely potential risk drivers. After the rapid response analysis has been completed, coverage is

broadened to include additional issues, scenarios, leading indicators, and performance measures to enable longer-term decisions to made with greater confidence.

- The level of the organizational entity. In general, organizational entities at lower levels in the organizational structure tend to be concerned with specific parts of a system or tasks within an activity, and so the emphasis is on quantitative analyses of the risks associated with specific identified scenarios or with specific, narrowly focused leading indicators. On the other hand, organizational entities at higher levels are concerned with integrated systems, entire missions, or activities at a high level, and so the emphasis is on qualitative understanding of aggregate risks and the status of broad leading indicators. Where feasible, the qualitative analyses are backed by quantitative analyses to obtain best results.

11.1.2 How Activity Importance and Timeframe Affect Choices Concerning the Scope, Inclusiveness, Completeness, and Rigor of Analyses that Support Risk Management

For purposes of assigning classifications for the scope, inclusiveness, completeness, and rigor of the analyses supporting risk management, NASA defines four graded approach levels, and labels them as Levels I through IV. They may be summarized as follows (see, for example, NASA, 2022, 2024):

- Graded Approach Level I (the highest level) stresses comprehensiveness and rigor in all the steps of risk management to ensure that the stakeholders' low risk tolerances for activities that are deemed to have high importance are satisfied.
- For Graded Approach Level II, the degree of comprehensiveness and rigor is scoped down from Level I so as to weed out or deemphasize the performance measures, issues, scenarios, and leading indicators that are deemed to be of lesser importance. This is done in a manner that is consistent with the stakeholders' higher risk tolerances for activities that are considered moderately important.
- For Graded Approach Level III, the degree of comprehensiveness and rigor is again scoped down to focus on performance measures, issues, scenarios, and leading indicators that have been demonstrated to be important by virtue of lessons learned from historical experience. This includes lessons learned not only from actual catastrophic occurrences but also from precursors that could have had the potential to develop into a catastrophe. The definition of Graded Approach Level III is consistent with the stakeholders' yet higher risk tolerances for activities that are of lower importance or that are very early in the development cycle.
- Graded Approach Level IV (the lowest level) applies only to Importance Class D activities, as defined in the following paragraph, which are themselves of lower value and for which the primary concern is that they may interface with items or activities of higher value. The minimum acceptable degree of comprehensiveness and rigor is low, except for scenarios where they produce risks to the items or activities of higher value.

The decision on which graded approach level to apply depends on all the factors mentioned earlier, but when talking about scope, inclusiveness, and completeness, there are two that stand out: (1) the importance of the activity and (2) the time available before a commitment has to be made. Regarding the first factor, the attributes involved in defining the importance of an activity can be illuminated using an example. The following example is based on the mission importance classifications adopted by NASA (see NASA, 2022):

- Mission Importance Class A: The highest activity importance classification, typically constituting all crewed missions plus un-crewed flagship activities with very high complexity, and a potential for loss of over about 6% of their annual budget.
- Mission Importance Class B: A high activity importance classification, but not as high as for Class A, typically representing un-crewed high priority activities with high complexity and a potential for loss of between 3% and 6% of their annual budget.
- Mission Importance Class C: A moderate activity importance classification, typically representing un-crewed medium priority activities with medium complexity, and a potential for loss of between 1% and 3% of their annual budget.
- Mission Importance Class D: A low activity importance classification, typically representing un-crewed low priority activities with low complexity, and a potential for loss of less than 1% of their annual budget.

Next, in addition to NASA's importance categories, I like to introduce timeframe categories and define them by comparing the time available to the time it would take to perform a comprehensive risk analysis.[1] I tend to use three timeframe categories, defined as follows:

- Timeframe Category 1: (least demanding) The timeframe for response is notably greater than the time required to perform a comprehensive risk analysis based on lifecycle-stage-appropriate modeling and simulation.
- Timeframe Category 2: The timeframe for response is approximately equal to the time required to perform a comprehensive risk analysis based on lifecycle-stage-appropriate modeling and simulation.
- Timeframe Category 3 (most demanding): The timeframe for response is notably less than the time required to perform a comprehensive risk analysis based on lifecycle-stage-appropriate modeling and simulation.

Each graded approach level is equated to different combinations of the importance class and the timeframe categories. The combinations that correspond to each particular graded approach level may be specified by the activity decision authority, in concert with the decision maker's knowledge of all the perturbing and mitigating factors that pertain to the activity. As a default, however, the decision maker may choose to use the following table (Table 11.1) which encapsulates the general

[1] NASA's recently published Risk Management Handbook (NASA 2024) does not include timeframe category as contributing to the graded approach level, although their risk analysis level of comprehensiveness is influenced by it in practice.

Table 11.1 Suggested activity-execution graded approach levels for various importance classes and timeframe categories

		Mission or activity importance Class			
		Class A (most important)	Class B	Class C	Class D (least important)
Timeframe category	Category 1 (least demanding)	I	II	III	IV
	Category 2	II initially, later I	III initially, later II	III	IV
	Category 3 (most demanding)	III initially, later II, then I	III initially, later II	III	IV

principle of expecting increasing coverage and completeness to go along with increasing importance and increasing time for response.

These criteria for the graded approach are intended to apply to all categories of risk management and all types of risk. In particular they are postulated to be applicable to all risk management activity domains (program/project, infrastructure/institutional, enterprise), all mission execution domains (safety, technical, security, cost, schedule, liability protection, public education, etc.), all stages along the mission timeline (concept development, design of the solution, implementation of the solution, conduct of the operation, decommissioning of the operation), and all different shades and gradations of risk (individual risks, leading indicators of unknown/underappreciated (U/U) risk, and aggregate risk to organizational objectives).

11.2 Analysis-of-Alternatives Screening Analysis Approach

One of the main purposes of screening analyses is to weed out decision alternatives that are clearly inferior, so that attention can be focused on alternatives that are more promising. This is different from graded analysis, where the main purpose is to scope the analysis to what is necessary and sufficient after the inferior alternatives have already been screened out.

For the purpose of screening analysis to weed out second-rate alternatives, it is usually sufficient to use the Pre-Phase-A analysis models defined in Sect. 8.3.2, in conjunction with the Level III graded analysis approach defined in Sect. 11.1.2. In that way, attention is focused on models that employ analogy estimating methodology, parametric estimating, engineering build up methodology, first order estimating methodology, similarity estimating methodology, and first order parametric estimation (Sect. 8.3.2), and on performance measures, issues, scenarios, and leading indicators that have been demonstrated to be potentially important based on lessons learned from historical experience including both actual occurrences and precursors (Sect. 11.1.2).

11.2.1 Method Overview

The overall Monte Carlo analysis approach depicted in Figs. 4.1 and 7.3, together with Fig. 4.3, works as well for screening analyses as for the more rigorous and comprehensive analyses that are exercised after the poorer alternatives have been screened out. Furthermore, it is not as expensive or time-consuming to set up and execute, because the models that determine performance measure distributions are less complex and less numerous.

For example, in activities involving complex systems, separate system response modules may be needed for different risk scenarios, since each risk scenario defines the state of the system or the environment it is exposed to, both of which are inputs to the response models. In addition, different response models are needed for different performance measures. All told, the number and complexity of performance models needed in a Level-I comprehensive analysis for a large high-tech activity can be daunting. On the other hand, the number of risk scenarios and complexity of the models will be greatly reduced for Level-III screening analyses, so the number and complexity of the performance models will correspondingly be much more amenable.

11.2.2 Simplifications to Performance Modeling and Analysis

The graphic labeled as "Chart B" in Figs. 4.1 and 7.3 provides a general depiction of the integrated modeling needed to determine performance measure values for all of the objectives being considered in the analysis. During screening analyses where model complexity is intentionally reduced, it is possible to replace Chart B by a set of equations that act as a surrogate for the more general flowchart and are relatively simple to conceive. The ability to express each performance measure model in equation form stems from the fact that in the screening analysis, the models are based on analogy estimation, parametric estimation, and other first-order estimation techniques, as defined in Section 8.3.2, rather than on detailed mathematical formulations containing differential equations, integral equations, or complex algorithms. Figure 11.1 illustrates the transformation from flow-chart format to a simpler equation format.

After looking at Fig. 11.1, some readers may be interested in learning about the origin of each equation on the right-hand chart, while others may not. For interested practitioners, the next subsection will address the math that is implicit in the equations. Those who are not interested in this level of detail, are not able to spend the time, or are just not equation nerds may want to proceed directly to Chap. 12. In other words, the equations themselves are interesting but are not an essential part of the concepts being developed in this book.

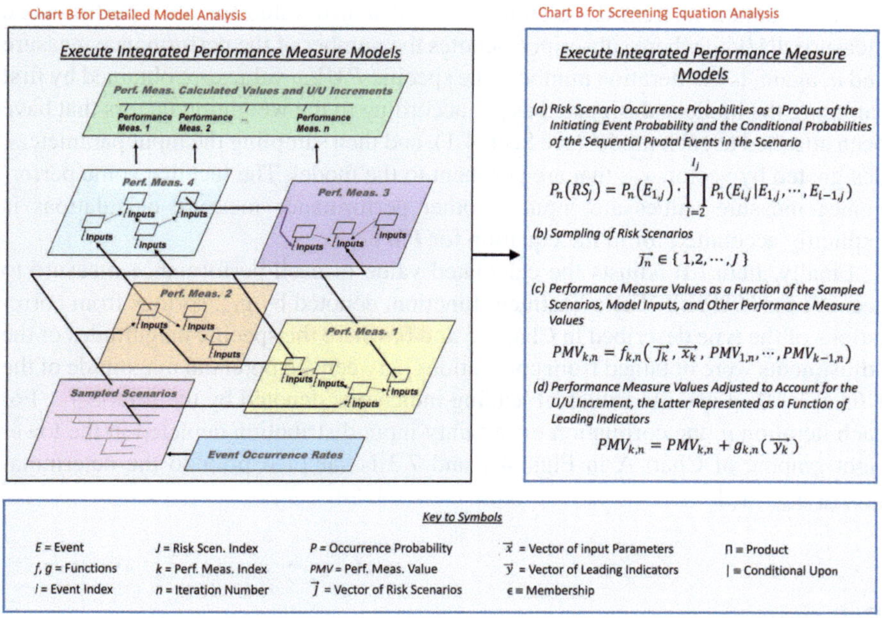

Fig. 11.1 An equation-based form of the integrated performance analysis flowchart that is suitable for screening analyses

11.2.3 For Equation Nerds Only

The equation in Item (a) of the right-hand version of Chart B establishes the occurrence probability, $P_n(RS_j)$, for each risk scenario that is defined for the screening analysis, where subscript j denotes the scenario and n denotes the current Monte Carlo iteration number. The scenario occurrence probabilities are determined by sampling the occurrence probabilities of the events $P_n(E_{i,j})$, that comprise the scenario, where i denotes the event number. For a given scenario j, the total number of relevant events is designated as I_j. Dependencies between the events are accounted for by allowing each event occurrence probability to be conditional upon the occurrence probabilities of all the events that precede it in the scenario.

After Item (a) is completed, there will be a total of J scenario occurrence probabilities, where J is the total number of scenarios designated for the analysis. Item (b) of Chart B on the right-hand side then establishes which of the J scenarios occur for Monte Carlo iteration n and denotes that set of scenarios by the vector $\overrightarrow{J_n}$. The inclusion or non-inclusion of a given scenario j during iteration m is determined by random sampling, with the likelihood of occurrence being $P_n(RS_j)$ and the likelihood of non-occurrence being $1 - P_n(RS_j)$.

The equation in Item (c) establishes a calculated value for each performance measure, $PMV_{k,n}$, where subscript k denotes the number of the performance measure and n, again, is the iteration number. The specific $PMV_{k,n}$ values are obtained by first sampling the models, designated as $f_{k,n}$, according to the weighting factors that have been attached to each model (see Sect. 4.1), and then sampling the input parameters, designated by vector $\overrightarrow{x_k}$, that are pertinent to the model. The fact that some performance measure values are input to other performance measure calculations is explicitly accounted for in the equation for $PMV_{k,n}$.

Finally, Item (d) adjusts the calculated value of each performance measure to account for U/U risk. The adjustment function, denoted by $g_{k,n}$, springs from correlations of the type described in Chaps. 5 and 6, where the specific magnitudes of the adjustments were obtained from correlations between the potential magnitude of the U/U risk effect and the values of leading indicators, denoted by the vector $\overrightarrow{y_k}$. For each iteration n, the correlation uncertainty input distribution depicted in the lower right graphic of Chart A in Figs. 4.1 and 7.3 is sampled prior to the determination of $g_{k,n}\left(\overrightarrow{y_k}\right)$.

References

NASA. (2022). *Risk classification for NASA payloads*. NASA NPR 8705.4C, Updated April 2022.

NASA. (2024, November). *NASA risk management handbook (Version 2, Part 1)*. NASA/SP-2024-3422.

Perrow, C. (1999). *Normal accidents: Living with high-risk technologies*. Princeton University Press.

Chapter 12
Example No. 1 on Accounting for Dependencies Between Risk Scenarios

12.1 Setup

The principal purpose of this short chapter is to demonstrate the importance of accounting for risk scenario dependencies during risk aggregation and suggest means for doing so.

Overlooking dependencies or underestimating them can lead to incorrect results. Demonstrating this requires some knowledge of Boolean algebra, which can be daunting, but it is worth pursuing to at least a limited extent to demonstrate the point. The example to be used here emanates from Fig. 8.6, which is repeated here for reference as Fig. 12.1.

As previously stated in Sect. 8.3.4, Objective O1 concerns the ability of the organizational unit to maintain a sufficient number of senior IT specialists to support Project X, O2 concerns its ability to hire a sufficient number of junior IT specialists fresh from college if O1 is not met, and O3 concerns its ability to provide in-house courses on the organizational unit's IT networks and processes for the newly hired junior IT specialists. If objective O1 is unsuccessful and either O2 or O3 is unsuccessful, then objective O4, concerning the overall level of IT expertise needed for Project X, is considered to be unsatisfied. As shown in Fig. 12.1, the failure to achieve objective O1 is mediated by the combined effects of risk scenarios RS1 and RS2, objective O2 by scenarios RS1 through RS5, and objective O3 by scenario RS6.

12.2 Analysis

Suppose a preliminary analysis of the various risk scenarios by the RM analysis team indicates that none of them individually is capable of causing a shortage of qualified and trained IT personnel. On the other hand, a combination of scenarios

A. S. Benjamin, *Integration of Project, Infrastructure, and Enterprise Risk Management*, Risk, Governance and Society 21,
https://doi.org/10.1007/978-3-031-85070-7_12

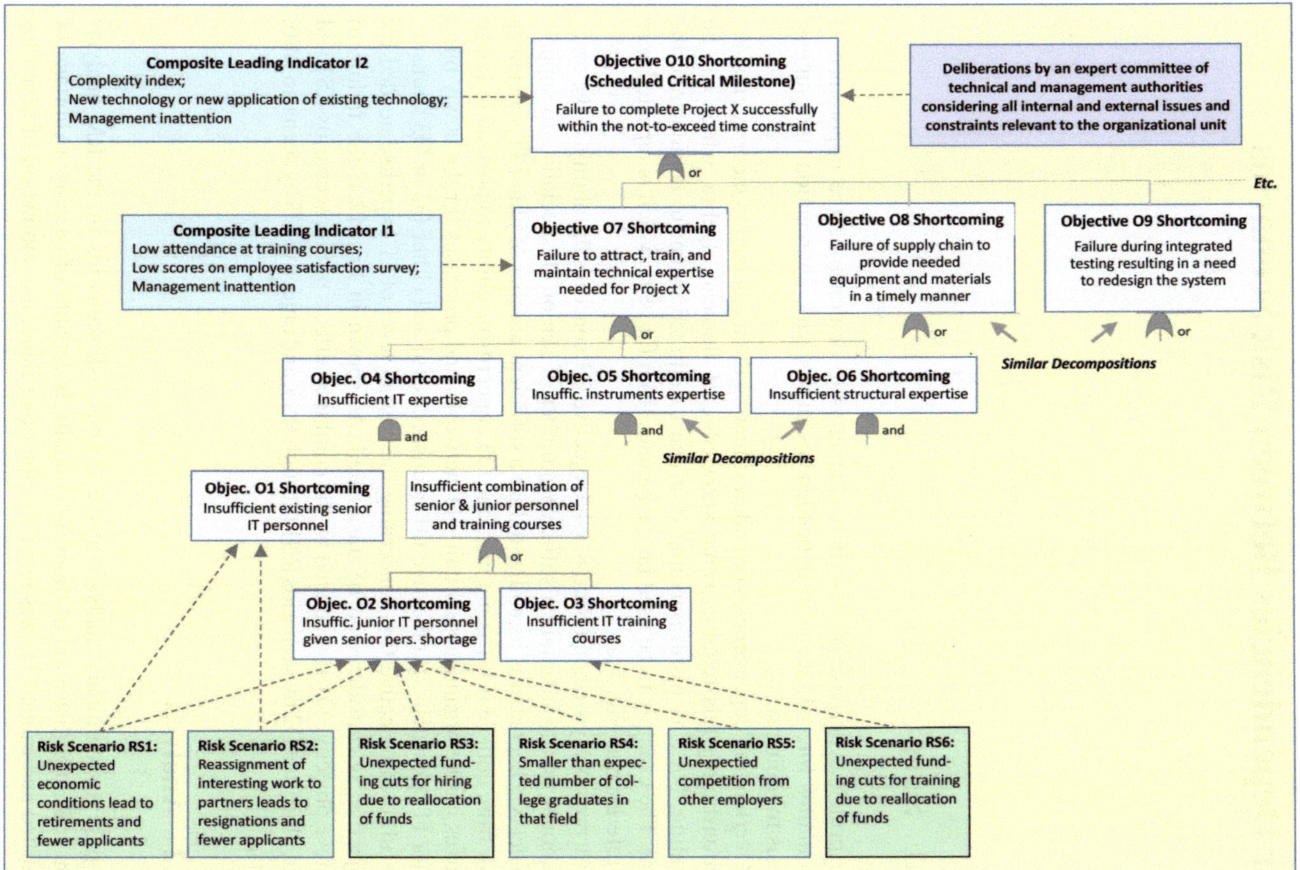

Fig. 12.1 Fault tree representation for the example

*RS*1 and *RS*3, or a combination of *RS*1 and *RS*6 are judged to have the potential for failing objective O4. *RS*1 (an economic recession causing early retirements) and *RS*3 (lack of funding for hiring) could reinforce each other to provide a shortage of qualified IT personnel, as could *RS*1 and *RS*6 (lack of funding for training courses).

To estimate the risk to O4 attributable to these combinations of risk scenarios, the analysis team defines the following performance measure:

- $PM_4 = N_1 + \alpha N_2$
- N_1 = the number of IT senior full-time equivalents (FTEs) available for Project X
- N_2 = the number of trained IT junior FTEs available for Project X
- α = the ratio of the productivity of junior IT personnel to senior IT personnel.

From experience, the team estimates that a reasonable value for α is 0.75, meaning that four junior IT personnel with training are considered to be equivalent in productivity to three senior IT personnel. (This particular value of α should be interpreted as hypothetical for this example, and not a universal rule of thumb.)

Suppose the constraint value, risk tolerance level, and risk acceptance level for performance measure PM_4 have been specified prior to the analysis to have the following values:

- $PMC_4 = 25$ FTEs, meaning that the quorum can be met with 25 senior IT personnel and no junior IT personnel, or 22 senior personnel and 4 trained junior personnel, or 19 senior personnel and 8 trained junior personnel
- $RTL_4 = 0.10$, meaning that the risk is intolerable if the probability of the performance measure value being less than 25 FTEs, symbolically referred to as $P(PMV_4 < PMC_4)$, is greater than or equal to 10%
- $RAL_4 = 0.05$, meaning that the risk is acceptable if $P(PMV_4 < PMC_4) < 5\%$

In the absence of any of the risk scenarios actualizing (i.e., the base case, or design-basis case, used for formulating the project plan), the expectation of the project team is that there will be 24 senior FTEs remaining on staff after normal retirements are considered and 4 junior FTEs will be hired and trained. Thus, the performance measure mean value in the base case is $PMV_4 = 24 + (0.75)(4) = 27$ FTEs. Since the constraint is 25 FTEs, the constraint is satisfied with 2 FTEs to spare.

If a major recession occurs, it is estimated based on historical experience (still hypothetical for this example) that 10 of the 24 existing senior IT personnel will retire earlier than planned, causing N_1 to reduce to 14 FTEs. However, in the absence of funding cuts for hiring and training, it will be easy to replace the loss of 10 senior personnel with 12 new hires that can be trained on the job, bringing the value of N_2 up to 4 + 12 = 16 FTEs. Thus, the calculated performance measure value for objective O4 is:

$$PMV_4 = 14 + (0.75)(16) = 26\,\text{FTEs} \tag{12.1}$$

which meets the requirement of at least 25 FTEs.

If the combination of risk scenarios RS1 and RS3 actualizes, there will still be a loss of 10 senior IT personnel, and because there will be no new hires due to the funding cut for hiring, the number of trained junior IT personnel will remain at $N_2 = 4$. Thus, the calculated performance measure value for objective O4 is:

$$PMV_4 = 14 + (0.75)(4) = 17\,\text{FTEs} \tag{12.2}$$

implying that the constraint of 25 FTEs will not be met.

The probability of RS1 and RS3 occurring simultaneously is estimated as follows. The probability of a major recession during the development time for Project X is estimated based on economic data such as the composite index of leading indicators (for example) to be 0.10, or 10%. Should a major recession occur, the probability of funding being cut for new hires is estimated to be 0.50, or 50%. Thus, the joint probability of occurrence of RS1 and RS3 is the probability that RS1 occurs times the probability that RS3 occurs given that RS1 occurs. Mathematically, this may be written as follows:

$$P(RS1 \cap RS3) = P(RS1)P(RS3 \mid RS1) = (0.10)(0.50) = 0.05 \tag{12.3}$$

If the combination of risk scenarios RS1 and RS6 actualizes, the same number of existing senior IT personnel will retire early and there will be no funding for training courses. Thus, the calculation results in the same values: $PMV_4 = 17$ FTEs and $P(RS1 \cap RS6) = 0.05$.

The probability of failure for Objective O4 has to take account of the overlap between the two composite scenarios, $RS1 \cap \text{RS3}$ and $RS1 \cap RS6$. Suppose it is estimated that the probability of funding for training being cut if funding for hiring has already been cut is 0.20, or 20%. The net probability for there not being enough IT specialists is therefore:

$$P(PMV_4 < 25\,\text{FTEs}) = 0.05 + 0.05 - (0.05)(0.20) = 0.09 \tag{12.4}$$

The full mathematical expression from which this derives, for those who are mathematically inclined, is as follows (see, for example, Yale, 1997; Mathematics, 2014):

$$P[(RS1 \cap RS3) \cup (RS1 \cap RS6)] = P(RS1 \cap RS3) + P(RS1 \cap RS6) - P(RS1 \cap RS3) \cdot P[(RS1 \cap RS6) \mid (RS1 \cap RS3)] = 0.05 + 0.05 - (0.05)(0.20) = 0.09 \tag{12.5}$$

Here the symbol "∪" translates to "union", "∩" translates to "intersection", and "|" translates to "conditional upon".

Since the risk tolerance and acceptance levels have been specified to be 0.10 and 0.05, respectively, and $0.05 \le 0.09 < 0.10$, the risk acceptability for objective O4 is deemed to be "marginally intolerable," meaning that it is marginal but closer to intolerable than to acceptable. One way to mitigate the aggregate risk so that it becomes acceptable might be for higher-level management to provide for a sharing of IT personnel across different projects.

To illustrate the importance of correctly treating the dependencies, consider what the result would have been if the risks were all considered to be independent. The calculation in that case is very simple: $P(PMV_4 < 25 \text{ FTEs}) = P(RS1) \times [P(RS3) + P(RS6)]$. Suppose that the unconditional probability is estimated to be 0.10 for all three risks (ignoring the fact that if risk *RS*1 actualizes because of a major recession, then risks *RS*3 and *RS*6 are more likely to actualize because of the same reason). Then the probability of *PMV*4 being less than 25 FTEs would be $0.1 \times (0.1 + 0.1) = 0.02$, a value that is 4.5 times less than the correct value of 0.09 and well within the risk acceptance level. The implication of ignoring the dependencies between the risks is clear: it leads to incorrect results.

12.3 Common Cause Treatment

In fault tree analysis, accounting for dependencies in the aggregation of risks can be a daunting challenge, particularly when there are many dependencies. For example, in the fault tree of Fig. 12.1, it could well be expected that there would be significant dependencies between Objectives O4, O5, and O6, since the risks leading to shortages in IT personnel, instrumentation personnel, and structural design personnel could emanate from the same or similar sources (e.g., a national recession that reduces funding for hiring or a political change of guard that reprioritizes how existing funding gets allocated). Likewise, at a higher level, there could be significant dependencies between Objectives O7 and O8. (For example, a national recession, a political change of guard, or an unexpected problem with a widely needed technology could affect both in-house staffing requirements and supply chain ability to deliver.) At a still higher level, there could be important dependencies between top-level Objective O10 (accomplishing Project X successfully and within schedule) and the same top level objective for other projects, affecting mission success risk and reputational risk at the very top level of the enterprise. Clearly, a sound treatment of dependencies is critical for any effort that addresses program/project, institutional/infrastructure, and enterprise risk management activity domains in an integrated manner.

Fortunately, in most situations, the problem of dependencies can be made tractable through the use of common cause methodology (Rasmuson & Mosleh, 2007; Stamatelatos & Dezfuli, 2011). As previously discussed in Sect. 8.3.4, common cause analysis identifies the modes of failure that have the potential of being triggered by a single, more basic root cause, and incorporates the root cause as the initiating event for all risk scenarios that are affected by it. Of course, as cited in Sect. 8.3.4, accounting for dependencies by decomposing the logic to independent common causes can itself become a complicated proposition if there are many potential common causes, but at least the dependencies will be resolved. That section of the book also cites several additional useful references pertaining to the formulation and implementation of common cause methodology (Worrell & Stack, 1977; NRC, 1981, 2007; Jones, 2012).

References

Jones, H. W. (2012, November). *Common cause failures and ultra reliability*. American Institute of Aeronautics and Astronautics, AIAA 2012-3602.

Mathematics. (2014, February). *Probability of the union of 3 events?* Mathematics Stack Exchange. https://math.stackexchange.com/questions/669249/probability-of-the-union-of-3-events

NRC. (1981, January). *Fault tree handbook*. Nuclear Regulatory Commission, NUREG-0492.

NRC. (2007, September). *Common-cause failure database and analysis system: Event data collection, classification, and coding*. Nuclear Regulatory Commission, NUREG/CR-6268, Rev. 1.

Rasmuson, D. M., & Mosleh, A. (2007, June). *A brief history of common-cause failure analysis*. IAEA Technical Meeting on CCF in Digitial Instrumentation and Control Systems for Nuclear Power Plants.

Stamatelatos, M., & Dezfuli, H. (2011, December). *Probabilistic risk assessment procedures guide for NASA managers and practitioners* (2nd ed.). NASA/SP-2011-3421.

Worrell, R. B., & Stack, D. W. (1977). *Common cause analysis using SETS* (pp. 77–1832). Sandia National Laboratories, SAN.

Yale. (1997). *Conditional probability*. Yale University Online Course 1997-98. http://www.stat.yale.edu/Courses/1997-98/101/condprob.htm

Chapter 13
Example No. 2 on Multi-Year Milestone Risk Analysis

It is a long-accepted practice for all enterprises, whether financial, small business, large business, government, low-tech, or high-tech, to review how many of their key milestones have been achieved over the past year, and to keep a running count year-to-year. Most also make at least a qualitative prognosis of how many key milestones will be met during the coming year (see, for example, NASA's most recent Volume of Integrated Performance (VOIP, 2024)). However, few if any actually perform a quantitative milestone risk analysis to extend the prognosis for future milestone success or failure beyond a year or so and to account for uncertainties in a rational manner.

The methods presented in Chaps. 4, 7, and 11 allow such an analysis to be performed, and they also provide the basis for using milestone risks to help determine the viability of the program portfolio. The following example is intended to demonstrate this.

13.1 Setup

The purpose here is to utilize the methods developed earlier to determine uncertainty distributions for key milestone slippages and to aggregate those slippage risks to organizational or portfolio objectives. The key milestones are defined for each objective and for each of several years. For example, let's assume that the objectives to be satisfied are those listed as A through I in Sect. 10.4.2 (a total of nine objectives that were abstracted from NASA 2022 and VOIP 2022). Objective A, for instance, was human exploration of Earth's moon and the planet Mars. Let's further suppose that the timeframe of interest is five years after the present year, which at this writing is 2024. Then there will be a separate set of key milestones for each objective for years 2025, 2026, 2027, 2028, and 2029.

A. S. Benjamin, *Integration of Project, Infrastructure, and Enterprise Risk Management*, Risk, Governance and Society 21,
https://doi.org/10.1007/978-3-031-85070-7_13

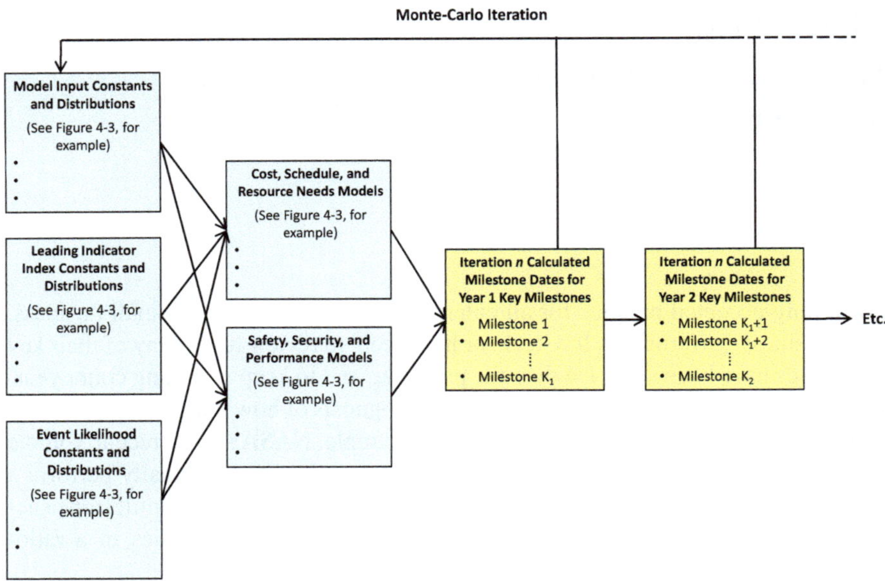

Fig. 13.1 Example inputs, models, and outputs to apply to the analysis of key milestone risks

By way of review, Fig. 4.1 in Chap. 4 illustrated the steps involved in performing a Monte Carlo analysis to determine the aggregate risks to the objectives of any organizational entity, while Fig. 7.3 in Chap. 7 did the same for making that determination with respect to a portfolio of programs at enterprise level. Figure 4.3 provided an example of the kinds of input parameter distributions and logical and phenomenological models that might need to be developed for this purpose. These figures are still applicable as examples, but the results of interest at the individual milestone level are the probability distributions for the dates on which each key milestone will be met, in place of the performance measures listed on the right-most chart of Fig. 4.3.

Figure 13.1, above, provides a more simplified version of Fig. 4.3 that concentrates on the determination of achievement date distributions for the key milestones. The distribution for each date of achievement may be compared to the date specified in the program or project plan, the collection of which is shown schematically in Fig. 13.2.

13.2 Analysis

The purpose of the analysis is to make a determination of risk undesirability scores pertaining to overall schedule, or what I will refer to herein as *schedule risk undesirability scores* (SRUS).

Year 1 from End of Present Year

Key Milestone Number	Planned Achievement Date
k = 1	-----
k = 2	-----
⋮	⋮
$k = K_1$	-----

Year 2 from End of Present Year

Key Milestone Number	Planned Achievement Date
$k = K_1+1$	-----
$k = K_1+2$	-----
⋮	⋮
$k = K_2$	-----

⋮

Year 5 from End of Present Year

Key Milestone Number	Planned Achievement Date
$k = K_4+1$	-----
$k = K_4+2$	-----
⋮	⋮
$k = K_5$	-----

Fig. 13.2 Schematic of key milestones and planned achievement dates

13.2.1 Calculation of Aggregate Schedule Risks

The calculation of the aggregate schedule risks has four dimensions, and to perform the analysis, each dimension is taken to have a set of possible discrete values. Table 13.1 provides a synopsis of the dimensions and the discrete values that are used in this example.

To evaluate aggregate schedule risks, it is necessary to define performance measures at the level of the organizational objectives. Each performance measure (one for each of the nine objectives and for each of the five evaluation years) should act as a reasonable surrogate for the cumulative effect of the key milestone slippages on the success of that objective for the year under evaluation.

There are various ways to define objectives-level performance measures. The most general approach (and most defensible one) is to elicit appropriate functional

Table 13.1 Itemization of dimensions and discrete values for the example

Value No.	Dimension No., corresponding subscript, and definition			
	1 (i) Organization objective	2 (j) Evaluation year (after current year)	3 (k) Key milestone arranged by year	4 (n) Monte Carlo iteration number
1	1 = Obj. A	1	1 (Yr. 1)	1
2	2 = Obj. B	2	2 (Yr. 1)	2
3	3 = Obj. C	3	3 (Yr. 1)	3
4	4 = Obj. D	4	4 (Yr. 2)	4
5	5 = Obj. E	5	5 (Yr. 2)	5
6	6 = Obj. F		6 (Yr. 2)	6
7	7 = Obj. G		7 (Yr. 3)	7
8	8 = Obj. H		8 (Yr. 3)	8
9	9 = Obj. I		9 (Yr. 3)	9
10			10 (Yr. 4)	10
11			11 (Yr. 4)	11
12			12 (Yr. 4)	12
13			13 (Yr. 5)	13
14			14 (Yr. 5)	14
15			15 (Yr. 5)	15
⋮				⋮
10,000				10,000

relationships from the organizational managers and technical leads, using an elicitation process similar to the ones described in Sects. 3.2.2 and 7.3.4. The intention is to reflect their consensus viewpoint regarding key milestones and their effects on objectives.

To facilitate an understanding of the general approach, it is useful to represent it in mathematical terms. Performance measure $(PMV)_{i,j}$ is evaluated as follows:

$$\left(PMV\right)_{i,j} = f_{i,j}\left(\overrightarrow{MS}_{k\epsilon j}\right) \tag{13.1}$$

where $f_{i,j}$ denotes the functional relationship for objective i in evaluation year j, and $\overrightarrow{MS}_{k\in j}$ is a vector of key milestone slippages comprising milestones applicable to year j. Each elicited function can be an equation or an algorithm.

In cases where a simple approximation is preferred, it may be sufficient to replace each functional relationship by a weighting factor, and then to add up all the slippages multiplied by their weights. The managers and technical leads would be asked to provide only weighting factors rather than full functional relationships. The mathematical representation is as follows:

$$\left(PMV\right)_{i,j} = \sum_{k\epsilon j} w_{i,k} \left(MS\right)_k \delta_k \tag{13.2}$$

where $w_{i,k}$ is the weighting factor for milestone k reflecting its importance to objective i in the year that the milestone is scheduled to occur; $(MS)_k$ is the calculated slippage (measured in days, for example) for milestone k; δ_k is a "Kronecker delta", having a value of 1 when $(MS)_k > 0$ and a value of 0 when $(MS)_k \leq 0$; and the summation is performed over milestones k that are members of evaluation year j. The weighting factors are defined such that $\sum_{k\epsilon j} w_{i,k} = 1.0$.

13.2.2 Calculation and Display of Schedule Risk Undesirability Scores

Once objective-level performance measures are defined, probability distributions for them may be readily calculated using the results obtained from the Monte Carlo milestone slippage analysis (Fig. 13.1). Thereafter, using the methods of Sects. 3.2.2 and 4.3.1, risk tolerance and risk acceptance levels may be defined and schedule risk undesirability scores may be deduced for each objective and each evaluation year. Figure 13.3 shows example results.

After the process has been completed, a spider chart similar to Fig. 13.4 can be prepared, portraying the schedule risk undesirability scores for all the organizational objectives for each evaluation year. The spider chart relates the degree to which the accumulation of the key milestone risks affects the risks to objectives and suggests how much time is available to take mitigative action.

As a final comment, it may be noted that the above analysis, which was presented in the context of a full-scale quantitative assessment with expert input, can also be performed in the context of a screening analysis, wherein the guidelines in Sect. 11.2 and its subsections apply. In the screening analysis approach, the events and conditions that are considered in the analysis of milestone slippages are ones that have been significant contributors to risk in the past, and the models used are first-order prediction models. Otherwise, the basic processes are the same as in the full-scale approach.

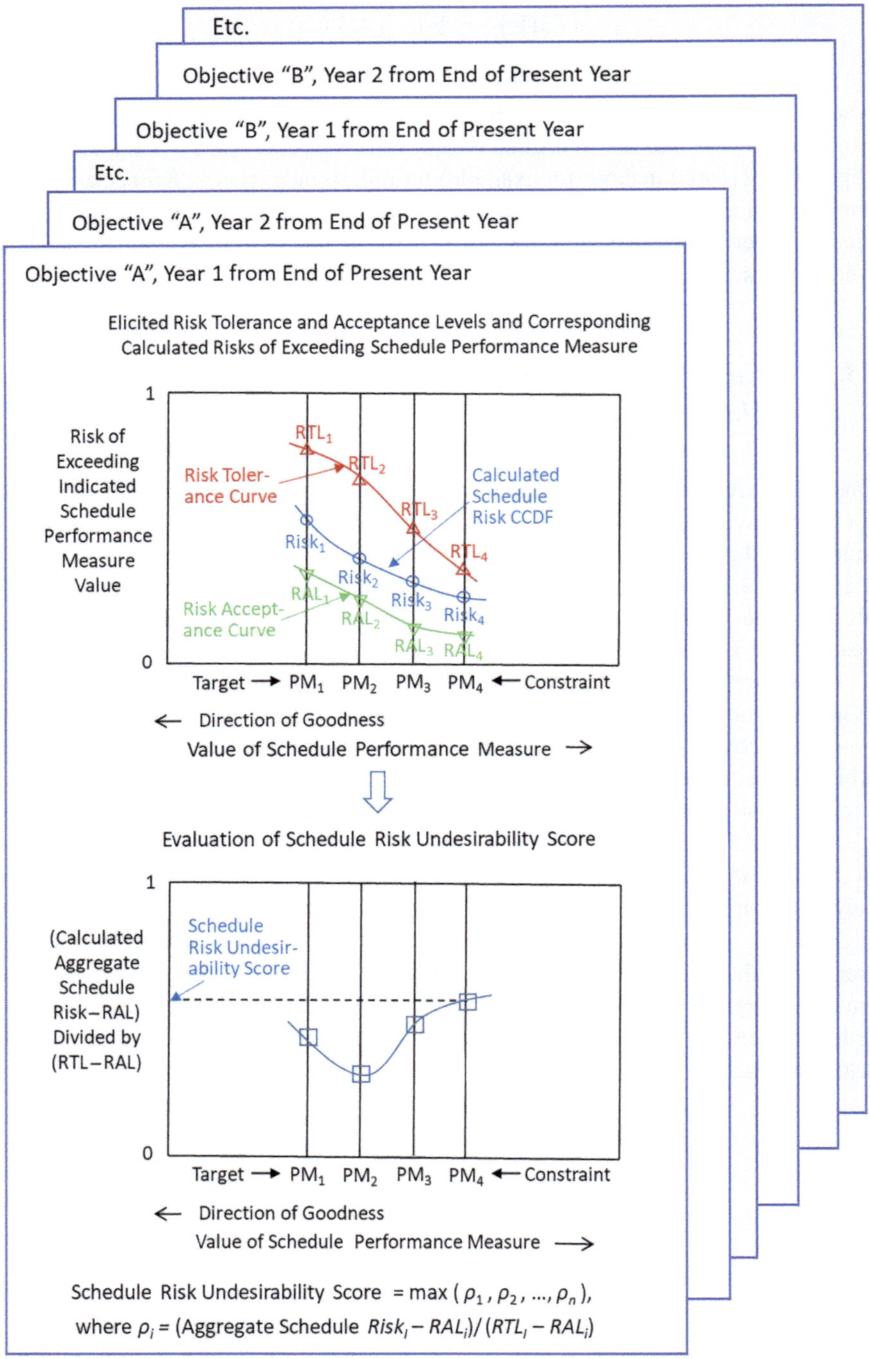

Fig. 13.3 Example risk posture results for aggregate schedule risk and evaluation of schedule risk undesirability scores

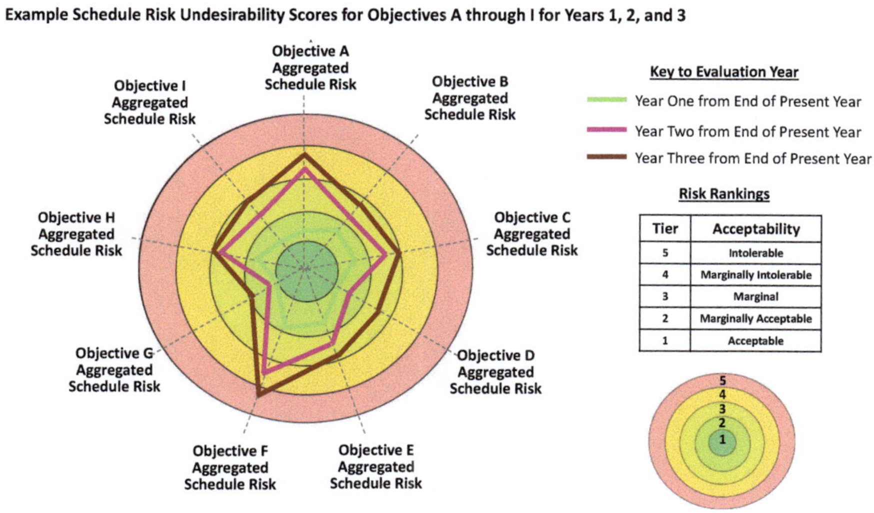

Fig. 13.4 Example spider chart display for the aggregate schedule risk to objectives caused by slippages of key milestones

References

NASA. (2022, March 28). *NASA strategic plan 2022*. NASA, Office of the Administrator.

VOIP. (2022). *FY2023 volume of integrated performance*. NASA, Office of the Chief Financial Officer.

VOIP. (2024, March 11). *FY2025 volume of integrated performance*. NASA, Office of the Chief Financial Officer.

Fig. 13.4

References

Chapter 14
Example No. 3 on Designing for Optimally Balanced Risks

This example concerns the design of a complex system in accordance with the risk leadership principle that all of the organization's top-level objectives should be satisfied within the organization's pre-established risk tolerance posture first and foremost, and given that constraint, that the aggregate risks should be as low as reasonably achievable (ALARA). The example could apply to any large, high-tech enterprise that pursues groundbreaking technology for which there are significant safety hazards. New energy systems, spaceflight systems, ground transport systems, mining systems, military systems, or petrochemical systems could be pertinent examples. An introduction to the subject was provided earlier in Sect. 2.3.

14.1 Flow of Activities within Design for Optimally Balanced Risks

The process of striving to reach the best balance of risks to objectives over all mission execution domains within the organization's risk tolerance posture, while simultaneously satisfying all mandated requirements, is referred to within the enterprise as Design for Optimally Balanced Risk, or DFOBR. DFOBR is defined as an iterative approach in which (1) management authorities allocate objectives, risk tolerance postures, and mandated requirements; and (2) an integrated technical team of systems engineers, safety and mission assurance engineers, and risk analysts performs detailed trade studies, considering all significant sources of uncertainty, including those from U/U risks, with the goal of optimizing the final design. Iterative cycles generally occur in tandem with design reviews so as to converge upon a design that is near-optimal with respect to minimizing and balancing risks across all the mission execution domains. A flow of activities consistent with this DFOBR strategy was previously presented in Fig. 2.4 and is reproduced here, for convenience, in Fig. 14.1.

Regarding the box labeled "Characterize Design Attributes for Known + U/U Risk Evaluation," Sect. 5.2.1 identified three general design factors that contribute to the potential for U/U risk: complexity involving the interfaces between different elements of a system or process, scaling beyond the domain of knowledge, and use of fundamentally new technology or a fundamentally new application of an existing

A. S. Benjamin, *Integration of Project, Infrastructure, and Enterprise Risk Management*, Risk, Governance and Society 21,
https://doi.org/10.1007/978-3-031-85070-7_14

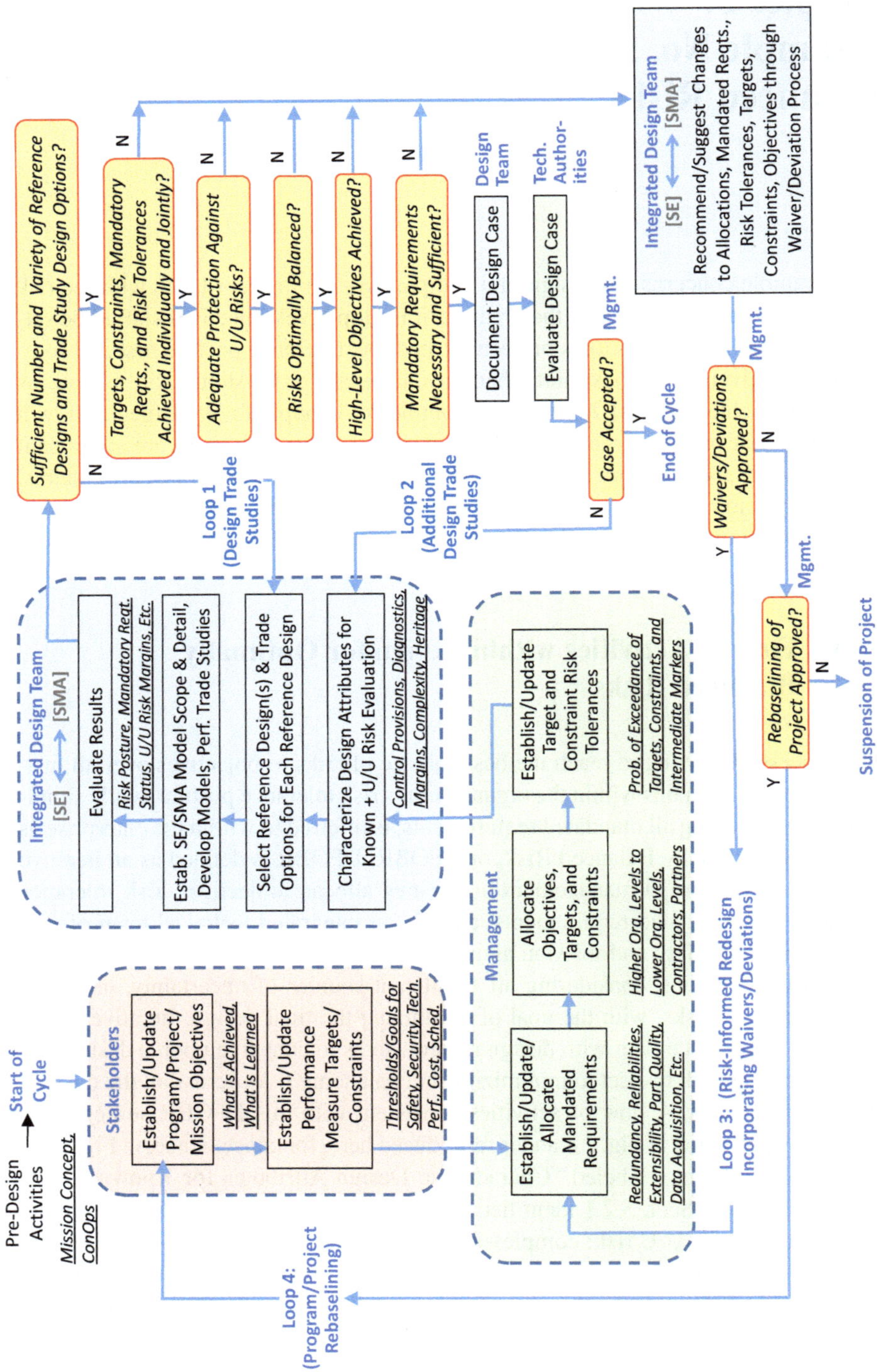

Fig. 14.1 DFOBR process flow

technology. When implementing DFOBR, it is useful and informative to decompose those general U/U risk-producing attributes to deeper levels applicable to the system being developed. The following list of specific leading indicators are examples:

1. Design margins that fail to account for variations in the environment the system will be exposed to beyond the design-basis environments
2. Design margins that fail to account for departures from the present understanding of the system's responses to such environments because of the test data being limited or only partially applicable
3. Insufficient diagnostics, particularly for uncovering unexpected damage or failures
4. Insufficient opportunities for positive human intervention from onsite operators or from offsite control personnel
5. Insufficient autonomous fault recovery, particularly from computer hardware faults and software errors
6. Insufficient opportunities for personnel emergency escape, such as an abort system

For example, it may be argued that the principle design factors contributing to U/U risks for the Space Shuttle during the Challenger and Columbia accidents were insufficient design margin and insufficient diagnostics. In this regard, it has been suggested that the temperature margin for the Challenger O-rings should have been larger so as to guard against the potential for cold temperature failure (Challenger, 1986), and for Columbia, that there should have been a means for astronauts to examine the condition of the thermal tiles before committing to undocking from the ISS and initiating reentry (Columbia, 2003).

For the box in Fig. 14.1 labeled "Establish SE/SMA Model Scope & Detail, Develop Models, Perform Trade Studies", there are many types of analysis models currently used within the safety and cost/schedule domains that can contribute to the integrated analysis needed for DFOBR. Some of the more important of these include accident precursor analysis (APA) (see, for example, NASA, 2011); failure modes, effects, and criticality analysis (FMECA) (e.g., DoD, 1980); hazard analysis (HA) (e.g., Ericson, 2005); probabilistic risk assessment (PRA) (e.g., Stamatelatos & Dezfuli, 2011), critical path methods (CPM) (e.g., Santiago & Magalon, 2009), program evaluation and review techniques (PERT) (e.g., Miller, 1963), Bayesian network cost estimation techniques (e.g., Khodakarami et al., 2007), and neural networking cost estimation techniques (e.g., Matel et al., 2022). Furthermore, the performance of trade studies normally includes the use of Monte Carlo sampling, as described and illustrated earlier in Sect. 4.1, in order to calculate probability distributions for the performance measures of interest and evaluate the risk posture associated with each design option.

The term "Design for Optimally Balanced Risks" may sound like an existing, related design approach called Design for Minimum Risk (DFMR), but it is in fact quite different. DFMR pertains to the minimization of safety risk only, while constraints in the other mission execution domains of technical performance, cybersecurity, physical security, cost, and schedule remain absolute and nonnegotiable (Wetherholt & Heimann, 2010). DFOBR, on the other hand, is an approach that seeks the best balance of risks over all the mission execution domains, not just safety, while also recognizing that there are targets, constraints, and minimum requisites to be promulgated and negotiated in the process. Additionally, DFOBR is holistic, applying to the system level and directly referring to the risk of not meeting stakeholder objectives and requirements. DFMR applies to specific items (i.e., those for which failure tolerance is impractical), and the risk is that of failure of the item. DFMR is applied selectively and locally, and does not ensure that the system as a whole is designed for minimum risk. The methodology for DFOBR may be viewed as a significant generalization from DFMR.

In practice, optimally balanced risk is a goal that is achievable only in an approximate sense. There are two main reasons for this. First, achievement of the goal in an absolute sense would require an inordinate number of design variations to be considered, which is not practical in the real world of limited time and budgets. Second, the optimal balancing of risks is dependent on a set of risk models that are not, in themselves, true reality but instead an abstraction of reality. Determination of how close the results are to true reality requires an ardent assessment of the robustness of the models and the degree to which design convergence has been reached.

14.2 Principles Concerning the Conduct and Use of Trade Studies in Design for Optimally Balanced Risks

To achieve the intent of DFOBR, the integrated analysis team selects one or more reference designs, develops synthetic models to analyze them, and then explores a variety of design modifications in an attempt to converge upon a best design: i.e., one that satisfies all objectives and requirements and achieves an optimal balance between the residual risks. Three questions to address are (1) how best to select the reference designs, (2) how best to select from among various design trade options, and (3) how best to develop synthetic models that are fast enough to analyze a large number of design variations but reliable enough to converge on a final design that is indeed near-optimal.

14.2.1 Starting from De-Minimis, De-Maximus, and Hybrid Reference Designs

The integrated analysis team first selects a de-minimus design and a de-maximus design to serve as starting points. A de-minimis design (Putney et al., 2010) is a minimum-cost design that satisfies minimum performance requirements and does not include any special safety provisions. Features are then selectively added to it to improve safety until the constraint on total cost is reached. A trade study that starts from a bare-bones reference design and makes sequential additions tends to result in a final design that is minimally functional and not very innovative.

A de-maximus design, as opposed to a de-minimis design, is a reference design that is formulated to include high technical performance capability, many safety features, and desirable attributes (like extensibility) without initially considering cost and schedule. Features are then selectively removed or modified until the cost and schedule constraints are met. Starting from de-maximus rather than de-minimis has analytical advantages in that it is easier to subtract features from an integrated analytical model that includes everything that may be in the final design plus more, than to add features to an analytical model that includes very little that will be in the final design. It also promotes innovative thinking from the beginning.

The team recognizes, however, that starting from any single reference design, whether de-minimis or de-maximus, does not guarantee that the final design will be optimally balanced with respect to the panoply of risks. Experience has shown that at least two reference designs (de-maximus and de-minimis) should be employed as starting points for trade studies before concluding that DFOBR has been achieved (Di Pietro, 2015). If the results from the trade studies emanating from the two reference designs are notably different, then a third reference design should be derived, based on interpolating between de-minimis and de-maximus guided by the results of the trade studies, and used as the starting point for another set of trades. Three reference designs should normally be sufficient, but the possibility of progressing to a fourth or fifth reference design should be entertained if needed.

14.2.2 Narrowing the Trade Space in the Search for Optimal Balance by Identifying and Acting upon Risk Drivers

The integrated team decides that the search for design modifications to pursue in a trade study needs to be explored from two directions: (1) by identifying those that best reduce *known* risks in any of the mission execution domains, and (2) by identifying those that best reduce U/U risks. Both directions are pursued in order to ensure that the final design is DFOBR.

To effectuate this type of search, the team infers that the best way to select the design modifications is to identify (1) the risk drivers in each mission execution domain using the synthetic performance models, and (2) the design changes that would be most effective in mitigating those risk drivers. A risk driver, as defined and developed in Sect. 4.4, is a significant source of risk to one or more organizational objectives or mandated requirements. Specific examples pertaining to system design might include:

- Lack of specific components or subsystems needed to adequately address mission execution objectives such as safety, technical performance, cybersecurity, and physical security
- Lack of provisions in the design to address high-priority enterprise objectives such as technical innovation (the promotion of new promising technologies) or extensibility (the applicability of the design to other missions)

- Unreliability of specific components, subsystems, or other provisions in the design leading to unacceptable failure rates
- Lack of sufficient workforce capacity to address design challenges in a timely manner
- Insufficient provisions to address design risks that cut across organizational boundaries
- Excessive hardware or software complexity
- Excessive integration complexity, particularly at subsystem interfaces
- Excessive testing complexity given the state of the organization's test facilities
- Lack of provisions for positive human intervention to manage unexpected challenges during operation
- Uncertainties in the human reliability models
- Uncertainties in the load capacity, extent of deformation, or thermal properties of certain materials due to environmental conditions
- Combinations of scenarios, leading indicators, model shortcomings, or parameter uncertainties that are individually of low concern but collectively cause the aggregate risk to change from acceptable to not acceptable

The team plans to determine the risk drivers after the integrated performance models have been created and executed by performing sensitivity analyses within the calculation of performance measures. The identification of risk drivers may sometimes need to be performed in two steps or more. The first step looks at each scenario, leading indicator, model shortcoming, or parameter uncertainty individually to determine whether it is a driver by itself. If no drivers are identified by this process, then combinations of scenarios, leading indicators, model shortcomings, or parameter uncertainties are considered.

14.2.3 Simplified Synthetic Models for the Trade Space

The team recognizes that using high-order synthetic performance models developed for the purpose of analyzing reference designs may prove to be impractical for performing all the design trades needed to search for a design that optimally balances the risks. As the design matures, the integrated system models become more detailed, and running time becomes an issue for performing trade studies. It therefore plans to develop relatively simple response surfaces and train them to approximate the results of the rigorous models sufficiently well to explore the necessary design variations. It plans to use the detailed, more rigorous models both to train the response surfaces and to verify the effectiveness of the final choice of design when the analysis has been completed.

14.3 Fundamentals Concerning Communication, Evaluation, and Assurance in Design for Optimally Balanced Risks

14.3.1 Coordination Between Designers and Risk Analysts

As mentioned earlier in Sect. 2.3, the derivation of design requirements and evolution of a design that achieves an optimal balancing of risks and satisfies all requirements requires a fully coordinated effort between the design teams and risk teams within and across participating organizations, in which decisions about design tradeoffs and risk tradeoffs are made after deliberative discussions. Once the final design requirements have been determined and the contents of the final design have been derived, a formal system design case will be prepared.

During the design process, the integrated team plans to collaborate and deliberate at many junctures, including:

1. When deciding what the reference design(s) should contain and what trade studies should be performed;
2. When deciding what analytical models to use for evaluating safety risk, technical performance, cost, and schedule and how to integrate them so that all assumptions and methods of analysis are consistent;
3. When deciding the level of detail to be incorporated into the reference-case analytical models, based on the importance of the mission, the complexity of the design, and the maturity of the design;
4. When deriving fast-running approximations to the more detailed analytical models if necessary to examine a large number of design variations;
5. When evaluating the results;
6. When deciding whether a successful design can be achieved that satisfies all stakeholder objectives and requirements within the specified risk tolerances and that balances the residual risks;
7. When deciding upon recommendations to make to management authorities in order to facilitate the achievement of success (to be taken up in the next subsection); and
8. When developing a system design case using the concept of optimally balanced risks.

14.3.2 Evaluation and Display of Results from the Trade Studies

The team decides that spider charts will be the principal means for illustrating aggregate risk rankings in a manner that facilitates comparisons between different designs. After performing its analyses using the methods and processes described in Sects. 4.1 and 7.3.3 and illustrated in Figs. 4.1 and 7.3, the team calculates aggregate risk undesirability scores for twelve performance measures and displays them as shown in Fig. 14.2. For illustration, results are shown for three designs: a *de-maximus* design, the next design in the trade progression, and the final balanced risk design that results from progressively iterating until balance is achieved.

Because the de-maximus design is formulated without regard to cost or design complexity, it tends not to do very well for items that involve cost and schedule containment but extremely well for all other items. The basically unlimited funding and schedule flexibility for the de-maximus design allow for U/U risks to be minimized through a defense-in-depth approach, despite the fact that the design tends to be complex. The optimally balanced design, on the other hand, does acceptably well for all items, but not extremely well for any one item.

In Fig. 14.3, the analysis team presents their risk rankings for the same twelve performance measures for a *de-minimis* design, the next design in the trade progression starting from de-minimis, and the final balanced risk design that results after a number of design iterations. Because the de-minimis design is formulated with substantial regard to cost and design simplicity, it tends to do extremely well for items that involve cost and schedule containment but not very well for all other items. Again, the optimally balanced design does acceptably well for all items. From their analyses, the risks resulting at the end of the iteration process turn out to be slightly lower when starting from the de-maximus design than when starting from the de-minimis design.

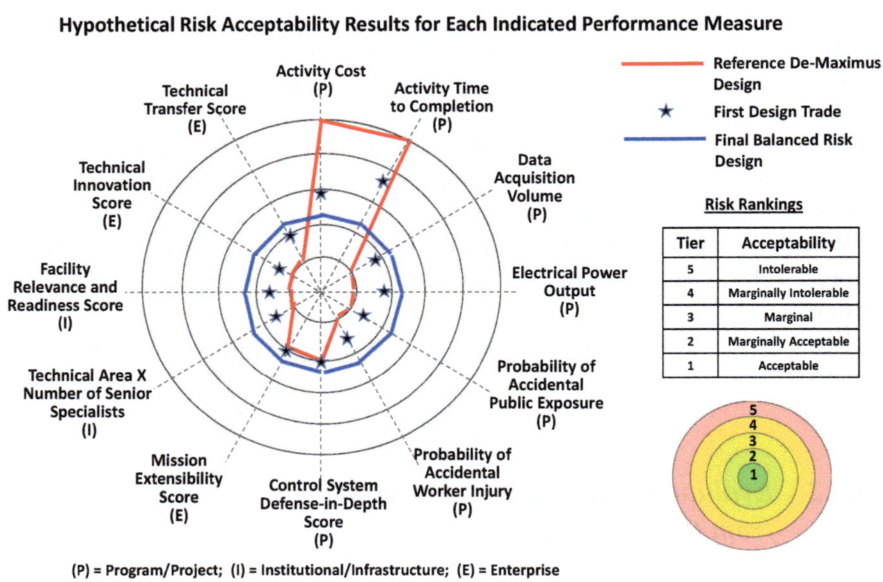

Fig. 14.2 Spider chart for the example comparing risk rankings for a de-maximus design, an intermediate design, and the final balanced risk design

14.3.3 Performance Metrics Considered Jointly

In addition to striving for a design that optimally balances risks to individual objectives or requirements, the team considers the probabilities of success on a joint-risk basis. For example, some agencies, including NASA implement a joint confidence level (JCL) for cost and schedule, which requires that the joint probability of a project's cost exceeding the cost constraint <u>and</u> the finish date exceeding the schedule constraint not be greater than a specified value (NASA, 2012, 2020). To handle the JCL requirement, the team combines the two performance objectives in Figs. 14.2 and 14.3 labeled "Meets Cost Constraint" and "Meets Schedule Constraint" into one performance objective labeled "Meets Cost and Schedule Constraints Jointly." This results in spider charts with 11 rather than 12 spokes, but otherwise the display of aggregate risks is identical to Figs. 14.2 and 14.3.

14.3.4 Formulation of a System Design Case for Optimally Balanced Risks

A system design case for optimally balanced risks is a set of arguments that provides one of the bases for design acceptance. It is similar in content and organization to a risk-informed safety case or RISC (as described in NASA, 2014, 2024), except that it focuses on optimally balancing risks across all mission execution domains rather than just minimizing safety risk without violating the stakeholders'

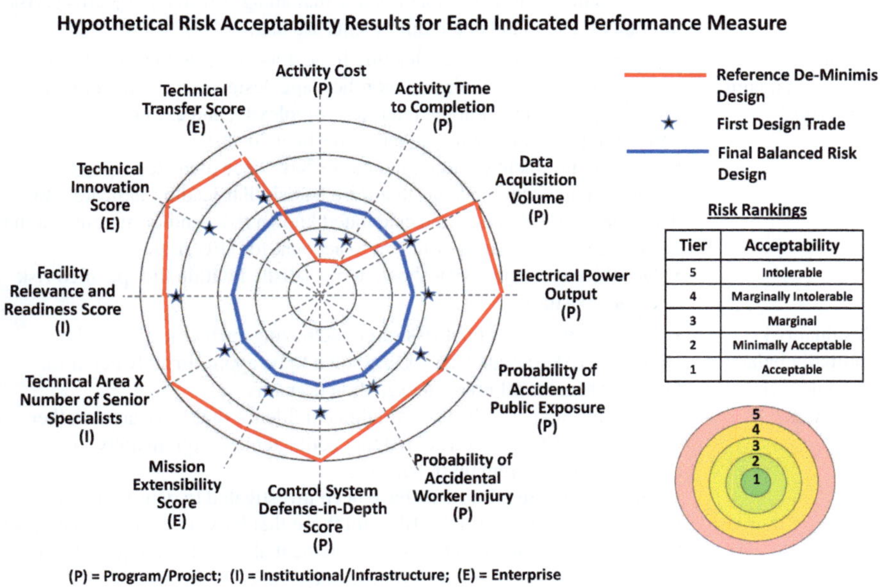

Fig. 14.3 Spider chart for the example comparing risk rankings for a de-minimis design, an intermediate design, and the final balanced risk design

constraints. Table 14.1 illustrates the list of questions that the team addresses and summarizes their associated arguments.

Table 14.1 Questions addressed and arguments developed for the system design case for optimally balanced risks

Questions to be addressed	Argument to be developed
Sufficient number and variety of trades on design options and reference designs?	• A sufficient variety of design tradeoffs starting from the initial reference design have been identified and analyzed to provide confidence that further design exploration would not uncover a more optimal design. – In this context, "optimal" refers to the achievement of all constraints within specified risk tolerances and balancing of residual risks with assurance that no other design achieves lower residual risks. – The term "exploration" includes consideration of design options exercised one at a time as well as in various combination. • In addition to the "initial" reference design, enough additional reference designs have been considered to provide confidence in the final design recommendations.
Objectives, risk tolerances, and mandated requirements achieved based on best model prediction?	• The models used to evaluate safety performance, technical performance, security, cost, and schedule have been verified and validated for the designs being investigated in the environments to which the system is expected to be exposed. • Known uncertainties have been accounted for and included in the modeling and simulation. • When simplified models, such as response surfaces, are used to examine the sensitivity of the results to design variations and to recommend changes to the baseline design, results for the final recommended design are updated using the more rigorous models. • The results from these models show that all agreed-upon objectives, risk tolerances, and mandated requirements are met.
Adequate protection against U/U risks?	• Design and programmatic leading indicators contributing to U/U risks, such as first-of-a-kind mission, non-heritage design of critical elements, use of unproven technology, interface complexity, and extremely demanding schedules and budgets, have been identified. • The U/U producing leading indicators have been analyzed using historical data from missions that have had similar leading indicators to determine adjustments to the calculated known risks and/or margins on the performance constraints sufficient to account for U/U risks. • The objectives have been shown to be satisfied within the specified risk tolerance posture.
Residual risks optimally balanced and within risk tolerances?	• The ratio of the residual risk of not achieving each objective to the respective risk tolerance has been shown to be approximately equal for objectives across all mission execution domains. • The trade studies indicate with high confidence that there are no other designs beyond those considered that could achieve significantly lower residual risks that remain in balance. • All mandated requirements have been investigated to determine how they affect the intent of DFOBR, and those that have a negative effect have been brought to the attention of management along with a request for a waiver of adjustment if deemed necessary.

References

Challenger. (1986). *Report of the Presidential Commission on the space shuttle challenger accident.*

Columbia. (2003). *NASA, Columbia Accident Investigation Board Report.*

Di Pietro, D. (2015, July 13–16). Techniques for conducting effective concept design and design-to-cost trade studies. In *NASA GSFC, 25th Annual INCOSE International Symposium.*

DoD. (1980, November). *Procedures for performing a failure mode, effects, and criticality analysis.* Department of Defense, MIL-STD-1629A.

Ericson, C. (2005). *Hazard analysis techniques for system safety.* Wiley.

Khodakarami, V., et al. (2007, June). Project scheduling: Improved approach to incorporate uncertainty using Bayesian networks. *Project Management Journal, 38.*

Matel, E., et al. (2022). An artificial neural network approach for cost estimation of engineering services. *International Journal of Construction Management, 22*, 1274–1287.

Miller, R. W. (1963). *Schedule, cost, and profit control with PERT—A comprehensive guide for program management.* McGraw Hill.

NASA. (2011, December). *NASA accident precursor analysis handbook (Version 1).* NASA/SP-2011-3423.

NASA. (2012, August). *NASA space flight program and project management requirements.* NASA NPR 7120.5E.

NASA. (2014, November). *NASA system safety handbook, Volume 2, System safety concepts, guidelines, and implementation examples.* NASA/SP-2014-612.

NASA. (2020). *NASA cost estimating handbook, Version 4*, Issued February 2015, Updated December 2020.

NASA. (2024, November). *NASA risk management handbook (Version 2, Part 1).* NASA/SP-2024-3422.

Putney, B., et al. (2010, June). Considering a cost constrained risk informed design paradigm for NASA. In *Probabilistic Safety and Management Conference, PSAM10.*

Santiago, J., & Magalon. (2009, February). *Critical path method.* Stanford University CEE 320 – VCC Seminar.

Stamatelatos, M., & Dezfuli, H. (2011, December). *Probabilistic risk assessment procedures guide for NASA managers and practitioners* (2nd ed.). NASA/SP-2011-3421.

Wetherholt, J., & Heimann, T. (2010, May). *Design for minimum risk.* NASA Marshall Space Flight Center, International Association for the Advancement of Space Safety.

References

Chapter 15
Advanced Concepts for Evaluating, Aggregating, and Managing High-Tech Performance Risks and Promoting Resilience

The practices of risk analysis and risk management, and their integration across program/project, institutional/infrastructure, and enterprise risk management domains, are in the process of being revolutionized by recent advances in information technology. Four of the most widely discussed recent advances pertain to (1) the methodology of predicting and reacting to tipping points and their effects on organizational and societal risk; (2) the use of artificial intelligence as part of a red teaming process to evaluate and protect against the risk from cyberattacks and other adversarial incursions; (3) the use of artificial neural networks and genetic algorithms (parts of AI) to derive more accurate predictions of the total aggregate risks (i.e., the summation of risks from known, unknown, and known but underappreciated scenarios); and (4) the use of AI to facilitate the establishment and maintenance of organizational and operational resilience, resulting in major efficiencies with respect to coping with disasters that could disrupt operations, undermine or sabotage organizational objectives, or cause widespread unacceptable hardship.

These four advances are undergoing rapid evolution and are not yet fully integrated into risk management, either at an organizational level or at a societal level. Therefore, it would be premature to discuss the intricacies of their formulation or implementation at the level of detail presented in the preceding chapters for the more established practices in risk management. Nonetheless, it is becoming increasingly important to incorporate these rapidly emerging practices into risk analysis and risk management to the maximum extent that is defensible, with the understanding that successive developments will result in subsequent improvements.

With that in mind, the purposes of this chapter are as follows:

- To provide guidance on the incorporation of extra-organizational risks from societal, political, economic, and environmental stressors into the integrated analysis of organizational risks;

A. S. Benjamin, *Integration of Project, Infrastructure, and Enterprise Risk Management*, Risk, Governance and Society 21,
https://doi.org/10.1007/978-3-031-85070-7_15

- To describe how the preceding purpose can be addressed by using agent-based modeling and empirically-derived leading indicators to examine the potential occurrence and impact of tipping points;
- To outline provisions for using artificial intelligence tools together with red-team exercises to assess the risks from cyberattacks;
- To discuss how the use of artificial intelligence in conjunction with red-teaming can not only resist cyberattacks by delaying an adversary's penetration time (the main cybersecurity performance measure per Sect. 9.2), but also improve recovery from cyberattacks by decreasing the time needed to detect and correct the damage;
- To outline the formative aspects of artificial neural networks and genetic algorithms within the context of Monte Carlo simulation processes, as they apply to the prediction of uncertainty distributions for organizational performance measures; and
- To describe current and likely future uses of AI aimed at facilitating the establishment and maintenance of organizational and operational resilience.

15.1 Evaluating Societal and Environmental Tipping Point Likelihoods and their Effects on the Aggregate Risks to Organizational Objectives

As discussed in Sect. 8.3.4, the likelihood of occurrence of many risk scenarios may depend, in part or in whole, on the likelihood of occurrence of various societal, political, economic, or environmental events or conditions. To cite three example, (1) funding for one or more programs may be influenced by changes in the economy (e.g., a worldwide economic boom or economic recession); (2) supply chain problems may be introduced by the occurrence of a natural disaster (abetted, for example, by the occurrence of global climate change); and (3) the prioritization of organizational objectives may be altered by changes in the national political landscape (e.g., leading to emphasis on different short-term and long-term goals). The third example could lead to changes in risk tolerance and risk acceptance levels for the different objectives.

To account for these and other extra-organizational factors in the integrated analysis of risks, the analysis team may need to include models for societal, political, economic, and/or environmental risks within the integrated performance modeling depicted in Figs. 4.1 and 7.3, Charts A and B.

15.1.1 Agent-Based Modeling (ABM)

Several categories of modeling can be utilized for this purpose, but the type of modeling most frequently used for societal, biological, and ecological risk studies is Agent-Based Modeling, or ABM. According to Wikipedia (Wiki ABM, 2025, with reference to Niazi & Hussain, 2011), "ABM is a computation model for simulating the actions and interactions of autonomous agents (both individual or collective entities such as organizations or groups) in order to understand the behavior of a system and what governs its outcomes. It combines elements of game theory, complex systems, emergence, computational sociology, multi-agent systems, and genetic algorithms. Monte Carlo methods are used to understand the stochasticity of these models. … The goal of ABM is to search for explanatory insight into the collective behavior of agents obeying simple rules, typically in natural systems."

In other words that are perhaps easier to fathom, ABM is a type of simulation where one creates virtual "agents" that act and interact with each other and with the overall environment according to sets of rules defined by the modelers. The rules are iteratively varied over the range of reasonable possibilities and the emergent behavior of the system of interest is computed. A probability can be assigned to each set of rules according to how well the emergent behavior for each rule set replicates historical experience and expert knowledge.

As a simplified conceptual exercise, consider how a group of normal people who under most circumstances act rationally and avoid conflict might get entrapped in an armed conflict. Each person is an individual agent. If I am one of those people, I might look around me and make a judgment of how many of those people tend to cheat and how many tend to be honest. My rules of behavior might include being honest if I judge that 10% or fewer of the people around me tend to cheat and 90% or more tend to be honest, but conversely, I might choose to cheat if I judge that 60% or more of the people around me tend to cheat and the remaining 40% or fewer tend to be honest. Obviously, cheating produces conflict, and so the chances of an armed conflict increase as the percentage skews toward more cheaters and fewer honest people. Considering that each person has his own set of rules, and that the number of possible rule variations for each person is extremely large, so too is the number of potential outcomes. Some of the outcomes will tend to mimic historical data pertaining to the development of armed conflict in various-sized populations better than others. The rule sets leading to those outcomes will be assigned higher probabilities (that is, higher degrees of belief) than the other rule sets.

15.1.2 Tipping Points

A *tipping point* is a set of conditions that, when surpassed, causes changes in part of a system to become self-perpetuating, leading to substantial, widespread, often abrupt and irreversible impacts (Lenton et al., 2023). It is a kind of threshold, in which a small change that causes a system to pass a tipping point becomes a trigger for the system to change phases from one equilibrium to another. Other terms that are frequently used interchangeably with tipping points include *regime shift* (Dakos et al., 2019) and *critical transition* (Scheffer, 2010).

Tipping points are frequently encountered in complex systems consisting of a large number of interconnected components or agents that interact with one another, often giving rise to feedback loops, nonlinearity, and emergent properties that cannot be reduced to the properties of the individual parts. Tipping systems are often societal, political, economic, environmental, or technological. Examples of the results of surpassing a tipping point in each of these categories include the occurrence of wars, upheavals in political ideology, widespread economic upturns or downturns, irreversible global climate change, and large technology breakthroughs or massive failures. As implied by these examples, tipping points can be positive or negative, with both being of concern in risk management.

While most tipping points of significance occur on a national or global level and cause risks that need to be dealt with at that level. They can obviously also cause risks to the major objectives of individual organizations. Within the domain of CRM, the roles of organizational risk management include tracking the leading indicators of tipping points that occur outside the organization, analyzing the risks they bring to the organization, and planning how to address those risks at the organizational level.

15.1.3 The Use of ABM to Predict Tipping Points

One of the purposes of ABM is to simulate complex systems that are prone to catastrophic shifts and major irreversible changes that occur near tipping points (Fabiani et al., 2024; Scheffer & Carpenter, 2003; Scheffer, 2010; Dakos et al., 2019; Armstrong McKay et al., 2022). Accordingly, the occurrence of tipping points under predictable conditions is inherent in the use of these models.

While stochastic analytical models like ABM can be used to predict the probability that a tipping point might occur, these models have practical limitations related to potentially high computational cost. To counteract that difficulty, some researchers have experimented with the construction of reduced-order models, trained to simulate the results of the higher-order ABM models. Fabiani, for example, had success using one-dimensional stochastic differential equations as a simplified model form that succeeded in simulating the higher-order models near tipping points (Fabiani et al., 2024). This approach saves significantly in the computational cost, which can be of great value given that the number of candidate rule sets may be very large.

15.1.4 The Use of Empirically Derived Leading Indicators as Monitoring Aids for Tipping Points

In addition to the potentially high cost of performing Monte Carlo analysis with agent-based models, these models may also have potential limitations related to incomplete coverage of the complex interactions that are involved as well as the applicability of the data used to develop probabilities for different rule sets. To compensate for these limitations, the models may be augmented by the consideration of U/U risk based on the identification and tracking of leading indicators. Ideally, these indicators should be straightforward to monitor and strongly correlated with the imminent occurrence of tipping points.

Based on the results of research reported in the literature, there are several empirical leading indicators that have been observed near tipping points. Among them are the occurrence of wider swings in the dynamics of key variables, slower return rates after a perturbation, and a shift of the system response towards lower frequencies (Carpenter et al., 2008). The second of these is typically characterized as a "critical slowing down" (CSD) in the system, and is the most commonly used leading indicator to forecast a tipping point event. As the system nears a tipping point, the state it occupies tends to lose its stability, and the restoring feedbacks that pull the system back to that state after it is perturbed start to degrade. This causes the system to respond more sluggishly to these perturbations and thus slow down, leaving signatures that a tipping point is imminent. More detailed information on the leading indicators of tipping points may be found in a number of references (e.g., Dakos et al., 2024; Wissel, 1984; Drake et al., 2020; Renn & Lucas, 2022; Lenton et al., 2023).

Careful monitoring of these leading indicators is needed to detect changes that might forecast a tipping point. As such changes are observed, the input distributions for the integrated models need to be adjusted and the simulation needs to be updated to reflect such adjustments.

15.2 Utilizing Artificial Intelligence to Better Evaluate and Manage Cybersecurity Risk

It is an undeniable fact of life today that artificial intelligence (AI) is being used by adversaries to launch faster, broader, and more effective cyberattacks. It is therefore increasingly common for organizations to respond by incorporating AI in their cybersecurity defense strategies (Costa, 2024, see also Rowe, 2025 and IBM, 2024).

As discussed in these references and others, AI-powered cybersecurity tools can be applied to combat AI-generated cyber threats by rapidly detecting anomalous activities in real time and by automatically adapting defenses to emerging threats. This use of AI, while critically important, is however basically *reactive* in nature, since it does not predict the risk and act upon potential future threats, but rather responds to currently enfolding threats. Also critically important is the ability to use AI in a *proactive* manner to help evaluate and protect against risk.

15.2.1 Using AI Proactively in Conjunction with the Use of Red Teams

As discussed previously in Sect. 9.3, I and others recommend the use of red teams to evaluate the risk from cyberattacks by determining conditional probability distributions for the time it would take for an adversary to penetrate an organization's cyber protections and inflict damage. If the adversary is using AI for offense and the organization's cybersecurity team is using AI for defense, then it stands to reason that the red teams should also use AI to be on the same par. Recently, the use of AI in red teaming has become a mainstream activity in cybersecurity protection, to the point where many now refer to that activity using the phrase "AI red teaming" as established terminology.

While AI red teaming has a strong robotic component, it also tends to have a strong human component. In a web-based discussion of the role of the human element in AI red teaming, actually generated by an AI application (in itself an example of irony), the following points are made:

- AI red teams are principally composed of human experts who leverage AI tools to simulate real-world attacks and assess the safety and security of AI systems.
- AI red teams rely heavily on human expertise to craft prompts, interact with AI models, and analyze results, as humans can identify a wider range of potential issues and attacks.
- AI tools can be used to automate tasks like generating prompts, orchestrating attacks, and scoring responses, but they are not a replacement for human expertise.
- Human expertise is crucial for understanding the nuances of AI systems, identifying creative attack vectors, and interpreting the results of red teaming exercises.
- Humans can design prompts that exploit vulnerabilities in AI models to generate harmful or inappropriate content.
- Humans can assess the outputs of AI models to identify biases, inaccuracies, or other issues that could lead to harm.
- Humans can simulate real-world scenarios to test the resilience of AI systems against various threats.
- The most effective AI red teaming approaches combine human expertise with AI tools, allowing for both broad and targeted testing.

As recently stated by David Bray of the Stimson Center (Bray, 2025), a hybrid approach to red teaming, which he calls "AI-enhanced red teaming," can pair AI's data processing and pattern recognition abilities with human strategic expertise to analyze potential impacts of decision alternatives that are not readily apparent.

Referring to analyses associated with the potential adoption of export controls as an example, he points out how AI could rapidly assess global supply chains and simulate adversarial responses to export controls, while human experts could evaluate the diplomatic and/or political implications. The synergisms between AI and human participation in red teaming are also highlighted in NIST Technical Series (2023), Microsoft AI Red Team (2024), OpenAI (2024), and Zhang et al. (2024).

Significantly (and thankfully), the role of humans in AI red teaming is not yet obsolete, and there are no indications that it is about to become so.

15.2.2 *Using AI to Improve Both Resistance and Response to Cyberattacks*

The use of AI red teaming makes it possible to define two adjunctive objectives with respect to cybersecurity: first, to impede/resist the adversary's goals by making it very difficult for them to find a way to breach the system and inflict harm; and second, to rapidly identify any intrusion once it has occurred and counteract the damage. The first objective can be thought of as a *resistance objective*, and was the basis of the analyses presented in Sects. 9.2 and 9.3. The second can be thought of as a *response objective*, which will be elaborated upon later in this subsection.

As discussed earlier, I and others believe that the most suitable performance measure for evaluating the strength of the *resistance* objective is the amount of time it takes for a knowledgeable adversary to (a) succeed in finding a way into the portion of the IT network that is applicable to the adversary's intent, and (b) inflict harm without being detected. In the text that follows, I will refer to this performance measure as the *penetration time*.

A corresponding performance measure for evaluating the strength of the *response* objective, also supported in the literature, is the amount of time it takes, once the adversarial act has been perpetrated and the system has been compromised, for the victimized organization to subsequently detect the breach and correct the problem. I will henceforth refer to this performance measure as the *recovery time*.

For example, extending the example for the penetration time provided in Sect. 9.2, assume that a constraint on the recovery time has been specified as one month, the associated risk tolerance level as 0.10, and the risk acceptance level as 0.05. The aggregate conditional risk associated with this performance measure would be intolerable if the probability of the recovery time being more than one month is greater than or equal to 0.10, marginal if it is between 0.05 and 0.10, and acceptable if it is less than 0.05.

The method described in Sect. 9.3 for synthesizing a probability distribution for the adversary's penetration time also applies to the synthesis of a probability distribution for the organization's recovery time. In the former case, the inputs to the distribution are the amounts of time it takes each of several AI red teams to succeed in penetrating a system's cybersecurity defenses undetected. In the latter case, the pertinent inputs are the amounts of time it subsequently takes for the organization's AI-assisted cyber protections to independently detect the intrusion and provide corrective action.

15.3 Utilizing Artificial Neural Networks and Genetic Algorithms to Derive more Accurate Correlations Between Leading Indicators and Performance Risks

One way that artificial intelligence strengthens risk management is by identifying and quantifying correlations and patterns in data that humans might miss. In particular, AI enables the development of better correlations between leading indicators of risk (such as design complexity, high pressure working environments, and overly hierarchical management structures) and affected measures of performance (such as program cost, completion date, accident frequency, resource availability, technical transfer success, customer satisfaction, etc.).

Such data-based correlations are particularly valuable for predicting the potential magnitude of unknown and/or underappreciated (U/U) performance risks. Even without the use of AI, as demonstrated in Chaps. 5 and 6 and in Sect. 8.3.5, it is possible to develop meaningful correlations relating performance measures to leading indicators, and it is further possible, as demonstrated in Tables 5.1 and 6.2, to derive meaningful *composite* leading indicators that improve the range of applicability of the correlations. The value of using AI is that it determines the correlations in less time, makes them more accurate, and is superior in providing verifiability.

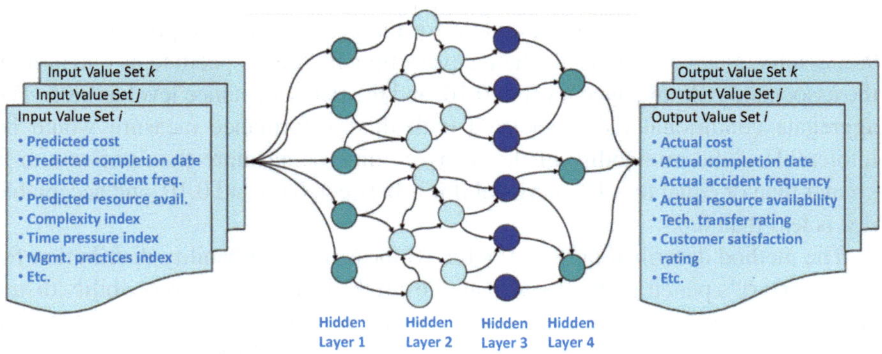

Fig. 15.1 Conceptual depiction of a neural network with inputs and outputs applying to an integrated analysis of program/project, institutional/infrastructure, and enterprise risk analysis

15.3.1 Neural Networks

One of the most widely used forms of AI relies on the use of *artificial neural networks* (Bishop, 1995; Aggarwal, 2003; Hardesty, 2017; Benjamin et al., 1997). A neural network (see Fig. 15.1) consists of a set of input variables (e.g., system attributes and leading indicators), a set of output variables (e.g., performance measures), and a collection of intermediate nodes and edges that determine how the input variables influence the output variables. The intermediate nodes (termed "hidden layers") do not have to have any conceptual interpretation, but can merely serve as the processing engine that determines how the input variables produce the outputs.

In the majority of neural networks, nodes are connected to one another using weights that determine the influence of one node on another. The relationship between each pair of nodes connected by an arrow is normally assumed to be linear, although nonlinear forms, such as radial basis functions (Benjamin et al., 1997) and polynomial expansions (Benjamin and Red-Horse, 2002), can be considered. In that case, weights are replaced by the adjustable constants in the nonlinear relationships. The weights or coefficients are adjusted during the training process to achieve improved model performance. As the data transfers from one node to another, the neural network learns more and more about the data which eventually leads to the output.

An important aspects of neural network development is the selection of data used to train it (Vaprik, 1998; Koch, 2025). For effective neural network training, provisions for selecting high-quality, relevant, and representative data are crucial. This involves focusing on data relevance, diversity, and quality, ensuring the training set mirrors the real-world scenarios the model will encounter. For example, for training a model to predict results for a mechanical system that has many human interfaces and uses new technology, the training data should come from other mechanical systems that have many human interfaces and use a new technology. If trying to predict a particular performance measure (e.g., system cost), the data should include characteristics that are relevant to that performance measure (e.g., system characteristics, supply chain contingencies, market conditions, etc.). The dataset should also include a wide range of examples to prevent the model from overfitting to specific scenarios, and examples should be included to cover boundaries and unusual cases.

The data itself is generally divided into three sets: training, validation, and testing. The training set is used to train the model, the validation set is used to tune parameters and prevent overfitting, and the test set is used to evaluate the final model's performance.

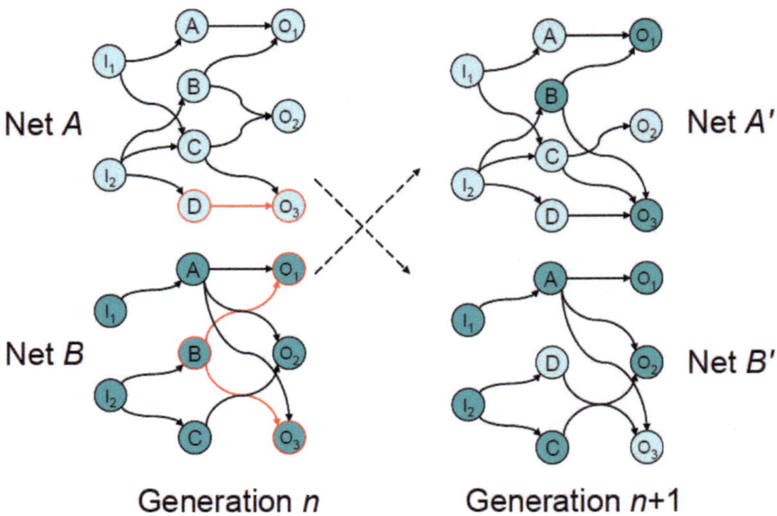

Fig. 15.2 Conceptual depiction of a genetic algorithm plus neural network crossover operation

15.3.2 Genetic Algorithms

A common limitation of neural networks is the need to impose a static structure on the network. In this regard, genetic algorithms (a.k.a., evolutionary programming, genetic programming) embody techniques that can be used to "evolve" a neural network so as to optimize its accuracy (Koza, 1992; Slowik & Kwasnicka, 2020; Abido & Elazouni, 2021). When used in combination with neural networks, a genetic algorithm consists of a family (called a population) of networks, each with its own hidden layer structure. A "goodness of fit" measure determines how well each of the neural networks predicts the historical outputs based on the historical inputs. As shown in Fig. 15.2, the genetic algorithm generates a new population of neural networks from the old population by allowing some networks to remain unchanged, some to change randomly (called mutation), and some to change by combining part of one neural network with part of another (called crossover). Those networks that have the higher goodness of fit score have a higher probability of surviving to the next generation and also have a higher probability of being involved in the crossover. Over time, this evolutionary process frequently produces networks whose goodness of fit is greatly improved from that of the initial population.

15.3.3 Accommodating Data Sparsity and Epistemic Uncertainty

There may be instances where only a limited amount of applicable data is available to train a neural network, such that epistemic uncertainty dominates and genetic algorithms have limited applicability. The use of fundamentally new technology in a complex system often introduces this situation. In such instances, it is highly advisable to account for the epistemic uncertainty by assigning different degrees of belief to different sets of node-to-node weights for the neural network edges (the arrows in Fig. 15.1), based on how well each set of weights appears to replicate the results that are available. This process is similar to the one described in Sect. 15.1.1 for assigning different degrees of belief to different sets of rules in the development of agent-based models. The result in both cases is a set of discrete model probabilities, one for each discrete model, that can be sampled during a Monte-Carlo simulation such as the ones previously illustrated in Figs. 4.1 and 7.3.

It may be noted that various special purpose methods are available for deducing different degrees of belief for different neural networks that are devised from a common but limited database. One of the most tenable of these can be derived from a technique used in machine learning called *L2 regularization*. (Hastie et al., 2009; Bishop, 2006; Goodfellow et al., 2016). In that scheme, overfitting of sparse data is discouraged by adding a penalty term to the loss function being minimized during training to produce an *amended* loss function. The penalty is represented as $C(w_1^2+w_2^2+...+w_n^2)$, i.e., a constant times the sum of the squared values of the edge weights. This prevents networks being favored purely on the basis fof goodness-of-fit when the number of data points is not much greater than the number of edge weights (a situation that encourages overfitting). In the present context, where analysts assign different degrees of belief to difference neural networks rather than attempting to converge on a single network, it would be natural to specify the degree of belief for each network as being inversely proportional to the amended loss function. The combination of different degrees of belief then defines a discrete probability distribution that can be used for the selection from among the devised networks during the Monte Carlo sampling process.

15.4 Use of AI in Support of Organizational and Operational Resilience

Organizational and operational resilience are forms of risk management that are keyed to adaptation more than prevention. Organizational resilience encompasses an organization's ability to adapt and thrive in the face of change and uncertainty, whereas operational resilience focuses on maintaining critical services, systems, and financial flow during disruptions. In combination, their purpose is to mitigate or cope with major disasters that could otherwise disrupt operations, undermine or sabotage organizational objectives, or cause widespread unacceptable hardship. Organizational and operational resilience are rapidly becoming cornerstones in private sector businesses, where adaptation is a key to success, and in government agencies that provide essential services and protect citizens during crises.

Resilience touches on many areas but principally concerns the following key practices:

- Adherence to best practices learned from prior experience (including accident precursors and near misses);
- Employment of adequate margins in all mission execution domains (cost, schedule, safety, physical security, cybersecurity, technical performance);
- Implementation of effective diagnostics during all activity phases (design, development, fabrication, testing, fielding, and operation);
- Design and implementation of supply chains, infrastructure, and business models that are robust, redundant, and adaptive;
- Training of personnel to improve readiness and response (for both anticipated and unanticipated occurrences);
- Certification of personnel qualification and the empowerment to act when needed;
- Recurrent reviews of designs, procedures, emergent risks, and results by qualified, unbiased overseers, experts and practitioners; and
- Fostering of a holistic and integrated culture of communication and cooperation.

Resilience (both organizational and operational) is directed toward the ability to respond to emerging leading indicators of U/U risk as well as to protect against black swan events (i.e., events with extremely low probability of occurrence and extremely high consequence). The importance of having resilience to black swan events, rather than just addressing risk uncertainty, is amplified by the fact that such events as a whole have increased in frequency due to the increasing complexity and interfacing of global events with business and government operations.

Historical instances where resilience was found to be lacking during risky operations abound. Some examples are as follows:

- The Space Shuttle Columbia accident could have been avoided if there had been adequate diagnostics for determining the condition of the orbiter's heat-resistant tiles prior to leaving the International Space Station, or if there had been adequate prior testing of the effects of impacts from sizable foam fragments on the tiles.
- The Space Shuttle Challenger accident most likely would not have happened if there had been a larger margin for the low-temperature capacity of the solid rocket booster O-rings, or if management had paid more attention to the concerns of staff and contractors concerning the launching of the flight during abnormally cold temperatures.
- The Three Mile Island nuclear reactor accident would likely not have resulted in core melting if there had been more adequate diagnostics for the water level in the pressurizer and the reactor core, and if the operators had received better training concerning awareness of water levels and pump behavior.

- The Fukushima Daiichi nuclear reactor accident resulting from a black swan tsunami event would not have resulted in core melting if the emergency electric generators had been sited at a higher elevation to prevent them from becoming flooded.
- The Bhopal pesticide plant chemical leak catastrophe could have been averted if there had been a more rigorous formulation and enforcement of safety rules, and the consequences would have been mitigated if the plant had not been sited near a high-density population center.
- The James Webb Space Telescope (JWST) history of cascading delays and cost overruns due to supply chain problems could largely have been avoided if there had been alternate suppliers or spares on hand to accommodate the occurrence of faulty parts and unexpected damage during testing.
- The 2001 World Trade Center attack could arguably have been defeated if there had not been missed warning signs and if there had been better sharing of information among Federal agencies prior to the attack.
- The 2008 US housing market collapse might have been completely averted were it not for the laxity of lending standards, excessiveness of financial deregulation in certain areas, and overly optimistic ratings of risky securities, the last of these arguably influenced by conflicts of interest between the rating agencies and the firms issuing the securities.
- The 2020 COVID pandemic could have been contained more successfully if there had not been a suppression of information exchange early during the crisis, slow responses to leading indicators, inadequate data collection, understaffing of hospitals, and shortages of protective equipment.

Organizations that have the highest potential for achieving gains in resilience (e.g., by factors of 10 or more in terms of response and restoration times according to ChatGPT) are those that tend to operate in data-rich environments, have complex or distributed systems, and face frequent high-cost disruptions. Such organizations have high risks of failure but also have the database needed to reduce that risk through application of AI in resilience planning and execution. Correspondingly, it will be harder to achieve this level of improvement for organizations that deal with new technologies that are complex, have complex interfaces with other systems, and are in an early stage of development. For such conditions, the supply of applicable data may be limited.

However, as highlighted in Sect. 15.3.3, there exist techniques specifically designed to accommodate AI network training and uncertainty accounting in the presence of sparse data. As discussed there, the use of L2-regularization together with Monte Carlo simulation provides a promising pathway, in that it provides an amalgam of two processes that have been demonstrated to be successful when used individually as well as in combination. Furthermore, these techniques can be combined with agent-based methods (see Sect. 15.1 and its subsections), which do not inherently require a lot of data other than to establish initial conditions. While not likely to achieve improvements in response or restoration resilience on the order of a factor of 10 compared to current achievement for organizations that develop and implement complex new technology, increased use of these methods appears to offer promise of substantial improvement over the status quo. This observation is supported by recent reported successes and the rate of progress that is being experienced in the development of advanced AI techniques.

References

Abido, M., & Elazouni, A. (2021, November). Modified multi-objective evolutionary programming algorithm for solving project scheduling problems. *Journal on Expert Systems with Applications, 183*, 115338.

Aggarwal, C. (2003). *Neural networks and deep learning: A textbook*. Springer.

Armstrong McKay, D., et al. (2022). Exceeding 1.5 C global warming could trigger multiple climate tipping points. *Science, 377*.

Benjamin, A., et al. (1997 January). Use of Artificial Neural Networks for Engineering Analysis of Complex Physical Systems. In Proceedings of the 30th Hawaii Conference on System Sciences, IEEE Computer Society.

Benjamin, A., & Red-Horse, J. (2002, June). Estimating uncertainties when there is little knowledge. In *Proceedings of the Probabilistic Safety Assessment and Management Conference, PSAM-6*.

Bishop, C. (1995). *Neural networks for pattern recognition*. Oxford University Press. first published 1995, subsequently reprinted 13 times.

Bishop, C. (2006). *Pattern Recognition and Machine Learning*. Springer Series in Information Science and Statistics.

Bray, D. (2025, March 3). *Hybrid AI and human Red teams: Critical to preventing policies from exploitation by adversaries*. Stimson Center Policy Memo, Red Cell Project Series. https://www.stimson.org/2025/hybrid-ai-and-human-red-teams-critical-to-preventing-policies-from-exploitation-by-adversaries/

Carpenter, S., et al. (2008). Leading indicators of trophic cascades. *Ecology Letters, 11*.

Costa, J. (2024, May 7). *Counter AI attacks with AI defense*. Palo Alto Networks.

Dakos, V., et al. (2019). Ecosystem tipping points in an evolving world. *Nature Ecology & Evolution, Nature Portfolio, 3*.

Dakos, V., et al. (2024). Tipping point detection and early warnings in climate, ecological, and human systems. *Earth System Dynamics, European Geosciences Union, 15*.

Drake, J., et al. (2020). Alternative stable states, tipping points, and early warning signals of ecological transitions. In *Theoretical ecology: Concepts and applications*. Oxford University Press.

Fabiani, G., et al. (2024, May 15). Task-oriented machine learning surrogates for tipping points of agency-based models. *Nature Communications, 15*.

Goodfellow, I., et al. (2016). *Deep Learning, the MIT Press*.

Hardesty, L. (2017, April). *Explained: Neural networks*. MIT News Office. https://news.mit.edu/2017/explained-neural-networks-deep-learning-0414

Hastie, T., et al. (2009). *The Elements of Statistical Learning: Data Mining, Inference, and Prediction*, 2nd edition, Springer Series in Statistics.

IBM. (2024). *Cost of a data breach report 2024*. ibm.com/reports/data-breach

Koch, R. (2025). *The value of data quality and data diversity in AI models*. https://www.clickworker.com/customer-blog/data-quality-and-diversity,

Koza, J. (1992). *Genetic programming: On the programming of computers by means of natural selection*. MIT Press.

Lenton, T., et al. (2023). *The global tipping points report 2023*. University of Exeter.

Microsoft AI Red Team. (2024). *Lessons from red teaming 100 generative AI products*. MS_AIRT_Lessons_eBook.pdf, Microsoft Corporation white paper, 2024, takeaways synopsized online by B. Bullwinkel and R. Kumar, January 13, 2025.

Niazi, M., & Hussain, A. (2011). Agent-based computing from multi-agent systems to agent-based models: A visual survey. *Scientometrics, 89*(2).

NIST Technical Series. (2023, January). *Artificial Intelligence risk mangement framework (AI RMF 1.0)*. National Institute of Standards and Technology, Publication No. NIST AI 100-1.

OpenAI. (2024, November 21). *Advancing red teaming with people and AI*. https://openai.com/index/advancing-red-teaming-with-people-and-ai/

Renn, O., & Lucas, K. (2022). Systemic risk: The threat to societal diversity and coherence. *Risk Analysis, 42*.

Rowe, A. *AI cyber defense: How to spot AI cyber attacks*. tech.co/news/how-to-spot-ai-cyber-attacks, updated March 3, 2025.

Scheffer, M. (2010). Foreseeing tipping points. *Nature, 467*, 411–412.

Scheffer, M., & Carpenter, S. (2003). Catastrophic regime shifts in ecosystems: Linking theory to observations. *Trends in Ecolology & Evolution, 18*.

Slowik, A., & Kwasnicka, H. (2020, August). Evolutionary algorithms and their applications to engineering problems. *Journal of Neural Computing and Applications, 32*.

Vaprik, V. (1998). *The nature of statistical learning theory*. Springer.

Wiki ABM. (2025). *Agent-based model*. https://en.wikipedia.org/wiki/Agent-based_model

Wissel, C. (1984). A universal law of the characteristic return time near thresholds. *Oecologia, 65*.

Zhang, A., et al. (2024, September 11). *The human factor in AI red teaming: Perspectives from social and collaborative computing*. arXiv open-access repository, Cornell University, arXiv:2407.07786.

Appendix A. Explanation and Characterization of Key Concepts

Appendix A elaborates upon the key concept introductory table at the beginning of the book. It explains and characterizes the following principal terms and concepts that pertain to the integration of risk management across the enterprise, infrastructure/institutional, and program/project activity domains, as they are used in this book and, when applicable, in other references:

- *Performance Measure* (*PM*)
- *Performance Measure Marker* (*PMM*)
- *Constraint*
- *Target*
- *Risk Tolerance Level* (*RTL*)
- *Risk Tolerance Posture* (*RTP*)
- *Risk Tolerance*
- *Risk Appetite*
- *Risk Acceptance Level* (*RAL*)
- *Risk Acceptance Posture* (*RAP*)
- *Individual Risk Scenario*
- *Aggregate Risk*
- *Cumulative and Complementary Cumulative Distribution Functions* (*CDFs and CCDFs*)
- *Known Risks*
- *Underappreciated Risk*
- *Unknown Risk*
- *Risk Posture*
- *Risk Undesirability Score*
- *Optimal Balancing of Risk*
- *Risk-Informed Decision Making* (*RIDM*)
- *Continuous Risk Management* (*CRM*)

A. S. Benjamin, *Integration of Project, Infrastructure, and Enterprise Risk Management*, Risk, Governance and Society 21,
https://doi.org/10.1007/978-3-031-85070-7

These terms appear and reappear throughout the book as foundational elements of risk management for large, high-tech organizations.

Performance Measure (PM), Performance Measure Marker (PMM), Constraint, and Target

A *performance measure* is a quantitative metric used to evaluate the extent to which a system, process, or activity fulfills an intended objective. Upon definition of an objectives hierarchy network that decomposes top-level objectives into a complete set of quantifiable or otherwise assessable performance objectives, a performance measure can be identified for each objective, as the primary metric by which its degree of fulfillment can be characterized and/or quantified. In most cases, the appropriate performance measure to use is self-evident from the definition of the objective itself. In other cases the choice may not be as clear, and work must be done in order to assure not only that the objective is assessable, but that the performance measure used to characterize it or quantify it is adequately representative of the objective to begin with. In cases where two or more performance measures are needed to characterize an objective, additional objectives are defined so that at the end, each objective is characterized by a single performance measure.

A *performance measure marker* (*PMM*) is a particular value of a performance measure that the organization sets as a peg point for defining a risk tolerance level and a risk acceptance level (as defined in he next paragraph). Examples of PMMs include *constraints* and *targets*. A constraint is a PMM that stakeholders, including managers, funding authorities, and others at risk, specify as not to be breached with a high level of confidence (e.g., the maximum allowable cost of a project, the minimum required service life of an engineered system, or the minimum acceptable revenue from a service). A target is a less restrictive PMM that can be interpreted as a relaxed constraint that includes a designated margin or reserve. Stakeholders generally accept a lower level of confidence for meeting targets than for meeting constraints.

Risk Tolerance Level (RTL), Risk Tolerance Posture (RTP), Risk Tolerance, Risk Appetite, Risk Acceptance Level (RAL), and Risk Acceptance Posture (RAP)

A *risk tolerance level* (*RTL*) is a risk threshold that expresses the *maximum limit* of probability of shortfall or loss the organization is willing to accept in order to pursue the achievement of a particular objective. If evaluation of a risk results in it being higher than the RTL, the organization tries to identify and implement control or mitigation actions so that it no longer exceeds the RTL. Control actions differ from mitigation actions in that the former emphasizes watchfulness and procedural rigor while the latter emphasizes changes in system design or operation. References to this distinction are made in Sects. 1.1.3, 4.4, 10.1, and 10.2.

A full set of RTLs comprises the operational definition of risk tolerance posture (see Sect. 1.1.2) that an organization seeks to apply across the range of organizational objectives and performance dimensions, and expresses the organization's view of how the likelihood of gains or shortfalls in the pursuit of any one objective balances against the corresponding likelihoods of gains or shortfalls in the pursuit of the other objectives. RTLs may be applied to objectives whose measure of success is ultimately observable (e.g., the objective of obtaining X years of useful data or a Y percent return on investment), as well as to objectives whose measure of success can only be estimated probabilistically but not directly observed (e.g., the objective of maintaining a probability of life-threatening accidents less than Z).

The specific term *risk tolerance level* generally refers to the risk unacceptability threshold for a specified performance measure marker value. The term *risk tolerance,* on the other hand, is more general than *risk tolerance level.* It can refer to the collection of risk tolerance levels defined as discrete values for each marker (e.g., an RTL for the constraint value and a different RTL for the target value), or it may refer to the entire curve of risk tolerance level values vs. performance measure values. The interpretation of *risk tolerance* as a continuous function of a performance measure may be found in Hubbard (2020, Chap. 4) and Smith (2021, Sect. 2.3.9).

In the form of a continuous function, a *risk tolerance curve* as defined by Hubbard or Smith may be viewed as the complement of a *utility curve* for a single attribute (i.e., the utility curve for a single organizational objective). In a financial context, a risk tolerance curve connotes what a decision maker is willing to pay to acquire various levels of protection from risk, and a utility curve reflects what he/she is willing to pay to acquire various levels of benefit. It should be noted that the use of the term *risk tolerance* in utility theory, however, is quite different from its usage by Hubbard, Smith, and others, and refers instead to the concavity of the utility curve (Myerson & Zambrano, 2019; Al-Karaeen, 2006).

There is considerable diversity in the literature as to what is meant by *risk tolerance* vis-à-vis *risk appetite.* Hubbard equates the two by saying that "a statement about how much risk an individual or organization is willing to endure may be called a *risk tolerance* or sometimes a *risk appetite,*" and then proceeds to explain the concept using *tolerance* instead of *appetite.* NASA also tends to use the term *risk tolerance* rather than *risk appetite.*

Norman Marks summarizes the use of the two terms by COSO (Marks, 2015). COSO defines *risk appetite* in COSO (2004) as "the amount of risk, on a broad level, an organization is willing to accept in pursuit of value." In a COSO ERM addendum (Rittenberg & Martens, 2012), the authors Larry Rittenberg and Frank Martens make the following distinction between terms: "Risk tolerance relates to risk appetite but differs in one fundamental way: risk tolerance represents the application of risk appetite to specific objectives." They go on to say that "operating within risk tolerances helps ensure that the entity remains within its risk appetite and, in turn, that the entity will achieve its objectives," implying that risk tolerance refers to an acceptable level of variation. Furthermore, "to be effective, risk appetite must be operationalized through appropriate risk tolerances." This last statement implies that the expression of risk appetite is more qualitative and that of risk tolerance is more quantitative. Marks says that he is "not a big fan" of risk appetite as defined by COSO, and would prefer for risk tolerance to be defined as "an acceptable likelihood of a defined level of variation."

The terminology *risk tolerance posture* seems to resolve the issues raised by Marks by expanding the COSO definition of risk tolerance from individual objectives to multiple objectives. It thereby defines it as a quantitative version of COSO's more qualitative conception of risk appetite.

A *Risk Acceptance Level* (*RAL*) is a different risk threshold that expresses the *minimum level* of probability of shortfall or loss the organization requires in order to retire the risk as an area of concern that requires additional control or mitigation. If the risk is not fully eliminated, the organization continues to monitor it so as to ensure that it does not rise above the RAL. A full set of RALs comprises the operational definition of risk acceptance posture.

If an evaluated risk lies between its RAL and its RTL, I label it as *marginal*. For purposes of discrimination concerning the level of the risk relative to the RAL and the RTL, the marginal region of risk may be further divided into two, three, or more sub-regions. In this book, I present examples using three sub-division of marginality, which I refer to as *marginally acceptable*, *marginal*, and *marginally intolerable*. The elicitation of stakeholders to establish RALs and RTLs for each performance measure is discussed in Sects. 3.2.1 and 7.3.4, and Sects. 4.3.1 and 4.3.2 elaborates upon the division of the marginal region into sub-regions.

Individual Risk Scenario

An *individual risk scenario* is a defined sequence of events, starting from an initiating event or perturbation, and leading after some set of pivotal events to an undesirable effect on one or more performance measures. The characterization of an individual risk includes the scenario itself (see Fig. A.1), the likelihood of the scenario occurring, and the consequence resulting from the scenario.

Below are four examples of individual risk scenarios applicable to different risk management activity domains:

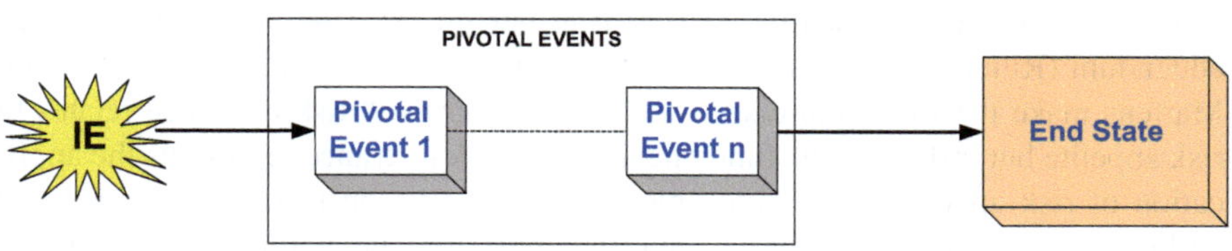

Fig. A.1 Schematic representation of an individual risk scenario

- Program/project example 1 (safety and mission assurance related): Random failure of a component in a control system during operation of System X leads to failure of the control system, excessive loading, structural failure, and loss of mission
- Program/project example 2 (cost related): Unexpected results during Project Y integrated system testing lead to concern about the ability of the system to meet mission requirements, resulting in a significant delay in the operational date with a commensurate unplanned cost increase
- Infrastructure/institutional example (core competency related): Unanticipated retirements in critical specialty Z, stiff competition for new hires, and lack of funding for training courses lead to a poor score from an independent assessor concerning the ability of the responsible department or division to maintain a strong core competency in that specialty
- Cross-domain example (cybersecurity): An adversary successfully executes a plan to locate a vulnerable point of entry to a secured but highly interconnected IT network and either steals sensitive information or plants malicious software that leads to failure of a critical system.

Aggregate Risk, CDFs, and CCDFs

Aggregate Risk is the cumulative risk associated with a given performance measure, accounting for all significant risk contributors, including known risks, underappreciated risks, and unknown risks (defined later in this appendix). An aggregate risk is determined from the results of integrated modeling of the individual contributors to the aggregate risk and their interactions with one another, leading to a performance measure probability distribution. If the "direction of goodness" for the performance measure is toward higher values (e.g., reliability), the risk of falling short of a specified performance marker value is the area under the curve to the left of the marker (see Fig. A.2). Similarly, if the direction of goodness is toward lower values (e.g., cost), the risk is the area under the curve to the right of the marker.

Below are four examples of aggregate risks applicable to different risk management activity domains:

- Program/project example 1 (S&MS related): The risk that the frequency of operational failure of critical system X is greater than once in ten years, considering all accidents that could lead to operational failure, is 10%. The evaluated performance measure is the frequency of operational failure, the performance marker is once in ten years, and the risk of exceedance is 10%.

- Program/project example 2 (cost related): The risk that the total expenditure on project Y will exceed the allocated funding, considering all potential contributors to cost overrun, is around 30%. The evaluated performance measure is the total expenditure, the performance marker is the allocated funding, and the exceedance risk is 30%.

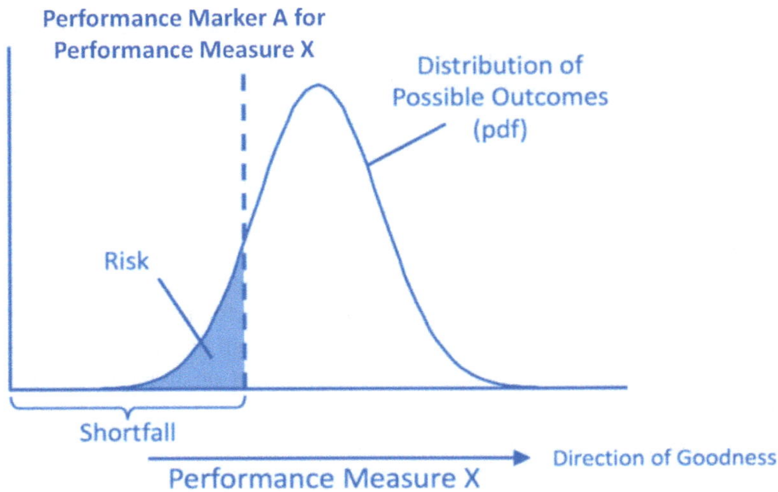

Fig. A.2 Schematic representation of the results from an aggregation of risk contributors

- Infrastructure/institutional example (core competency related): The risk that the required staffing to maintain core competency in critical specialty Z, considering all potential contributors to staff attrition and replenishment difficulties, is between 15% and 25%. The performance measure is the number of qualified staff in the specialty of interest, the performance marker is the number required to maintain core competency, and the shortfall risk is around 20% with a variability of ±5%.
- Cross-domain example (cybersecurity): The cumulative *conditional* probability (given an attack attempt) that an adversary locates a vulnerable point of entry and successfully plants malicious software, all within one year of initiating the effort, is less than or equal to 50%. The performance measure is the time for an adversary to gain entry and plant malicious software, the performance marker is one year, and the shortfall is not greater than 50%.

To consider and display aggregate risks most effectively, it is important to be aware of the relationship between probability density functions (pdf's), cumulative distribution functions (CDFs), and complementary distribution functions (CCDFs). CDFs and CCDFs integrals of the probability density functions and are useful for determining the probabilities of under-shooting or exceeding a performance measure marker value. Figure A.3 conceptually illustrates the relationships between pdf's, CDFs, and CCDFs.

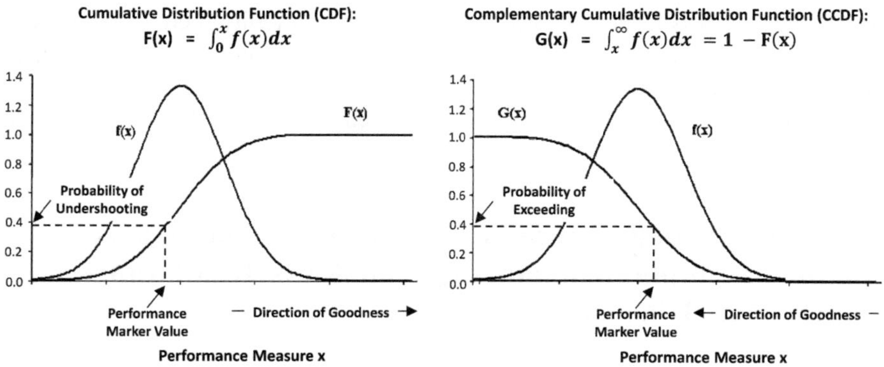

Fig. A.3 Schematic representation of the relationships between probability density functions, cumulative distribution functions, and complementary cumulative distribution functions

Risk Posture, Risk Undesirability Score, and Optimal Balancing of Aggregate Risks

The term *risk posture* is used by NASA in its governance policy directive (NASA, 2020) and in its risk management handbook (NASA, 2024), as noted in Sect. 1.1.5, as well as by several other US Government agencies with respect to cybersecurity risk. Among them are the National Institute of Standard and Technology (NIST, 2021), the Government Accountability Office (GAO, 2019), and the Department of Homeland Security (DHS, 2018). Its definition in these references, while not explicitly stated, implicitly encompasses a combination of risk tolerance posture and aggregate risk status. A satisfactory risk posture, then, implies that all of the aggregate risks lie within their corresponding risk tolerance levels.

The aggregate risks can be considered to be *optimally balanced* when the value of the aggregate risk divided by the risk tolerance level is the same for all risk tolerance levels over all objectives and that ratio cannot be further reduced by introducing new risk mitigation options. For example, if the aggregate risk for not meeting the total cost constraint for a project is 10% when the risk tolerance level is 15%, and at the same time the aggregate risk for not meeting the operating life requirement is 20% while the risk tolerance level is 30%, those two risks would be considered to be balanced with a ratio of 2/3 for both. If that ratio could not be reduced further through mitigation, the two risks would be optimally balanced.

In this book, I use a slightly different normalization of the aggregate risk to define what I mean by *optimally balanced*. I introduce the term *risk undesirability score* to characterize the normalization and define it as follows:

$$\textit{Risk Undesirability Score} = \frac{\textit{Aggregate Risk} - \textit{Risk Acceptance Level}}{\textit{Risk Tolerance Level} - \textit{Risk Acceptance Level}}$$

An aggregate risk is labeled as acceptable if the undesirability score is less than or equal to zero, marginal if it is between zero and one, and intolerable if it is greater than one. The concepts of undesirability scores and optimal balancing for aggregate risks are elaborated upon further and demonstrated in Sects. 4.3.1, 4.3.2, and 13.2.

Known Risks, Underappreciated Risk, and Unknown Risk, and their Incorporation into Aggregate Risks, Risk Posture, and Optimal Balancing

Three types of risk contributors are considered as essential components of the overall aggregate risk, namely known risks, underappreciated risk, and unknown risk. *Known Risks* comprise the category of individual risks for which there is (1) a defined scenario leading to degraded performance with respect to one or more performance measures, plus (2) a known occurrence likelihood for the defined scenario (either single-valued or with a well-characterized uncertainty distribution), and (3) a known consequence with respect to the severity of performance degradation (with a well-characterized uncertainty distribution).

This type of risk is roughly equivalent to what former Secretary of State Donald Rumsfeld prototypically once referred to as "known knowns," commenting during a press conference on the war in Iraq and the lack of evidence linking the Iraqi government with the supply of weapons of mass destruction to terrorist groups (DoD, 2002). In Rumsfeld's idiomatic lexicon, known knowns refer to "things we know we know." In the context of known *risk*, we don't know with certainty what the outcome will be because there are aleatory and epistemic uncertainties (i.e., uncertainty due to inherent randomness that cannot be explained away, and uncertainty due to a lack of information or understanding). But we have enough solid information to characterize a reliable probability distribution for the outcome that incorporates both sources of uncertainty.

Underappreciated Risk comprises the category of individual risk contributors for which there is again (1) a well-defined scenario leading to degraded performance, but for which (2) either the scenario likelihood or the accompanying consequence, or both, are not well characterized. The incomplete or erroneous characterization is caused usually by a lack of dependable information about the realm of possibility, but may also be caused by a misinterpretation of available information. For example, the Fukushima nuclear reactor accident and the Space Shuttle Challenger and Columbia accidents can be argued to fit within this category. The amount of underappreciation can best (perhaps only) be estimated from leading indicators that are known to correlate with shortfalls in performance.

This category of risk is roughly equivalent to Rumsfeld's characterization of "known unknowns," namely "things we know we don't know." However, in the context of risk, it also includes "things we know exist (the scenario) but don't know the full magnitude of (the likelihood and/or the consequence)."

Unknown Risk refers to the category of risk contributors for which there is no well-defined single scenario leading to the degraded performance, but rather a set of unknown scenarios whose existence is implied by a set of *leading indicators*. For example, we may know that complexity and poor management oversight are correlated with increased risk of unwanted occurrences, for example as a result of human error (Perrow, 1999; Benjamin, 2016, 2017), but not know the particulars of the scenarios that may lead to the increased risk. For instance, the Three-Mile Island and Chernobyl nuclear reactor accidents fit within this category, as both resulted from particular human errors, compounded by system deficiencies, that had not been previously dissected. As was the case for underappreciated risk, the potential magnitude of unknown risk can be estimated from leading indicators that are known to correlate with shortfalls in performance. Thus, the operational means for accounting for unknown risk is similar to the operational means for accounting for underappreciated risk.

The category of unknown risk is roughly equivalent to Rumsfeld's definition of "unknown unknowns," namely "things we don't know we don't know." In the context of risk, what is known is that there is a correlation between certain leading indicators and underestimated shortfalls in performance, but the specific scenarios leading to that shortfall and their individual likelihoods and consequences are unknown.

The aggregate risk of not satisfying an objective includes the cumulative effect of not just the known risks but also the underappreciated and unknown (U/U) risk. Thus it is evaluated using a combination of scenario-based models (the known risks) and leading-indicator-based correlations (the U/U risk). The specification of risk tolerance levels and risk postures (including risk tolerance postures), and the optimal balancing of aggregate risks are all based on the calculation of total aggregate risk, inclusive of known risks and U/U risk.

The evaluation of U/U risk from leading indicators and its subsequent utilization is taken up in more detail in Chaps. 5 and 6.

Risk-Informed Decision Making (RIDM) and Continuous Risk Management (CRM)

Risk-Informed Decision Making is the process of evaluating both individual and aggregate risks for the purpose of informing decision making regarding the selection between alternative initiatives, designs, processes, and modes of operation. The six steps of RIDM occur within and across the PRM, IRM, and ERM activity domains and include: (1) formulating objectives and associated performance measures to support decision making, (2) formulating decision alternatives recognizing both the risks and the opportunities that they bring to the table, (3) conducting an integrated analysis of risks for each alternative, (4) developing the technical basis for deliberations and conducting the deliberations, (5) selecting an alternative and accepting the associated risks informed by the risk analysis results, and (6) documenting the decision and its rationale (NASA, 2011, 2024). RIDM supports the principles of risk leadership by helping ensure that deliberations on the selection between alternatives takes full account of the risk tolerance posture that has been established, both at the top level of the enterprise where risk tolerance posture is initially specified and at the lower levels to which the risk tolerance posture has been flowed down.

Continuous Risk Management is a systematic and iterative process that (1) identifies, (2) analyzes, (3) plans responses to, (4) tracks, (5) controls, and (6) communicates and documents all risks associated with the implementation of initiatives, designs, and processes within and across the PRM, IRM, and ERM activity domains (Dorofee et al., 1996; NASA, 2011, 2024). The six steps of CRM apply in like measure to the management of individual risk scenarios, leading indicators of underappreciated and unknown risks, and aggregate risks to objectives. CRM supports the principles of risk leadership by ensuring that the aggregate risks to objectives, at all organizational levels, remain responsive to the risk tolerance posture throughout the timeline of the program, project, or activity. When coordinated with RIDM during the execution phases of an activity, it helps to ensure that decisions concerning which risk mitigation option to pursue from among various proposed alternatives, or about whether or not to pursue a proposed opportunity that seems promising, are made in a sound and timely manner.

Figure A.4 depicts the relationships between RIDM, CRM, and organizational management at a 50,000-ft level.

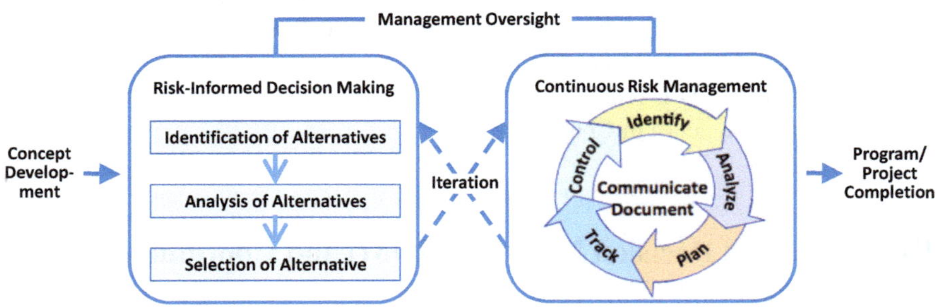

Fig. A.4 High-level conceptualization of the relationship between RIDM, CRM, and management

References

Al-Karaeen, F. (2006). *Characterizing battlefield human decision making with value focused thinking and reliability modeling*. PhD Dissertation, Wright State University.

Benjamin, A. (2016, January). Developing probabilistic safety performance margins for unknown and underappreciated risks. *Journal of Reliability Engineering and System Safety, 145*, 329–340.

Benjamin, A. (2017). *Enterprise risk and opportunity management: Concepts and step-by-step examples for pioneering scientific and technical organizations* (Finance series). Wiley.

COSO. (2004). *Enterprise risk management – Integrated framework*. Committee of Sponsoring Organizations of the Treadway Commission (updated in 2017).

DHS. (2018, May). *US DHS cybersecurity strategy*. Department of Homeland Security.

DoD. (2002, February 12). *Defense.gov News Transcript: DoD News briefing – Secretary Rumsfeld and General Myers*. U.S. Department of Defense.

Dorofee, A., et al. (1996, January). *Continuous risk management guidebook*. Carnegie Mellon University, Software Engineering Institute, Rept. No. 19970108 045.

GAO. (2019, July). *Cybersecurity: Agencies need to fully establish risk management programs and address challenges*. Government Accountability Office, GAO-19-384.

Hubbard, D. W. (2020). *The failure of risk management: Why it's broken and how to fix it* (2nd ed.). Wiley.

Marks, N. (2015, June). Chapter 13: Risk evaluation, appetite, tolerance, and criteria. In *World-class risk management*. CreateSpace Independent Publishing.

Myerson, R. B., & Zambrano, E. (2019, December). Chapter 3: Utility theory with constant risk tolerance. In *Probability models for economic decisions*. MIT Press.

NASA. (2011, November). *NASA risk management handbook (Version 1)*. NASA/SP-2011-3422.

NASA. (2020, January). *NASA governance and strategic management handbook*. NASA NPD 1000.0C.

NASA. (2024, November). *NASA risk management handbook (Version 2, Part 1)*. NASA/SP-2024-3422.

NIST. (2021, February). *NIST Cyber Risk Scoring (CRS) Program Overview*. National Institute of Standards and Technology.

Perrow, C. (1999). *Normal accidents: Living with high-risk technologies*. Princeton University Press.

A. S. Benjamin, *Integration of Project, Infrastructure, and Enterprise Risk Management*, Risk, Governance and Society 21,
https://doi.org/10.1007/978-3-031-85070-7

Rittenberg, L., & Martens, F. (2012, January). *Enterprise risk management: Understanding and communicating risk appetite*. Committee of Sponsoring Organizations of the Treadway Commission.

Smith, C., et al. (2021, September). *Treatment of uncertainties for security-related design aspects of advanced reactors when using a risk-informed licensing approach*. Idaho National Laboratory, INL/EXT-21-64565.

Index

A

Accident precursor analysis (APA), 104, 153
Achievement measures, 79, 81, 86
Activity importance, 131–133
Aerospace Corporation complexity index, 54, 104
Aerospace Corporation cost uncertainty analysis methodology, 78
Agent-based modeling (ABM), 164–166
Aggregate risks, 11, 23, 29, 31, 35, 40, 42, 45–47, 49, 50, 73, 76, 78, 82, 89, 91–93, 96, 99, 101, 107, 111, 115, 116, 119–123, 126, 129–131, 133, 140, 144, 151, 156, 157, 159, 163–167, 179, 183–188
Aggregate schedule risk, 145–147
Analysis-of-alternatives (AoA), 92, 133–136
Analytical hierarchy process (AHP), 34
Artificial intelligence (AI), 2, 121, 163, 164, 167–171, 173–176
Artificial neural networks, 163, 164, 170–173
Aspirational objectives, 76, 77, 79–81, 83–87
Augustine Committee, 73–87

B

Benefit significance scores, 73, 79–81, 84, 85
Bhopal accident, 175

C

Challenger accident, 61, 62, 174
Chernobyl accident, 4, 65, 175, 187
Columbia accidents, 52, 61–64, 68, 153, 174, 186
Committee of Sponsoring Organizations of the Treadwell Commission (COSO), 11, 181, 182
Common-cause analysis, 101, 141
Complementary cumulative distribution functions (CCDFs), 42, 179, 183–184
Conditional probabilities, 107–108, 168, 184
Confidence levels, 25–28, 31, 32
Constraints, 3, 25–28, 31, 32, 52, 53, 61, 76, 79, 85, 92, 93, 99, 103, 108, 111, 119, 123, 139, 140, 151, 153–155, 159, 160, 169, 179–181, 185
Continuous risk management (CRM), 89–105, 115–128, 166, 179, 187–188
Control loops, 11, 116–118
COVID pandemic, 175
Cross-organizational interaction, 13–23
Cumulative distribution functions (CDFs), 183–185
Cybersecurity, 6, 9, 40–42, 107–109, 111, 112, 121, 124, 125, 153, 155, 164, 167–170, 183–185

D

De-minimis and de-maximus reference designs, 154–155
Design for Optimally Balanced Risks (DFOBR), 19–21, 151–161

A. S. Benjamin, *Integration of Project, Infrastructure, and Enterprise Risk Management*, Risk, Governance and Society 21,
https://doi.org/10.1007/978-3-031-85070-7

E
Enterprise risk management (ERM), 8–11, 14, 25, 28, 46, 141, 163, 181, 187, 188
Evaluation year, 145–149
Evolutionary programming, 172
Expert calibration, 33–34
Expert elicitation, 33–34, 81

F
Failure modes, effects and criticality analysis (FMECA), 104, 153
Fault tree based risk aggregation models, 89, 99–101
Fukushima accident, 65, 175

G
Genetic algorithms, 163–165, 170–173
Genetic programming, 172
Governance, 1, 9–11, 116, 185
Graded analysis approaches, 5, 129–133

H
Hazard analysis (HA), 104, 153
Housing market collapse, 175
Hubbard, D.W., 7, 13, 29, 30, 33, 181
Human reliability, 46, 52, 59, 67–68, 70, 156

I
Infrastructure/institutional risk management (IRM), 8–10, 14, 25, 28, 118, 187, 188
Integrated modeling, 41, 134, 183
Internal controls, 1, 9–11, 20, 46, 105, 115–119

J
James Webb Space Telescope (JWST), 28, 53–57, 104

K
Key milestone slippage, 143–149
Known risks, 50, 61–63, 65–68, 93, 155, 160, 179, 186–187

L
Launch vehicle failures, 59–62
Leading indicators, 4, 5, 23, 36, 40, 45, 46, 49–56, 59, 60, 68, 70, 81, 92, 93, 99, 100, 103, 104, 116, 129–131, 133, 136, 140, 144, 153, 156, 160, 164, 166, 167, 170–173, 186–188
Leveson, N.G., 10, 116
L2 regularization, 173, 175

M
Mandated requirements, 19, 25–28, 31, 45, 91–93, 151, 155, 160
Milestone risk analysis, 143–147
Mission objectives, 8, 125–127
Model-based mission assurance (MBMA), 13, 23
Model-based risk posture assessment, 23
Model-based system engineering (MBSE), 13, 23
Model rigor, 130
Model scope, 153
Monte Carlo sampling, 7, 35, 81, 82, 164, 173
Multi-attribute utility theory (MAUT), 7, 33, 84
Multi-criteria decision analysis (multi-criteria decision-making), 7, 34
Multi-program risk aggregation, 6, 101–104

N
NASA, 2, 4, 7–9, 16, 28, 30, 31, 54, 55, 57, 59, 62, 63, 68, 73–77, 80, 96, 108, 125, 126, 131, 132, 143, 159, 181, 185
Nelson complexity index (NCI), 56
Neural networks, 170–173
NotPetya ransomware attack, 41, 111

O
Optimal balancing, 2, 126, 154, 157, 179, 185–187
Organizational and operational resilience, 164

P
Penetration time, 164, 169
Performance measure histogram, 37
Performance measure markers (PMMs), 27, 42, 108, 179–181, 184
Performance measures, 6, 16, 27–30, 42, 44, 45, 49, 50, 70, 74, 76–82, 86, 92, 95, 96, 104, 107, 109–111, 119,

122, 129–131, 133, 134, 136, 139, 140, 144, 156–158, 164, 169, 171, 179–184, 186, 187
Performance modeling and simulation as a function of activity phase, 96–99
Performance shaping factors, 67–68
Programmatic objectives, 8, 76, 77, 80, 81, 86
Program/project risk management (PRM), 8–10, 13, 14, 25, 28, 187, 188

R
RACI matrices, 11, 118
Re-baselining, 19, 123–128
Recovery time, 40, 169
Red teams, 40–42, 104, 107, 109, 110, 112, 164, 168–169
Requirements, 9, 19, 20, 25, 30, 46, 53, 56, 90, 91, 97, 123, 126, 139, 141, 154, 157, 159, 183, 185
Resilience (organizational and operational), 163–164, 173–176
Risk acceptance levels (RALs), 25, 29–32, 42, 73, 76, 79, 85, 108, 119, 139, 141, 147, 164, 169, 179–182
Risk acceptance posture (RAP), 123, 179–182
Risk appetite, 4, 179–182
Risk drivers, 35, 45–47, 115, 116, 119–121, 123, 130, 155–156
Risk-informed decision making (RIDM), 92, 125, 179, 187–188
Risk leadership, 1, 7–8, 50, 70, 151, 188
Risk management communication, 14, 23
Risk mitigation options, 27, 115, 121, 185, 188
Risk posture, 3, 4, 8, 11, 14, 20, 23, 46, 86–87, 108, 123, 124, 179, 185–187
Risk scenario dependencies, 89, 137
Risk scenario diagrams, 89, 93–96, 104
Risk scenario/individual risk, 49, 91, 99, 100, 116, 179, 182–183, 188
Risk tolerance levels, 7, 25–33, 73, 76, 79, 85, 108, 111, 119, 139, 169, 179–182, 185, 187
Risk tolerance posture (RTP), 3, 4, 7, 92, 151, 160, 179–182, 185, 188
Risk types, 9, 10, 74, 94
Risk undesirability scores, 35, 42–45, 81, 86, 87, 122, 126, 127, 129, 144, 147, 148, 157, 179, 185–186

S
Schedule risk undesirability score, 147–149
Screening analysis, 129, 133–136, 147
Solar Winds hacking attack, 41
Space Shuttle, 57, 61–64, 66, 68, 75, 153
Spider charts, 44, 73, 76, 77, 86, 87, 122, 126, 127, 147, 149, 157–159
Strategic portfolio planning, 73, 74, 81–85
Systems engineering integration with safety assurance, 21

T
Tactical and strategic opportunities, 124–125
Targets, 25–28, 32, 76, 79, 85, 92, 119, 124, 154, 179–181
Technology readiness level (TRL), 5
Three-Mile Island accident, 65, 68, 174, 187
Tipping points, 163–167

U
Unknown and/or underappreciated (U/U) risk, 4, 5, 23, 30, 31, 36, 49–53, 59–61, 66–68, 70, 71, 92, 93, 99, 100, 103–104, 123, 125, 133, 136, 151, 153, 155, 158, 160, 167, 187
Utility theory, 7, 181
U/U risk adjustment, 40, 81

W
World Trade Center attack, 175

MIX
Papier aus verantwortungsvollen Quellen
Paper from responsible sources
FSC® C105338

If you have any concerns about our products,
you can contact us on
ProductSafety@springernature.com

In case Publisher is established outside the EU,
the EU authorized representative is:
Springer Nature Customer Service Center GmbH
Europaplatz 3, 69115 Heidelberg, Germany

Printed by Libri Plureos GmbH
in Hamburg, Germany